BENJAMIN LOGAN

CHARLES GANO TALBERT

Benjamin Logan

Kentucky
Frontiersman

UNIVERSITY OF KENTUCKY PRESS

TO DOROTHY JARETT TALBERT

PREFACE

THE HISTORY OF KENTUCKY from 1775 to 1803 may be divided into three periods. From 1775 through 1783 the Kentuckians were engaged in a struggle with the Indians, who were encouraged, aided, and at times led by British officers. From 1784 to 1792 the leading men of the District of Kentucky were seeking separation from Virginia and the creation of a new state. Indian troubles continued during this period, but they can hardly be compared in importance to such questions as statehood and the desire to use the Mississippi River as a commercial outlet. From 1792 to 1803 a new state was writing and rewriting its constitution and enacting essential legislation. The Mississippi question, which almost caused a filibustering expedition in 1794, was finally solved by the American purchase of Louisiana.

The first of these periods required leaders who above all else were good woodsmen and Indian fighters. The second and third periods called for leaders with an understanding of law and of constitution making, and with the ability to speak and write fluently. In all three periods the name of Benjamin Logan appears very frequently. The purpose of this study has been to investigate the career of this frontiersman and to portray him against a background of frontier history.

Indispensable aid has been rendered by many persons. Enough credit can never be given to Dr. Robert S. Cotterill of Tallahassee, Florida. Beginning with the author's doctoral dissertation at the University of Kentucky, "The Life and Times of Benjamin Logan," Dr. Cotterill made numerous and detailed suggestions without which this revision might never have been attempted. Help and encouragement have been provided by Dr. Thomas D. Clark and Dr. Will D. Gilliam of the department of history at the University of Kentucky, and by Dr. Jacqueline Bull and Mrs. Frances Dugan of the Margaret I. King Library, University of Kentucky. Carol Honeycutt and Dorothy Roberts have been diligent and accurate typists. Janice Holt Giles, in three of whose novels Benjamin Logan appears as a character, has responded graciously to questions regarding the methods which she employs in bringing a historical figure to life. I only regret that I lack her talents.

Valuable assistance has been given by librarians, archivists, and curators at the Library of Congress, the Virginia State Library, the Pennsylvania State Library, the Kentucky Historical Society, and the Filson Club. At the University of Michigan's William L. Clements Library, William S. Ewing, curator of manuscripts, provided guidance in the use of the Josiah Harmar Papers. At the University of Chicago's William R. Harper Library, Robert Rosenthal, curator of special collections, made the Durrett Manuscript Collection available. At Washington and Lee University's McCormick Library, the librarian, Henry Coleman, furnished photostatic copies of the William Fleming Papers. County and circuit court clerks in Kentucky, Virginia, and Pennsylvania have helped in using the wealth of historical materials which their offices contain. The collecting of information necessitated a considerable amount of travel, much of which was made possible by a grant from the University of Kentucky Research Fund.

Richard H. Hill, editor of the *Filson Club History Quarterly*, and Charles F. Hinds, former editor of the *Register of the Kentucky Historical Society*, have granted permission to incorporate into this work portions of articles by the author which have appeared in those journals.

The Draper Manuscript Collection, owned by the State

Historical Society of Wisconsin, has been drawn upon extensively through the medium of microfilm. The peculiar pagination employed by Lyman C. Draper would have required the use of superior characters in some citations. This has been avoided by placing these symbols in parentheses and in line with the base numbers.

CHARLES GANO TALBERT

CONTENTS

CHAPTER I

WESTERING TRADITION

IN THE SPRING OF 1775 a Virginian from the Holston River settlements was planting corn near a large spring which sent its water to the Kentucky tributary already known to the Holston people as Dick's River. The activity in which he was engaged provides some indication as to the intentions of this seasoned frontiersman Benjamin Logan. He would return to the Holston for his wife and small son, for his four slaves, and for such personal belongings as could be carried on the backs of horses. Together they would make a two hundred mile journey into the sunset.

Benjamin Logan was heir to a long tradition of westering. Early in the seventeenth century, when James I of England was settling portions of Northern Ireland with natives of the lowland areas of Scotland, from Ayrshire went certain members of the Logan family. A century later David Logan, his wife Jane, and their children Mary and William were on their way to America. Landing at Philadelphia, they, like most of their Scotch-Irish compatriots, migrated westward. They may have tarried briefly in the Cumberland Valley of Pennsylvania, where others of the Logan name had settled. If so, they did not remain long enough for their names to appear in the court records.[1]

The line of settlement advanced quickly to the Allegheny Mountains. Within twenty years after the first mass exodus from Ulster the Scotch-Irish together with some of their Ger-

man neighbors were spilling over into Maryland and on into
the Shenandoah Valley of Virginia. The Virginia Council, in
1730, granted to a Pennsylvania German, Jost Hite, 100,000
acres of land lying west of the Blue Ridge Mountains. In 1736
a grant of 500,000 acres, also in the Great Valley, was made to
Benjamin Borden. Both grants were contingent upon their
being settled within specified time limits. In the case of
Borden's grant the Scotch-Irish were to be encouraged. This
part of Virginia became a portion of the new county of Orange
in 1734.[2]

The name of David Logan first appeared in the court
records of Orange County, Virginia, on June 22, 1738, when
he was one of the defendants in a libel suit brought by a
Presbyterian minister, William Williams. It appeared a second
time on October 26 of the same year when he received the
fixed bounty for a wolf head. On May 22, 1740, Logan,
Alexander Breckinridge, and twelve other heads of families
were present at a session of the Orange County Court. Here
he testified that he had brought himself, his wife, and his
oldest two children from Ireland to Philadelphia and on into
Virginia at his own expense. He took an oath to the effect that
this importation had not on any previous occasion been used
for the obtaining of land.[3] Additional land in Virginia's Great
Valley was purchased by the Logans on November 26, 1742,

---

[1] Wayland F. Dunaway, *The Scotch-Irish of Colonial Pennsylvania* (Chapel
Hill, N. C., 1944), 17-20. William H. Egle (ed.), *Notes and Queries Historical
and Genealogical,* Annual Volume 1900 (Harrisburg, Pa., 1901), 209. Thomas
M. Green, *Historic Families of Kentucky* (Cincinnati, 1889), 117-18. Draper
MSS. 12 C 45(1-3), 47; 3 S 140; 18 S 144.

Green describes the Logans as having been "plain people in Ireland,
accustomed to rely upon themselves for their individual respectability as well
as for the means of subsistence." His suggestion of a close kinship with
Pennsylvania's James Logan, secretary of the province, is unproved.

[2] Dunaway, *The Scotch-Irish,* 102, 105. Thomas K. Cartmell (comp.),
Shenandoah Valley Pioneers and their Descendants (Winchester, Va., 1909),
6-7. Joseph A. Waddell, *Annals of Augusta County, Virginia* (Staunton, Va.,
1902), 27.

[3] Orange County Court Order Book 1, pp. 331, 397. Order Book 2, p. 158.
The headright system which allowed fifty acres of land for each person
transported was of long standing in Virginia.

from the original grantee, Jost Hite. This tract of 860 acres lay on the west side of Buffalo Meadow.[4]

Thus it was on the waters of the Shenandoah and near a tributary of its south fork called North River that the fifth child and second son of David and Jane Logan was born. He was given the name Benjamin in honor of his maternal grandfather, Benjamin McKinley. Young Benjamin had been preceded by Mary, William, Elizabeth, and Margaret. Although his own children did not know the exact date of his birth, a baptismal record kept by John Craig, one of the first Presbyterian ministers in the Valley, provides a fair approximation and shows the relative ages of Benjamin and some of his brothers and sisters. Craig, who ministered to the congregations of the "Old Stone" or Augusta church and the church at Tinkling Spring, baptized Margaret Logan on July 5, 1741, Benjamin on May 1, 1743, Hugh on March 24, 1745, and John on May 10, 1747. It seems evident that the Logan's first son, William, did not live long, because another son of the same name was baptized on July 16, 1749. This record, which covers the years 1740 through 1749, does not include the oldest three children or the youngest son, whose name was Nathaniel.[5]

The region where the Logans lived soon became Augusta County. Carved out of the county of Orange, it held its first court in 1745. The Augusta people were on the edge of the settled portion of Virginia, separated from their eastern neighbors by the Blue Ridge. Indian attacks were not uncommon, and defense was largely in the hands of the Augusta County militia. David Logan served in this organization as a member of Captain James Cathey's company.

On May 18, 1749, James McCarroll told the county court that he feared bodily harm or even loss of his life as a result of a dispute with David Logan and James Underwood. At the

---

[4] Orange County Deed Book 7, pp. 42-44.

[5] Draper MSS. 12 C 45(3); 9 J 184; 3 S 140; 18 S 144. Robert Davidson, *History of the Presbyterian Church in the State of Kentucky* (New York, 1847), 23-24. Florence W. Houston, *Maxwell History and Genealogy* (Indianapolis, 1916), 587-88. Waddell, *Annals*, 38-41, 49-51, 128.

next session of the court each of the accused was placed under a twenty pound peace bond for a year and a day. The trouble seems to have arisen in connection with a debt of about five pounds which the court eventually ordered McCarroll to pay to Logan as the assignee of Underwood. Early in 1750 Logan appeared in court to ask that his method of marking his live-stock be recorded. The justices agreed, listing his mark as a piece cut out of the lower side of the right ear and another out of the upper side of the left ear.[6]

The precarious situation of the people who had settled west of the Blue Ridge was brought more forcibly to their attention in the summer of 1755 when they learned of Braddock's defeat. Hugh McAden, a Presbyterian clergyman who was traveling through the Valley at the time, wrote in his diary that "this, together with the frequent accounts of fresh murders being daily committed upon the frontiers, struck terror to every heart." Pastor John Craig recorded that "people were in dreadful confusion, and discouraged to the highest degree. Some of the richer sort . . . were for flying to a safer part of the country." Although some may have resorted to this method of escape, there were many who did not. At Craig's suggestion the Augusta church, which was built of stone, was converted into a fort by the addition of a surrounding wall.[7] The Logans seem to have been among those who held their ground.

Early in 1757, David Logan died. Benjamin, the oldest living son, was not quite fifteen years of age, and the Logan family remained in Augusta County for several years.[8]

Conditions in the Valley of Virginia at this time did not encourage the acquisition of an education. In the words of

[6] Augusta County Court Order Book 2, pp. 117, 156, 347, 529. Draper MSS. 31 S 482. Lyman Chalkley, *Chronicles of the Scotch-Irish Settlement in Virginia* (Rosslyn, Va., 1912), II, 507-508. Henry Howe (ed.), *Historical Collections of Virginia* (Charleston, S. C., 1845), 177. Joseph A. Waddell, "Militia Companies in Augusta County, in 1742," in *Virginia Magazine of History and Biography*, VIII (1900-1901), 279. Waddell, *Annals*, 36-37, 45-49.

[7] Quoted in William H. Foote, *Sketches of North Carolina* (New York, 1846), 163. Waddell, *Annals*, 105.

[8] Draper MSS. 18 S 145. Chalkley, *Chronicles*, I, 76.

one who knew Benjamin Logan as an adult: "His mind was
not only unadorned by science, but almost unaided by letters."
Nevertheless, it is impossible to follow his career without
finding some basis for the opinion that "at home he was trained
in the principles of morality, religion and self-reliance."[9]

It is likely that Logan would have been enrolled in a militia
company at the age of sixteen. In 1764 he participated in
Colonel Henry Bouquet's Indian campaign as a sergeant.[10]

When Benjamin Logan became of age, he as the eldest son
inherited the entire estate of his father. Because the land was
not subject to division, he sold it and shared the proceeds with
the other members of his family. He then purchased 160 acres
of land on North River near the mouth of Cook's Creek from
William Brown for thirty pounds. Three years later, on November 19, 1766, he sold this tract to Jacob Hornbarrier for forty
pounds.[11]

In 1765 he purchased 400 acres of land from John McMahan
for one hundred pounds. It too lay on North River on "the
next spring branch below the mouth of Cook's Creek." He is
said to have joined with one of his brothers in the purchase of
a home for their mother on a branch of the James River. The
Augusta County records show Hugh Logan's buying 115 acres
of land on the James on October 18, 1768, and John Logan's
buying 200 acres on August 12, 1769. It is probable that Jane
Logan lived with Hugh, as he remained in this area until near
the end of the American Revolution, while John soon followed
Benjamin to more sparsely settled regions.[12]

Those members of the Logan family who moved to the
James soon found themselves in the new county of Botetourt,

[9] Humphrey Marshall, *The History of Kentucky* (Frankfort, 1824), I, 29.
Bessie T. Conkwright, "A Sketch of the Life and Times of General Benjamin
Logan," in *Register of the Kentucky State Historical Society*, XIV (1916), 22.

[10] Draper MSS. 18 S 145. Waddell, *Annals*, 198. Marshall, *Kentucky*, I, 29.

[11] Augusta County Deed Book 11, pp. 288-90; Deed Book 13, pp. 100-103.
Draper MSS. 12 C 45(3).

[12] Augusta County Deed Book 12, pp. 243-45. Chalkley, *Chronicles*, III,
432. Marshall, *Kentucky*, I, 29. F. B. Kegley (ed.), *Kegley's Virginia
Frontier* (Roanoke, Va., 1938), 347-48.

but Benjamin remained in Augusta for the time being. On March 1, 1771, the records of the latter county show that for fifteen pounds Henry Davis bound himself to Benjamin Logan for one year and ten months.[13]

In the fall of the same year Logan visited the new settlements on the Holston River. He obtained lodging at the home of Alexander Montgomery and inspected a tract of land belonging to Edmund Pendleton of Caroline County. He found the property very desirable and wrote to William Preston, Pendleton's agent, expressing a desire to buy it. The arrangements were not completed at this time, and Logan returned to Augusta County. He either was undecided about moving to the Holston or was speculating on a small scale. In February, 1772, he purchased another piece of Augusta land, which he sold in three tracts, 108 acres to David Nelson, Sr., on March 17, 1772, 110 acres to James Donnald on the following day, and 50 acres to Wendle Butt on March 18, 1773.[14]

In the summer of 1769 a Scotch-Irish couple William and Jane Montgomery had sold their farm on the South Branch of the Potomac and moved southward to the Holston. Their family included a daughter named Ann, then seventeen years of age. She is said to have rejected one suitor, James Knox, who had been one of the first settlers in the Holston region. Shortly afterward, perhaps to allow his feelings to heal, Knox left for Kentucky at the head of a party which came to be known as the Long Hunters.[15]

Benjamin Logan and Ann Montgomery may have met when he visited the Holston Settlements in the fall of 1771. It was in 1772 that they were married. Ann was twenty years old and Benjamin was thirty. In 1845 one of their daughters expressed

[13] Botetourt County Court Order Book for 1770-71, Part I, p. 1. Augusta County Deed Book 17, pp. 160-61.

[14] Deposition of John Montgomery, quoted in Chalkley, *Chronicles*, II, 145. Benjamin Logan to William Preston, October 11, 1771, Draper MSS. 2 QQ 127-28. Augusta County Deed Book 18, pp. 146-48, 153-55; Deed Book 19, pp. 204-206.

[15] Draper MSS. 12 C 45(3-4); 18 S 163-64. Waddell, *Annals*, 319-21.

the belief that the marriage took place in Rockingham County, which was not founded until 1778. They may have been married at the home of one of Ann's relatives in that part of Augusta County which afterward became Rockingham. The Holston region in which they established their home was soon included in the new county of Fincastle. It was founded in the year of their marriage and held its first court at Fort Chiswell on January 5, 1773. The next day Logan presented and had recorded his deed to the land which he had bought from Edmund Pendleton. It lay on Beaver Creek, a Holston tributary, and contained 309 acres. The price was £82 5s. 7d.[16]

One other member of Logan's family was living on the Holston at this time. His oldest sister Mary, her husband Samuel Briggs, and their children were living near Black's Station at the site of present-day Abingdon, Virginia. His younger brother John soon brought his bride Jane, whose maiden name was McClure, to the same community.[17]

There were two Presbyterian congregations on the Holston at this time, one at Ebbing and the other at Sinking Springs. On January 5, 1773, these two united in issuing a call to Reverend Charles Cummings. He had been licensed as a clergyman at Tinkling Spring nine years earlier and may have been known to Benjamin Logan, who was one of the 120 heads of families whose names appear on the petition. The call was accepted, and Cummings soon moved to the new community.[18]

The order books of the Fincastle County Court contain several references to Benjamin Logan. The Virginia government was encouraging the raising of hemp, and Logan produced a crop in 1772. On May 4, 1773, he presented to the court a certificate for 1,579 pounds of winter rotted hemp,

[16] Draper MSS. 12 C 45(1-4); 9 J 184(1)-185; 18 S 145; 32 S 67. Fincastle County Deed Book A. pp. 15-16. Fincastle County Court Order Book 1, p. 1. The Fincastle County records are in the Montgomery County Courthouse at Christiansburg, Virginia. Chalkley, *Chronicles*, II, 95. Howe, *Virginia*, 385n.

[17] Draper MSS. 12 C 46; 9 J 184(1); 18 S 144.

[18] Draper MSS. 9 DD 75. Lewis P. Summers (ed.), *Annals of Southwest Virginia, 1769-1800* (Abingdon, Va., 1929), 1354-55. Waddell, *Annals*, 92.

which was "ordered to be certified to his Excellency the
Governor."[19] On September 8, 1773, Logan, together with
several other residents of the county, was ordered to "clear the
nearest and Best way from Saml. Briggs on the Eighteen Mile
Creek to James Bryant's on the Eleven Mile Creek." On March
2, 1774, he was named to a similar group which was ordered to
consider the possibility of a road "from the Town House to
the Eighteen Mile Creek," and to "view the Several ways
proposed for said Road and make a report of the Convenience
and Inconveniences attending the same respectively and the
distances to the next court." At the May session of the court
Logan served on the grand jury. At the same session the court
considered petitions from some of the inhabitants of the Beaver
Creek section for a road in that part of the county and ordered
"that Benj. Logan open a Road from James Fulkerson's to the
Wagon Road at James Blacks the Best and most convenient
way." He also was to be overseer of this road. The court
ordered "that he with the Tithables thereof keep the same in
good repair according to Law."[20]

    In the summer of 1774 the governor of Virginia, Lord
Dunmore, called upon the militia commanders in the Valley
to furnish men for a campaign against the Indians. The
Fincastle militia was commanded by Colonel William Preston,
who held the commission of county lieutenant, and consisted
of a single regiment with John Byrd as colonel, William
Christian as lieutenant colonel, and Arthur Campbell as major.
Benjamin Logan, who had served as a sergeant under Bouquet
in 1764 and who may have acquired additional experience in
minor frontier engagements in the intervening ten years, was
the lieutenant in Captain William Cocke's company.[21]

    In March, 1774, Cocke had been invited to Williamsburg by

    [19] Fincastle County Court Order Book 1, p. 35. Draper MSS. 32 S 68.
    [20] Fincastle County Court Order Book 2, pp. 1, 3. Summers, *Annals*, 597,
615, 623-24.
    [21] Draper MSS. 32 S 68-69. William Preston to Evan Shelby, September 2,
1774, in Reuben G. Thwaites and Louise P. Kellogg (eds.), *Documentary
History of Dunmore's War, 1774* (Madison, Wis., 1905), 107. Waddell,
Annals, 219.

Lord Dunmore, who treated him politely but at the same time questioned him about the course that he would follow in the event of a rebellion against the Crown. The governor apparently had been impressed by the young frontiersman, who three months earlier had been tried by Dunmore and his council on a charge of treason and had won an acquittal. According to his own statement, Cocke told Dunmore that in the event of war he would be found defending the liberties of the colonists. Although he may not have been so outspoken as he afterward claimed, Cocke's subsequent actions show his loyalty to the American cause to have been above question. At the time, however, Colonel Preston may have had some doubts. It is not likely that invitations to visit the governor were received often by captains of militia in frontier counties. Perhaps the governor, with promises of promotion or gold, had won Cocke's allegiance. And so when orders were prepared for drafting a portion of Cocke's company for service on Dunmore's expedition they were sent, not to Cocke, but to Logan. In a letter to Colonel Preston, Cocke complained about this procedure. He pointed out that the other captains had been allowed to go on this campaign or at least to select the officers and men who were to go. "It is Mr. Logan," he wrote, "that is Captain in fact & I only Serve to See him Command." With a frontiersman's disregard for military subordination, he added: "[I] hope his command will meet with Success tho Shall Expect for the Future that my company will be commanded by me."[22]

The Fincastle militiamen who were drafted for this campaign were placed under the command of Lieutenant Colonel William Christian. They were to join the men from Botetourt, led by Colonel William Fleming, and the men from Augusta, commanded by Colonel Charles Lewis, at the Big Savannah near the present-day town of Lewisburg, West Virginia. There

[22] Draper MSS. 5 B 72-73; 32 C 84(a-b). William Cocke to William Preston, Draper MSS. 3 QQ 87. The date on this letter has been destroyed. A notation on the back, which appears to have been made by Lyman C. Draper, says: "Aug. or Sept. 1774 Ben Logan Lieut of Cocke's Company & goes on Expedition."

General Andrew Lewis was to assume command of the three
groups. The Fincastle companies were scattered over a large
area, and so considerable time was spent in collecting men and
supplies. Early in July, Colonel Christian marched from the
Holston, going through Moccasin Gap to Captain William
Russell's fort on the Clinch River. Flour was brought to
this point on packhorses, but meat was so scarce that Christian
may have wished that he had accepted Logan's offer to drive
forty cattle from the Holston. While at Russell's, Christian's
men were joined by one more Fincastle company, that of
Captain William Campbell.[23]

Before the Fincastle detachment could reach the meeting
place, Andrew Lewis had received orders from Dunmore to
move his men to Point Pleasant at the junction of the Kanawha
and the Ohio. Lewis reached that place ahead of Dunmore,
and on October 10, before the governor could arrive with
reinforcements, the Indians struck. Losses were heavy on
both sides, but the white men held their ground and the
enemy retreated across the Ohio. The Fincastle men reached
the scene of the battle about midnight. They took part in
Dunmore's invasion of the Indian country, but no more fighting
occurred. The governor's treaty with the red men, made at
his camp on the Scioto River, was criticized by some of the
frontiersmen, but was praised by others as opening the way
for the settlement of Kentucky. The Shawnee, nearest Indians
to the northward, seemed to have given up their claim to the
region, and the Cherokee to the southward were distant.[24]

Logan returned to the Holston in early October to find that
all was well with Ann and their son David, who had been born
on April 10.

Soon after the Fincastle men returned to their homes, Major
Arthur Campbell received a copy of the nonimportation,
nonexportation, and nonconsumptive agreement which had

[23] Draper MSS. 59 J 309. William Christian to William Preston, July 12,
1774, Draper MSS. 3 QQ 63.
[24] Draper MSS. 59 J 310. John Floyd to William Preston, October 16, 1774,
Draper MSS. 17 CC 161-64. Waddell, *Annals,* 222.

been approved by the Continental Congress on October 20. Thirty-eight Fincastle residents expressed their opposition to British colonial policy by signing this agreement. One of these was Benjamin Logan.[25]

[25] Arthur Campbell to William Preston, October 13, 1774, Draper MSS. 3 QQ 120. Draper MSS. 12 C 44; 18 S 145; 48 J 8.

CHAPTER II

ST. ASAPH'S, KENTUCKY

VIRGINIANS HAD LONG BEEN interested in the region known as Kentucky. In 1750 Thomas Walker, representing the Loyal Land Company, had led a party of explorers to this new country by way of the Cumberland Gap. Down the Ohio in the following year came Christopher Gist representing the Ohio Land Company. Although Kentucky had become something of a buffer state separating the northern and the southern Indians, Gist found a few Shawnee still living on the south bank of the Ohio opposite the mouth of the Scioto. The Indian trader John Finley encountered Shawnee in central Kentucky as late as 1753, but their camp seems to have been more of a trading post than a permanent settlement. It was Finley who, meeting Daniel Boone on General Edward Braddock's ill-fated expedition, told Boone about Kentucky. In 1767 Boone left his home in the Yadkin Valley of North Carolina with a desire to see this new land. He became "confused" in the valley of the Big Sandy and did not reach the "great meadow" that Finley had described, but in 1769 with Finley as his guide Boone's wishes were fulfilled. From the Holston Settlements, James Knox led his Long Hunters to Kentucky in 1770 and visited the valleys of the Kentucky, the Cumberland, and the Green rivers.

The British Proclamation of 1763 forbidding settlement west of the Appalachian divide may never have been intended as a permanent policy, for within a few years British agents were negotiating with the Indians for territory, much of which lay in the Ohio Valley. At Fort Stanwix in 1768 the Iroquois surrendered extensive claims, including those to lands lying to the south of the Ohio. At Hard Labor in the same year the Cherokee gave up their claims lying north of a line crossing the Valley of Virginia from Tryon Mountain in the Blue Ridge to Chiswell's Lead Mines on New River and east of the New and Kanawha rivers. White men already had settled on the Cherokee side of this line, and so in 1770 another change was made. In the Treaty of Lochaber the Cherokee agreed to a line running from a point six miles east of the Long Island of the Holston River to the mouth of the Kanawha. When this line was run by John Donelson in 1771, it went instead, apparently with the connivance of some of the Cherokee chiefs, to the Kentucky River and down that stream to its confluence with the Ohio. This created the impression among Virginians that settlement of that area which lay east of the Kentucky River would not be opposed by the Cherokee.[1]

Virginia surveyors were in Kentucky in 1773 and 1774 marking off military grants as well as claims for themselves and for others who had employed them for that purpose. Some of these men returned to their homes in time to participate in Dunmore's War. Among those who took part in this Indian campaign were James Harrod and some of the men who in June, 1774, had been with him in the founding of Kentucky's first settlement, Harrodstown. This was located on the waters of Salt River, but only six miles from the Kentucky River.

Letters and journals indicate that there was much talk about Kentucky among Dunmore's men. Those who had been there were plied with questions, and many who had not seen this region expressed a desire to visit it in the following spring, "not doubting but they would be deemed proprietors by occupancy of at least some valuable tracts."[2]

[1] Robert S. Cotterill, The Southern Indians (Norman, Okla., 1954), 34-35.
[2] William Christian to William Preston, July 12, 1774, Draper MSS. 3 QQ 63. Draper MSS. 15 CC 157-58; 60 J 383.

One party, led by captains Evan Shelby and William Russell, considered the possibility of returning from the campaign by way of Kentucky. These men had spoken to Daniel Boone about bringing horses and meeting them at the mouth of Dick's River, a tributary of the Kentucky, about November 15. The project was abandoned, but Major Arthur Campbell, who saw to the defense of the frontiers of Fincastle while Dunmore's expedition was in progress and who had not learned of the change of plans, wrote to Colonel Preston to ask his advice about allowing Boone to go. Campbell suggested, with obvious reference to William Cocke's complaint about Logan being selected to command his company, that Cocke be substituted for Boone, "as he is so hot for the fatigues of marching."[3]

Although Logan may have heard Kentucky discussed during Dunmore's War, he did not have to depend entirely upon this source of information. He had been on the Holston when James Knox and his Long Hunters returned as if from the grave. Knox had spoken so favorably of this new country that Logan had decided to see it for himself. He, like so many others, may have assumed that Dunmore's Treaty following those with the Iroquois and the Cherokee made this venture reasonably safe.[4]

In the meantime some North Carolinians were displaying an interest in Kentucky, and on August 27, 1774, the Louisa Company was formed by Richard Henderson, John Williams, Thomas Hart, Nathaniel Hart, John Luttrell, and William Johnston. With the addition of three more stockholders, James Hogg, David Hart, and Leonard Bullock, early in 1775, the name was changed to the Transylvania Company. About the same time Daniel Boone was hired as the company's explorer and guide.

In March, Henderson met with some of the Cherokee chiefs

[3] Arthur Campbell to William Preston, October 9, 1774, in Thwaites and Kellogg (eds.), *Dunmore's War*, 240. The spelling of Dick's River has been shortened to "Dix."

[4] Draper MSS. 12 CC 22-22(1); 8 J 146; 9 J 184(1), 202; 17 J 87(1); 15 CC 157-58.

at Sycamore Shoals on the Watauga River. There he purchased the claim of that tribe to a tract of land bounded by the Cumberland, Ohio, and Kentucky rivers and the crest of Powell's Mountain. An additional deed was obtained to a strip of land leading from the Holston to the border of the company's purchase.[5]

Boone with twenty axmen was sent ahead to cut a road to the Kentucky River. Beyond Powell's Valley the best that they could do was to blaze a trail. Henderson soon followed with about thirty men. After some delay in Powell's Valley, this group on April 8 passed through Cumberland Gap and entered Kentucky. They met several small parties which were fleeing from reported Indian hostility, and only a few individuals could be persuaded to join with Henderson and return.

Before Henderson left Powell's Valley, a messenger from Boone had arrived telling of an Indian attack on March 25 in which two of his men had been killed and a third wounded. Henderson's journal and the letters that he wrote to those of his partners who had remained in North Carolina reveal his constant fear that the next party encountered would be that of Boone in full retreat. But Boone held his ground, and on April 20 the two groups met on the bank of the Kentucky River at the mouth of Otter Creek. It must have been in appreciation of the job which Boone had done that Henderson decided to call the site Boonesborough.[6]

One of the early historians of Kentucky, Humphrey Marshall, stated that Henderson was joined in Powell's Valley by Benjamin Logan. According to this account Logan traveled with Henderson for a time, but, not approving of Henderson's plans, he veered to the westward and established his own settlement

---

[5] Draper MSS. 6 S 9; 1 CC 2-9, 17. Before the end of the following year some of the Cherokee are said to have stated that it had been their belief that Henderson had been sent by the government to purchase their lands. (See William Christian to Patrick Henry, October 23, 1776, Draper MSS. 13 S 207-12.)

[6] "Richard Henderson's Journal," Draper MSS. 1 CC 21-170. John Floyd to William Preston, April 15, 1775, Draper MSS. 17 CC 165-66. Draper MSS. 1 CC 198, 208-14.

on the waters of Dick's River.[7] This story has been repeated many times, often with additions. The Hazel Patch on the trail to the Kentucky River is named as the scene of the parting, a quarrel is said to have occurred, and the name of Logan's settlement is given as St. Asaph's. Unfortunately, the journals of Henderson and of William Calk, a member of his party, throw no light on the question.

Contemporary accounts of the founding of St. Asaph's read quite differently from that of Marshall. On April 15, the day on which Logan and Henderson are supposed to have disagreed at the Hazel Patch, a group of surveyors and adventurers was ready to leave the Holston for Kentucky. The leader was John Floyd, a deputy surveyor of Fincastle County, who had surveyed in Kentucky in the summer of 1774. In this group were John Todd, Alexander Spotswood Dandridge, Jacob Baughman, Thomas Carpenter, Joseph Drake, Matthew Jouett, Patrick Jordan, and twenty-three others. By April 21 they had reached Powell's Valley. In spite of reports of Indian hostility to white settlement in Kentucky, they decided to continue. These men certainly would have followed the trail of Boone and Henderson as far as possible, but it is evident that they left it soon after crossing Rockcastle River. On May 1 they camped at a spring in the valley of Dick's River near the present town of Stanford, Kentucky. Deciding to make this their base of operations, they gave to the place the name St. Asaph's. It was the name of a Welsh saint, of a cathedral town in Wales, and of King David's chief musician, supposed author of some of the Psalms.

Benjamin Logan also came to Kentucky in the spring of 1775. He could have come with Henderson, but he started from the upper Holston region as did Floyd and ended his journey at St. Asaph's rather than at Boonesborough. It is likely that he was a member of Floyd's party. He raised corn at St. Asaph's that year, as did several of Floyd's men. On the basis of this he

---

[7] Marshall, *Kentucky*, I, 30. Marshall is said to have interviewed Logan (see Draper MSS. 18 S 167). Nevertheless, his account of Logan's career is not sufficiently accurate to warrant accepting this portion without question.

later proved his claim to 1,400 acres of land at that site. Richard Henderson's journal shows very clearly that he considered John Floyd as the leader at St. Asaph's and John Todd as his second-in-command. The position of leadership which Logan later attained at this place has caused some writers to assume that he was in command there from the very beginning.[8]

There were several reasons for the raising of corn at St. Asaph's and elsewhere in Kentucky. It could be grown with very little clearing of the land, and it provided food which could be prepared in various ways. There also was reason to believe that the growing of corn could be used as a basis for establishing a title to land, and in this belief the settlers were not disappointed.

In the meantime there was the claim of the Transylvania Company to be considered. Two days after his arrival at St. Asaph's, Floyd went to Boonesborough to discuss matters with Henderson. The head of the Transylvania Company, whose huge land claim was questioned by Colonel William Preston and other prominent Virginians, naturally was suspicious of Floyd and his associates. He believed, however, that it would be wise to gain their friendship, as the claims which they wished to make would lie for the most part in the region which Henderson considered the property of his company. Although he considered it rather late for planting corn, he agreed to recognize their land claims on that basis.

If the raising of corn should not be sufficient to establish a claim either under the government of Virginia or under the proprietary government which Richard Henderson hoped to establish, Benjamin Logan had yet another possibility. The

[8] Floyd to Preston, April 15, 1775, Draper MSS. 17 CC 165; April 21, 1775, Draper MSS. 17 CC 167-69; and May 30, 1775, Draper MSS. 17 CC 180. Deposition of Patrick Jordon in Mrs. William B. Ardery (ed.), *Kentucky Court and Other Records* (Lexington, 1932), 106. "Certificate Book of the Virginia Land Commission of 1779-80," in *Register of the Kentucky State Historical Society*, XXI (1923), 15. Draper MSS. 3 B 184-213; 12 C 45(1); 6 J 89-108; 59 J 24; 60 J 385; 32 S 68; 33 S 270-75; 1 CC 21-170, 198-99; 26 CC 76.

Royal Proclamation of 1763 had promised land for service in the French and Indian War. On March 15, 1774, Lord Dunmore issued a certificate for such a grant to Sergeant William Bell, who was to receive 200 acres. On May 4, 1774, Bell, who had asked that his land be located in Fincastle County, decided to sell his certificate to Logan. On June 7, 1775, John Floyd surveyed the 200 acres that Logan had selected. It lay about two miles from the Kentucky River on a branch of Floyd's Creek.[9]

The total population of Kentucky at this time was estimated at three hundred. James Harrod had returned with forty-two men to the Salt River tributary on which he had started a settlement the year before. There were four settlements or camps which were looked upon by Richard Henderson as towns, Boonesborough, St. Asaph's, Boiling Spring, which Harrod had just established, and Harrodstown, now beginning to be known as Harrodsburg, where the current leader was a North Carolinian, Thomas Slaughter. Scattered over a wide area other men were planting corn and building cabins. Some of these were associated with one or another of the four settlements, while others were operating alone. Isaac Campbell and Benjamin Pettit were near St. Asaph's, Richard Calloway, his nephew Flanders Calloway, and James Estill were on Otter Creek, John Hinkston and John Martin were on the South Fork of Licking River, William Gillespie was on Boone's Creek, and James Knox was on Beargrass Creek. Squire Boone, Daniel's brother, left Harrodsburg long enough to mark a claim in what is today Shelby County.[10]

When John Floyd made his first visit to Boonesborough, Henderson explained the plan of government which he had in mind for his Transylvania Colony. A few days later James

[9] Draper MSS. 1 CC 34, 41-44. "Kentucky Land Office Military Surveys," 278 pp., bound photostats, Margaret I. King Library, University of Kentucky, 136-37, 139, 220.

[10] Draper MSS. 1 CC 203. Floyd to Preston, May 30, 1775, Draper MSS. 17 CC 180-81. "Preemption Books of Virginia Land Commission of 1779;" Draper MSS. 60 J 379-89. Deposition of Squire Boone in Shelby County Court Depositions, p. 5. "Certificate Book," 27.

Harrod and Thomas Slaughter visited Boonesborough and received a similar explanation. Each settlement was asked to elect delegates to a convention which would be held at Boonesborough beginning on May 23. Those chosen to represent the men at St. Asaph's were John Floyd, John Todd, Alexander Spotswood Dandridge, and Samuel Wood. Those historians who have treated Logan as the founder of St. Asaph's and as the leader of that settlement from 1775 on have been faced with the problem of explaining the failure of the residents to elect him as one of their delegates to the Boonesborough Convention. Their usual procedure has been to mention the quarrel that he is supposed to have had with Henderson and to imply that he could have been elected but refused to be a candidate because of his opposition to the type of government which Henderson was trying to establish. The story of the quarrel at the Hazel Patch seems to have little foundation and may have been invented to supply a needed link in a chain of proof.[11]

Those delegates who did go to Boonesborough, falling under the spell of Richard Henderson, established for the proprietary colony of Transylvania a government which one historian has described as "democratic in form but not in reality." The executive power was vested in the proprietors, and they retained control of the legislative branch as well. In a three house assembly, the members of the lower house would be chosen by the people. The middle house was to consist of not more than twelve members, all of whom must be landowners. Because there was no indication to the contrary, it is assumed that these men would be chosen by the proprietors. The upper house would consist of the proprietors themselves. Thus, as Richard Henderson's brother, Nathaniel, afterward explained, the Transylvania Company could kill any laws passed by the settlers.[12]

[11] Floyd to Preston, May 30, 1775, Draper MSS. 17 CC 180. "Henderson's Journal," 45-46, 55(1-2), 78-81. Draper MSS. 1 CC 202-206.
[12] John D. Barnhart, *Valley of Democracy* (Bloomington, Ind., 1953), 52. William S. Lester, *The Transylvania Colony* (Spencer, Ind., 1935), 97-98.

After planting his corn, Logan started early in June for his home on the Holston. He may have gone by way of Boonesborough, as Henderson recorded in his journal that a party from St. Asaph's arrived there on June 3 en route to their homes. If these people expected to increase their number at Boonesborough before undertaking the trip through the wilderness, they probably were not disappointed. Henderson's journal for June 9 states that many of his people were selling their lots and leaving, and a group of young men left that day after refusing his offer to allow them to enter claims to land without the usual requirement of raising corn.

While Logan was at home with his wife and son, he went to Fort Chiswell to have entered in the records of Fincastle County the 200 acres of Kentucky land that John Floyd had surveyed for him. This would seem to indicate that he was in the group which left Boonesborough on June 9, for it was not until June 7 that the survey was made. Logan also took the time to visit those members of his family who still lived near the forks of the James. There he saw his young cousin, Ebenezer McKinley, and tried without success to persuade McKinley to return to Kentucky with him.

Logan's intention to make his home in Kentucky was further demonstrated on June 26 by the sale of his 309-acre farm to John Teeter for 100 pounds. This land, on a tributary of the Holston called Beaver Creek or Shallow Creek, had been purchased from Edmund Pendleton in January, 1773.[13]

During the summer the population of Kentucky was greatly reduced, and St. Asaph's may have been deserted except for occasional campers. On June 5 Henderson was still thinking in terms of four settlements—Boonesborough, Harrodsburg, Boiling Spring, and St. Asaph's—and made out civil and military commissions accordingly, but in a letter written on June 12 he listed the known settlements in Kentucky and made no mention

---

13 Fincastle County Court Order Book 2, p. 143. Fincastle County Deed Book A, p. 138; Fincastle County Land Book, 1774-75, p. 48. Draper MSS. 4 B 13-14; 3 S 140-41; 32 S 69; 1 CC 84. Summers, *Annals*, 643, 670.

of St. Asaph's. Floyd and his surveyors were at this time northeast of the Kentucky River. Floyd may have considered St. Asaph's to be his base of operations, but it is unlikely that he returned often to so distant a point.

James Nourse, who visited Kentucky in June, 1775, thought that Harrodsburg and Boonesborough were the only settlements then occupied. He traveled from one of these to the other by a route that would have taken him very close to Boiling Spring and St. Asaph's, but he made no mention of either in his journal. In July, Richard Henderson made a similar trip, visiting St. Asaph's, Boiling Spring, and Harrodsburg. He was not specific about the condition of these places except in the case of Harrodsburg, where he recorded having found only five men, who had been left to look after the corn. It may be that a similar situation existed at the other two settlements, for it is certain that many men had returned to their homes as Logan had done, and others were members of surveying and exploring parties such as Floyd's on the Kentucky and the Elkhorn, and Thomas Slaughter's on Green River. By September, however, families were moving to Kentucky. Daniel Boone, Richard Calloway, and William Poage took their wives and children to Boonesborough, while Hugh McGary, Richard Hogan, and Thomas Denton chose Harrodsburg.[14]

By the fall of 1775 Logan and his former company commander, William Cocke, were commanding separate companies of Fincastle militia. On November 8 he was instructed by the Committee of Safety for Fincastle County to prepare a list of the names of the men in his company and to submit this to Major Anthony Bledsoe or Captain Isaac Shelby. This was an order from the Virginia Convention at Williamsburg which had started the process of transforming the colony into a state.

Logan did not return to Kentucky until late in the fall. A

[14] Draper MSS. 4 B 17-18, 23-25; 1 CC 85, 198-99; 26 CC 76. James Nourse, "Journey to Kentucky in 1775," in *Journal of American History,* XIX (1925), 121, 259-60. See also a statement of a daughter of William Poage quoted in Archer B. Hulbert, *Boone's Wilderness Road* (Cleveland, 1903), 117-18.

letter which he carried to John Floyd was delivered on
November 28. He is said to have brought livestock on this trip
and to have left it in the care of William Gillespie. It is likely
that this included both cattle and hogs, as Logan is known to
have had cattle in Kentucky in 1777, and a traveler reported
eating ham at his cabin at a very early date. The idea that
William Gillespie was the one to whom Logan's property was
entrusted may have been based on the fact that Gillespie later
proved his claim to 1,400 acres of land adjacent to Logan's.
This land, however, was on Boone's Creek, a few miles from
the Kentucky, and the Logan land that it touched was the
200-acre military tract which Floyd had surveyed and not his
claim at St. Asaph's.[15]

The date of Logan's second return to the Holston is uncertain.
He certainly would have remained in Kentucky long enough
to harvest the corn that he had planted in the spring, but it is
probable that he was back with his family by Christmas. Late
in February, 1776, they started for Kentucky, arriving at St.
Asaph's on March 8. With the Logans came Benjamin Pettit,
his wife and children, and Logan's Negro woman Molly, with
her three sons, Matt, Dave, and Isaac, the youngest of whom
was a little older than David Logan.

At St. Asaph's there were two springs between 200 and 300
yards apart. It was near the smaller spring that Logan had
built his cabin. The Pettits located about ten miles away
near the headwaters of Hanging Fork of Dick's River. Both
men were anxious to get their crops started and to clear more
land, and they made a practice of trading work. Logan, with
the Negro boys Matt and Dave, would spend a week at
Pettit's, and Pettit in turn would bring his two older boys and
work at Logan's. This left Ann and David and the Negroes
Molly and Isaac without protection for half of the time. As
yet their cabin had no door, a blanket serving the purpose.

---

[15] Draper MSS. 1 CC 199; 11 CC 273; 26 CC 76. Fincastle and Montgomery
County Revolutionary War Records, 1775-1783, p. 1. Marshall, *Kentucky*, I,
30. "Certificate Book," 27.

Plenty of food was available in the woods. Logan often killed a buffalo, a deer, or a turkey within fifty yards of the cabin. Wolves, attracted by the scent of fresh meat, sometimes frightened the women and children on the nights when they were alone. Even after the weather became warm, a fire was kept burning all night as a precautionary measure.

Besides attending to his own interests, Logan marked tracts of land for his brothers and planted corn on each tract. Hugh Logan's claim lay near the Hanging Fork, three or four miles south of St. Asaph's. John's was to the east on a tributary of Dick's River which came to be known as Logan's Creek. This land lay at the mouth of a branch that was fed by the springs at St. Asaph's. William Logan's tract was next to Benjamin's, and Nathaniel's lay on Logan's Creek about two miles below the mouth of St. Asaph's Branch.

Other settlers were building their cabins and raising their corn in Kentucky in the summer of 1776. William Whitley was on Cedar Creek about two miles west of the Crab Orchard, and his brother-in-law, George Clark, was nearby. The Bryans— Joseph, George, Morgan, William, Samuel, and James—were on the North Fork of the Elkhorn. Jesse Benton was on Silver Creek, and John Todd, who had been at St. Asaph's the year before, was building a cabin on the West Branch of Hickman's Creek. John Strode was near the headwaters of the South Fork of Licking, and James Strode was on Howard's Creek. Among the others were John Floyd, John Bowman, and Leonard Helm.[16]

By this time opposition to the pretensions of Richard Henderson and the Transylvania Company had become strong. In December, 1775, a petition had been drawn up and signed by eighty-eight residents and intended residents of Kentucky. In May of the following year it was presented to the Virginia Convention. This petition spoke of the hardships which the settling of the country had involved and raised strenuous

[16] Draper MSS. 4 B 64; 12 C 44; 60 J 379-86; 18 S 146-47. "Certificate Book," 14-15, 43.

objection to the claims and practices of the Transylvania Company. It charged also that the delegates to the Boonesborough Convention of May, 1775, had been "overawed by the presence of Mr. Henderson" and had approved measures which they now heartily disliked. The petitioners asked that the people living in Kentucky "be taken under the protection of the honorable Convention of the Colony of Virginia, of which we can not help thinking ourselves still a part."

The movement against Henderson was furthered at a meeting held at Harrodsburg on June 6, 1776. It had been called by George Rogers Clark, who expected to urge the election of deputies to go to Williamsburg and treat with the Virginia Convention. If favorable terms could be secured, the Kentucky settlements might throw in their lot with Virginia. If not, an independent government which could handle its own defense might soon be attainable. There certainly was ample land in Kentucky and it could be given free of charge to those who would come and settle upon it.[17]

Unfortunately for Clark's plan, he did not reach Harrodsburg until the voting was completed. Instead of deputies with power to negotiate, he and John Gabriel Jones had been elected as delegates to the convention from the western parts of Fincastle County. They would have authority to do no more than to ask for Virginia's protection and to urge that the region known as Kentucky be formed into a new county. A petition was prepared which criticized the pretensions of the Transylvania Company, expressed the belief that the Kentucky settlements lay within the charter limits of Virginia, and begged that Clark and Jones be accepted as members of the convention. A committee of twenty-one members was elected to maintain law and order. On June 20 this committee, of which Jones was chairman, drew up an additional petition. This one declared

[17] "George Rogers Clark's Memoir," Draper MSS. 59 J 2-4. Draper MSS. 4 B 71-72. Thomas P. Abernethy, *Western Lands and the American Revolution* (New York, 1937), 162-63. James Hall, *Sketches of History, Life and Manners in the West* (Philadelphia, 1835), II, 236-40. George W. Ranck, *Boonesborough*, Filson Club Publications No. 16 (Louisville, 1901), 241-44.

that the creation of a county government would help to prevent Kentucky from becoming a haven for Loyalists. It added that it would be unwise to allow "such a respectable body of prime riflemen to remain even in a state of neutrality."

Benjamin Logan played no direct part in this movement. Resistance to Henderson centered at Harrodsburg, and St. Asaph's was nearly twenty miles away. Its consequences, however, were to bring him gradually to a position of leadership both in civil and in military affairs.[18]

In the meantime the Kentucky people had more immediate worries. In the afternoon of July 14, 1776, the daughters of Richard Calloway, Betsy and Frances, and Daniel Boone's second daughter, Jemima, took the only canoe at Boonesborough and set out for a short ride on the waters of the Kentucky. In a bend just below the settlement the current carried them close to the opposite shore. There they were seized by six Indians, three Shawnee and three Cherokee. A party was formed to go in pursuit, but the lack of a boat caused some delay in crossing the river. By nightfall the pursuers had covered only five miles. They continued at daybreak, but the trail often was lost in the thick growth of cane. The Indians and their prisoners were overtaken before they reached the Licking River. The three Shawnee were killed, but the Cherokee made their escape. Of greater importance was the fact that the girls were rescued unharmed.[19]

At this time there were three forts in the process of construction. The one at Boonesborough had been started soon after the arrival of Henderson and his settlers. After many months of neglect the work had been resumed and now was nearing completion. A fort at Harrodsburg and one at the Royal Spring on the Elkhorn were well along. The incident at

[18] "Clark's Memoir," 4-5. "Levi Todd's Narrative," Draper MSS. 48 J 10(1). Draper MSS. 14 S 2-12. John W. Wayland, *The Bowmans, A Pioneering Family in Virginia, Kentucky and the Northwest Territory* (Staunton, Va., 1943), 45-46.

[19] Floyd to Preston, July 21, 1776, Draper MSS. 17 CC 172-73. Draper MSS. 8 J 115-16; 6 S 94-96; 12 CC 75.

Boonesborough, although it had involved only six Indians, caused consternation in Kentucky. If this could happen at Boonesborough, it could happen at any of the other settlements. Then too, there was the possibility that the Revolution, which already was in progress in the East, would spread. The people in Kentucky, caught between the northern and the southern Indians and separated from the other settled portions of Virginia by two hundred miles of wilderness, were not in an enviable position. In less than a week after the Boonesborough incident the people of John Hinkston's settlement on the South Fork of Licking River were on their way to safer regions. Those Kentuckians who had "settled out" began to gravitate toward one or another of the three forts.

William Whitley, George Clark, and a few other settlers from the Crab Orchard region stopped at St. Asaph's on their way to Harrodsburg with their families. Logan pointed out to them that by working together they soon could complete a small fort which they might be able to defend. The others were not convinced and continued on their way. This may have caused Logan to give more thought to the danger threatening his family. The boy David was only two years of age, and another child was expected in December. If more were needed to persuade him to move to a safer place, the news that Ben Pettit brought proved sufficient. Pettit had found numerous signs of Indians in the woods nearby. The two decided at once that their families should be taken to Harrodsburg. All of their possessions were packed, with the exception of the rough furniture which their own labor could replace, and the move was accomplished at night. At Harrodsburg the Logans, the Whitleys, the George Clarks, and William Manifees occupied cabins along the south wall of the fort.

The problem of food demanded immediate attention. Meat still could be obtained in the woods. It had been a good corn year in Kentucky, and the crop was ready to be harvested. Some was brought into the fort and the remainder was cribbed in the fields.

Logan had not given up the idea of building and maintaining his own fort at St. Asaph's. He went back and forth frequently during the winter. At times he was aided in his clearing and building by others from the St. Asaph's and Crab Orchard regions whose families were at Harrodsburg.[20]

In October this routine had been interrupted by a mission the importance of which can hardly be overemphasized. The fort at Harrodsburg by this time seemed fairly secure, but there was a dangerous shortage of powder and lead. It was decided that Logan and James Harrod should go to the Holston settlements for a fresh supply. The two set out on horseback, leading one packhorse. On reaching the Holston they found that powder had been scarce there also, but the situation had been relieved when the Virginia government sent a supply, most of which was intended for use against the Cherokee. Though Colonel William Christian had started on an expedition against that tribe when Logan and Harrod arrived, the two Kentuckians did not mean to return empty handed. They followed Christian and overtook him at the Long Island of the Holston, where they persuaded him to let them have 100 pounds of powder and 176 pounds of lead. With this they arrived at Harrodsburg only twenty days after their departure.[21]

Logan had learned that all had not been quiet on the Holston that summer and fall. In July a small group of men who had taken their families into Black's Fort for safety ventured out to secure the household goods of the Presbyterian minister, Charles Cummings. In addition to Cummings, the group included Benjamin Logan's brother John, James Caswell, James Piper, William Creswell, and Cummings' Negro servant Job. About two miles from the fort they were attacked by

[20] Floyd to Preston, July 21, 1776, Draper MSS. 17 CC 173-74. "Todd's Narrative", 10(1-2). "William Whitley's Narrative," Draper MSS. 9 CC 18. Draper MSS. 4 B 101; 12 C 26-29, 44-45(1); 9 J 185; 18 S 146-48; 15 CC 159.
[21] William Christian to Patrick Henry, October 23, 1776, Draper MSS. 13 S 207-212. Draper MSS. 4 B 105-106. Lincoln County Court Order Book 3, pp. 3-4.

Indians. When the attackers were driven off, Caswell was dead and Piper and John Logan had been wounded, the latter suffering the loss of a finger.[22]

While the other Kentuckians were strengthening their forts and procuring ammunition, George Rogers Clark and John Gabriel Jones were endeavoring to complete the task that had been assigned to them at the Harrodsburg meeting on June 6. The journey proved difficult, and they were too late to present their petitions to the Virginia Convention, which also was an interim assembly. So they decided to wait for the fall meeting of the newly constituted Virginia Assembly. In the meantime, when Clark visited Governor Patrick Henry at his home in Hanover County, he found the governor to be very favorable to the Kentucky settlers. At Williamsburg, Clark finally persuaded the Executive Council to spare 500 pounds of powder for the defense of Kentucky and to transport it as far as Fort Pitt, and a messenger was started to Kentucky with the word that the powder could be picked up at that point.[23]

The Virginia Assembly opened its first session at Williamsburg on October 7. On the following day Clark and Jones presented their petitions. They were not accepted as delegates on the ground that Fincastle was represented already, and there was no county of West Fincastle. Nevertheless, the assembly agreed to consider the request for the establishment of a new county. Richard Henderson was present to lobby against this proposal, which was opposed also by Arthur Campbell, one of the delegates from Fincastle, who objected to any division of his county. The opponents met defeat on December 7 when an act was passed abolishing Fincastle County and creating in its place three new counties, Montgomery, Washington, and Kentucky, the division to take effect on December 31, 1776. Although the Transylvania Company's purchase was not declared null and void until two years

[22] Draper MSS. 12 C 46(1); 9 J 198-99(1). Lewis P. Summers, *History of Southwest Virginia, 1746-1786* (Richmond, 1903), 230-31.

[23] "Clark's Memoir," 5-17. Excerpts from "Journal of the Virginia Council," Draper MSS. 60 J 354.

later, the company for all practical purposes was now dead.

The county of Kentucky was to consist of that portion of Fincastle which lay to the west of a line "beginning on the Ohio, at the mouth of Great Sandy Creek, and running up the same . . . to the . . . Cumberland Mountain, thence south westerly along the said mountain to the line of North Carolina." The law provided also that free white males who owned twenty-five acres of improved land or one hundred acres of unimproved land in the county should be allowed to vote for their representatives in the assembly and should be eligible to hold that office.[24]

The Virginia Council appointed a full set of militia officers for each county. Those for Kentucky were David Robinson, county lieutenant; John Bowman, colonel; Anthony Bledsoe, lieutenant colonel; George Rogers Clark, major; and John Todd, Benjamin Logan, Daniel Boone, and James Harrod, captains. Civil commissions were prepared for Logan as sheriff and for Robinson, Logan, Clark, Isaac Hite, Robert Todd, and several others as justices of the peace.[25]

The message which Clark sent to Kentucky concerning the procuring of the powder was never received. Not until he and Jones had finished their work at Williamsburg did they learn that the powder was still at Fort Pitt; so they decided to

[24] *Journal of the House of Delegates of the Commonwealth of Virginia, 1776* (Richmond, 1828), 3-9. William W. Hening (ed.), *The Statutes at Large of Virginia*, IX (Richmond, 1821), 257-60. "Clark's Memoir," 17-18. Draper MSS. 4 B 108(1).

[25] Draper MSS. 4 B 108, 115-115(1); 17 J 16; 60 J 350-53, 413; 13 S 107-108.

David Robinson was born in Ireland, but came to Augusta County, Virginia, at an early age. He served as a lieutenant in the French and Indian War and as a captain under Bouquet in 1764. He held a military warrant for two thousand acres of land. On May 16, 1776, John Floyd surveyed for him one-half of this amount on a tributary of the Kentucky River. Both this and his militia appointment would seem to indicate his intention of moving to Kentucky. Nevertheless, he did not do so until many years later and thus never acted in the capacity of county lieutenant. Anthony Bledsoe was a native of Culpeper County, Virginia. He served as a major in Fincastle County but, choosing not to move to Kentucky, he refused the commission as a lieutenant colonel in the new county. Bledsoe later settled in Tennessee. (See Draper MSS. 4 B 108 and "Kentucky Land Office Military Surveys," 123, 224.)

return by that route and to deliver it personally. Leaving Fort Pitt in a canoe with a party of seven, they journeyed to the mouth of Limestone Creek, the present site of Maysville, Kentucky. They arrived there after several indications that they were being followed and watched. The powder was hidden at several different spots, the canoe was set adrift, and the men started overland for Harrodsburg. On reaching the abandoned Hinkston's Station on the South Fork of the Licking, it was decided that Clark and two others should push on and obtain aid, while five would remain at that place. While Clark was away, another party under the leadership of John Todd arrived at Hinkston's, and it was thought that the two groups combined would be sufficient to get the powder and take it to Harrodsburg. With Todd in command, they set out by way of the Blue Licks. Shortly after passing that point they were attacked by a band of Indians. John Gabriel Jones was killed, and William Craden, Joseph Rogers, and Josiah Dixon were captured. The attack occurred on December 25.

The Indians did not discover the location of the powder, and on January 2 a party of about twenty-five men under James Harrod set out from Harrodsburg and retrieved it without incident. In the meantime, McClellan's Fort at the Royal Spring had been attacked on December 29 by a large band of Indians. They were finally repulsed after having wounded John McClellan, Charles White, Edward Worthington, and Robert Todd. White died on the following day, and McClellan on January 6.[26]

[26] "Clark's Memoir," 18-24. "George Rogers Clark's Journal," Draper MSS. 48 J 12(1). "Todd's Narrative," 10(2-3). Deposition of Jacob Sandusky, a member of Harrod's party, Draper MSS. 18 J 59. McClellan's was at the present site of Georgetown, Kentucky.

CHAPTER III

WAR IN THE WEST

KENTUCKY IN THE OPENING phases of the Revolution was not in immediate danger of a British invasion. It was, on the other hand, exposed to attacks by the Indian tribes from north of the Ohio. Some of these tribes were openly allied with the British, while many others were under British influence. The year 1777 found the Kentuckians living in three forts, Harrodsburg, Boonesborough, and McClellan's. Of these, McClellan's was the smallest, and, located northeast of the Kentucky River, it was in a more dangerous position than the other two. The remainder of the region on that side of the Kentucky already had been abandoned. The attack on December 29, followed by the death of John McClellan on January 6, made it unlikely that his fort could be maintained for long. It soon was agreed that the strength of this garrison should be added to that of Harrodsburg, and on January 30 the move was made.[1]

Benjamin Logan, with the aid of others who had marked their claims in the southern part of Kentucky's Bluegrass region, had been working on a fort for several months. It was situated on a very slight elevation about fifty yards west of the smaller spring at St. Asaph's. Although not so large as those at Boonesborough and Harrodsburg, it was adequate for the number of people it was expected to shelter. Blockhouses were constructed at three corners of a rectangle 150 feet long and 90 feet wide, but at the fourth corner a conventional cabin was built. Only seven cabins were constructed, three, flanked by two blockhouses, were on one side of the enclosure, while four, together with the third blockhouse, completed the other side. The stockade between the buildings and along the ends was formed by logs set in the ground vertically and sharpened at the tops. Gates at the ends, raised by leather thongs, could be lowered quickly if danger threatened. The problem of obtaining water during a siege was solved by digging a ditch about three feet wide and four feet deep from inside of one of the blockhouses to the spring. Puncheons were placed over the top, and these were covered with dirt, making a tunnel through which a person might crawl to bring water.[2]

The geographical position of St. Asaph's gave it a certain amount of protection by the other two forts. Lying eighteen miles southeast of Harrodsburg and thirty-five miles southwest of Boonesborough, it was south of an imaginary line joining them. Northern Indians passing this line would run a slight risk of being cut off, especially if the garrisons of Harrodsburg and Boonesborough should increase in size. On the other hand, if the southern Indians became dangerous, St. Asaph's probably would be the first to suffer.

The Logans' second son, William, who was born at Harrodsburg on December 8, 1776, was barely two months old when the new fort was occupied. With the Logans went five other families, the Ben Pettits, the William Whitleys, the William Manifees, the George Clarks, and the James Masons. Six single men accompanied them and occupied the blockhouses. Shortly afterward the family of Samuel Coburn arrived. This family included a daughter, Ann, and her baby son. Ann's husband, James McDonald, had been killed by Indians while making salt at Drennon's Lick.[3]

The situation in Kentucky at this time was critical. The total fighting strength did not exceed 140 men in the three forts,

---

[1] "Levi Todd's Narrative," Draper MSS. 48 J 10(3). "George Rogers Clark's Journal," Draper MSS. 48 J 12(1).

[2] Draper MSS. 9 J 183(1); 18 S 147-48.

[3] Draper MSS. 4 B 115; 12 C 22-22(1); 9 J 185; 59 J 24; 18 S 148; 9 CC 5-6, 21.

and more than half of these were at Harrodsburg. There were about forty families to be protected and fed, including several widows and orphans. On February 27 a committee of safety for the region, with Hugh McGary of Harrodsburg as its chairman, addressed a petition to Governor Henry and his council. It listed the recent Indian atrocities, confessed the inability of the settlers to handle the situation, and asked the executive to "devise some method to guard us against the attacks of our merciless enemy."[4]

Although this petition could have had no effect so soon, help did arrive early in March in the form of an opportunity for better organization. The militia commissions for those officers who had been named shortly after the establishment of Kentucky County were finally delivered by William Bush, who often acted as an "express." The highest ranking officer actually present in Kentucky was the major, George Rogers Clark. On March 5 the militia was mustered at the three forts by the four captains, John Todd, James Harrod, Daniel Boone, and Logan. This did not increase the numerical strength of Kentucky, but it made the existing strength more effective. Frontiersmen were highly individualistic, and while they might take orders from self-appointed leaders in time of extreme danger, they would not continue to do so when the threat was less immediate. Now the Kentuckians were commanded by officers whose authority came from Williamsburg. Each company, as was the custom, selected its own lieutenant and its ensign, and each of the forts chose two scouts who were to range over the now abandoned region between the Kentucky and the Ohio and, if possible, give warning of the approach of an enemy. Logan's selections for this task were John Kennedy and John Martin.[5]

The day after the first militia muster was held, and before the scouts had time to become effective, Indians arrived at the Kentucky settlements in considerable strength. St. Asaph's,

---

[4] "Todd's Narrative," 10(3)-11. Draper MSS. 4 B 111-12; 4 CC 29-30.
[5] "Clark's Journal," 12(2). "Todd's Narrative," 10(3). Draper MSS. 4 B 115-15(1).

commonly called Logan's Fort, had a little more time to prepare than the other forts. The first blood was shed at Harrodsburg. William Coomes, Thomas Moore, and two stepsons of Hugh McGary—William and James Ray—were surprised while working at the Shawnee Spring about five miles from the fort. James Ray escaped and gave the warning. A party of about fifty men went to the scene of the attack, where they found that Moore and William Ray had been killed, but Coomes had hidden himself and was rescued. The following morning the Indians set fire to an abandoned cabin outside of the Harrodsburg stockade. Some men who went out to investigate were fired upon and four were wounded. One of these men, Archibald McNeal, died several days later. Boonesborough also had two casualties on March 7, one killed and the other wounded.

The men of the three forts concentrated upon bringing in the corn that had been raised and cribbed in the fields the year before. Because it was assumed that the savages were still in the region, the corn that was near at hand was secured first. Hunters made a practice of leaving the forts by night to obtain buffalo and other meat. Logan's Fort went through the months of March and April without serious trouble, but Harrodsburg was visited by the enemy on three more occasions and Boonesborough once more. On March 18 Hugh Wilson was killed and scalped about a half mile from the fort at Harrodsburg, and on March 28 Garret Pendergrass and Peter Flinn were the victims. Another attack on April 29 resulted in the death of a militia ensign named McConnell. In the meantime an attack at Boonesborough on April 24 had left one man dead and Daniel Boone, John Todd, Isaac Hite, and Michael Stoner wounded.[6]

Civil commissions for Kentucky County did not arrive with the militia commissions. As a result the organization of the county government was delayed. The highest local authority

[6] "Clark's Journal," 12(2-5). "Todd's Narrative," 10(3)-11. "George Rogers Clark's Memoir," Draper MSS. 59 J 24-26. "John Cowan's Journal," Draper MSS. 4 CC 32(3). Draper MSS. 4 B 115(1); 31 C 54.

in the meantime was a council of war which included Captains Todd, Harrod, Boone, and Logan, with Clark as president. Courts martial were sometimes held, and on these lieutenants and ensigns were eligible to serve. Men were fined for such offenses as "quitting their arms," sleeping at their posts, and failing to report for duty. The council favored defensive measures and avoiding contact with the enemy when possible. Logan did not always agree with this policy. On at least one occasion he put his ideas into writing, and his letter was presented to the council by Clark at a meeting held at Harrodsburg on April 29. Logan expressed the opinion that a sufficient force could be collected from the three stations to repulse the Indians and perhaps to recover some of the plunder which they had taken. The council, replying to his request for an opinion, pointed out that the enemy's strength was thought to be very great. A general engagement, the other members felt, would be perilous and might result in the loss of all of Kentucky.[7] That Clark did not always take the other members of the council into his confidence is evidenced by his action in sending Ben Linn and Samuel Moore to the Illinois country as spies. These men were chosen on April 20 and departed on April 25, but no one in Kentucky, or so Clark afterward claimed, knew the full purpose of their mission.[8]

Kentucky County should have elected her delegates to the Virginia Assembly on the first Tuesday in April, but at that time no civil commissions had arrived, and no one was authorized to hold an election. This situation was remedied by the arrival of the commissions a few days later. Not enough magistrates were yet available to hold court, but Logan, who received the appointment as sheriff, named April 18 as the new election date. The balloting took place at Harrodsburg and was continued through the following day so that most of the landowners in the county had an opportunity to vote. The choice fell upon John Todd and Richard Calloway. When they

[7] Draper MSS. 18 J 23-24, 56.
[8] "Clark's Journal," 12(4). "Clark's Memoir," 32-33. "Cowan's Journal," 32(3). Draper MSS. 5 S 130.

started for Williamsburg late in May, they carried with them the results of the election, certified by Logan, and a statement from him explaining why it had been delayed. Because they had not been chosen on the day prescribed by law, the Committee of Privileges and Elections of the House of Delegates decided that "the election of delegates for the said county of Kentucky was not made according to law," but the right of Todd and Calloway to be seated was affirmed by the passage of a special bill validating their election, as it appeared to a majority of the other delegates "that a representation, from their peculiar circumstances, is highly interesting to the inhabitants of the said County of Kentucky, at this critical period." Logan's explanation was a major factor in producing this very satisfactory decision.[9]

By May 1 the fighting strength of the three Kentucky forts was only 121 men out of a population of about 280. At Harrodsburg there were eighty-four men capable of bearing arms, at Boonesborough twenty-two, and at Logan's only fifteen. Indians were seen near Logan's on Sunday, May 18, but in such small numbers that the men of the garrison ventured out from time to time in the hope of taking them by surprise. Such a party went to the Flat Lick, about two miles from the fort, on the following Thursday and remained there all night and through most of the next day. It was while Logan's men were thus engaged that the Indians struck again at Boonesborough. The attack began on Friday morning, May 23, shortly after Todd and Calloway had set out for Williamsburg. John Kennedy, one of Logan's scouts, and another man saw from a distance what was taking place and hurried to St. Asaph's with the news. The men at the Flat Lick were sent for, and the fort was prepared for an attack. Some Indians appeared in the evening, but there was as yet no attempt to lay siege to the fort. There were times during the next few

[9] *Journal of the House of Delegates of the Commonwealth of Virginia, [May Session], 1777* (Richmond, 1827), 47. Hening (ed.), *Statutes,* IX, 316-17. "Cowan's Journal," 32(3-5). "Todd's Narrative," 11. "Clark's Journal," 12(4-6). Draper MSS. 31 C 56; 13 S 181.

days when the fort was not being watched by the savages. News arrived from Boonesborough that the enemy had departed on Sunday morning, and an express, who must have left Logan's on Monday evening carrying this information, arrived safely at Harrodsburg on Tuesday morning, May 27.[10]

The women of the fort assisted in its defense by molding bullets, even using the few available pewter dishes when the supply of lead was exhausted. Two of the wives, Jane Manifee and Esther Whitley, were proficient with rifles and could take their turns at the loopholes. Ben Pettit, who had been a trader among the Indians and learned their methods, was considered good in the treatment of wounds. The Logan, Pettit, and Clark families occupied three of the cabins along the north side of the fort, and the Whitleys, Manifees, and Masons were on the south side. It is not certain that the Coburn family was in the fort at this time. If not, the single men may have used the cabin at the northeast corner as well as the blockhouses at the other three corners. The single men were John Martin, John Kennedy, James Craig, William Hudson, John King, Azariah Davis, Burr Harrison, William May, and a free mulatto named Daniel Hawkins.

There was occasional firing for several days without any casualties in the fort. The damage to the enemy would have been difficult to ascertain. One Indian was observed to be firing from behind a tree which stood about two hundred yards to the west. By lying on the ground and resting his gun on a protruding root, he was able to be fairly effective even at that distance. This situation was brought to the attention of John Martin, who fired once and succeeded in lodging a ball in the root upon which the Indian was supporting his gun, causing the savage to withdraw to safer territory.[11]

By the morning of May 30, twelve days after the Indians

[10] "Cowan's Journal," 32(2-6). "Todd's Narrative," 11. "Clark's Journal," 12(5-6). "William Whitley's Narrative," Draper MSS. 9 CC 21. Draper MSS. 4 B 125.

[11] "Whitley's Narrative," 22-23. Draper MSS. 4 B 129; 12 C 10(4); 9 J 183(1), 186; 18 S 148, 151-52, 170; 9 CC 3-4.

had first arrived, there were none to be seen and they were thought to have withdrawn. Milk was needed and there were some cows not far from the fort. With James Craig, William Hudson, John Kennedy, and Burr Harrison acting as guards, Ann Logan, Esther Whitley, and the Negro woman Molly went out to milk. The Indians had concealed themselves and must have been waiting for such an opportunity. The group hardly had reached its destination when several guns were fired. Harrison and Hudson fell, but Kennedy, although wounded, was able to flee to the fort with Craig and the three women. Firing was continued by both sides, cattle and hogs being the only new casualties.

Hudson had been scalped by the warriors, but Harrison, who had fallen somewhat closer to the fort, had not been mutilated in any way. Nevertheless, it was assumed by those in the fort that he was dead. In the afternoon, however, he was seen to move slightly, and this information was taken to Logan. The victim obviously was weak from loss of blood and for a time there was doubt as to whether or not he was conscious. But when told to move his foot as an indication that he could hear the men calling to him, he did so. Logan made plans at once for bringing him into the fort. In broad daylight the risk was too great, but if he were still outside after nightfall he would certainly be scalped and tomahawked. It was agreed that the attempt should be made at twilight. Slipping out at dusk, Logan crawled toward Harrison rolling a large bag of wool before him as a shield. He was not discovered until he had abandoned the bag, lifted Harrison to his shoulders, and started for the fort. One shot was fired, the bullet striking the wall near the gate. Before another attempt was made the two men were inside the stockade.

One of the defenders, John King, claimed later that John Martin, who had come to Logan's after abandoning his own station on Stoner Creek, offered to assist in the rescue. He was said to have started through the gate with Logan and then to have changed his mind. William Whitley, who first discovered

that Harrison was still alive, did not mention Martin in this
connection when he later dictated his memoirs. It is interesting
to note that, while others treated Logan's action as heroism,
King accused him of rashness.

After killing most of the livestock, the Indians departed
before daylight on Sunday morning, June 1. Spits on which
they had roasted their meat were counted, and it was decided
that the party had numbered fifty-two. If any warriors were
killed their bodies had been removed. Evidence of long splints'
having been made indicated that one had sustained a broken
leg. On the side of the whites, Kennedy had received only
flesh wounds, Hudson had been killed instantly, and Harrison
died of his wounds on June 13. Both he and Hudson were
buried inside the fort.[12]

There was doubt at this time whether the small garrison
could withstand another attack, and conditions at the other two
forts left much to be desired. Logan decided to go to the
Holston Settlements for aid. Much has been written of his
daring and rapid trip, which he is said to have made entirely
alone. However, there is reason for doubting that he was by
himself except possibly on the return trip. James Harrod and
a small group of men started from Harrodsburg on June 5 and
headed for Boone's Wilderness Trail. It is likely that they
would have been at St. Asaph's on June 6, which was the day
that Logan's trip began. Logan was back at his fort by June
25, but Harrod did not return until July 11.[13]

No immediate aid was forthcoming, but the critical situation
in Kentucky already was known to the Virginia executive.
Early in the year John Bowman, who was colonel of the

[12] "Clark's Journal," 12(6-7). "Cowan's Journal," 32(6-7). "Whitley's
Narrative," 21-23. Draper MSS. 4 B 90(1), 129; 12 C 10(4), 44(1); 31 C
54; 18 S 148-51, 157, 191; 9 CC 5-6; 17 CC 199.

The story of John Martin's change of heart has been repeated by many
people, including Logan's daughter, Mary Smith. Whether she obtained it
from her father, described by her as "taciturn," or from someone who had
heard it from King has not been determined.

[13] "Cowan's Journal," 32(8-9). "Whitley's Narrative," 23. Draper MSS.
4 B 131; 5 XX 54.

Kentucky County militia even though he was still living in Botetourt County, had written to the governor's council about the matter. As a result, the council on March 10, 1777, requested the governor to direct the raising of one hundred men in the counties of Botetourt and Montgomery to go to the aid of the Kentuckians. If these men could provide the necessary protection they were to remain in Kentucky pending further instructions. If, on the other hand, their officers considered the situation sufficiently serious, they were to escort the inhabitants to "some interior and secure parts of the country."[14]

On May 7 the council voted to allow James Barnett, the commissary for this expedition, one thousand pounds for the procuring of supplies, but it is uncertain how much recruiting had been done by that time. The council's intentions were known in Kentucky, and Harrod's trip to the Holston was partly for the purpose of meeting Bowman and his men. Logan had returned first, evidently to carry the news that help soon would be available. Harrod remained about three weeks longer, probably with the intention of accompanying Bowman, but he returned without him.[15]

In the meantime the council took additional steps for the protection and better government of Kentucky County. On June 4 notice was taken of the fact that of the justices of the peace who had been appointed in the preceding December only four—Clark, Logan, Isaac Hite, and Robert Todd—actually had transferred their residences to this region. Without five justices present no court could be held. This situation was corrected by the naming of some known residents as justices. The new appointments included Richard Calloway, James Harrod, Daniel Boone, John Kennedy, and Nathaniel Henderson. David Robinson, who had been named as county lieutenant, had not moved to Kentucky at this time, and on June 14 he was replaced by John Bowman. Richard Calloway, then

[14] Draper MSS. 60 J 351; 13 S 108; 32 S 48.
[15] "Cowan's Journal," 32(8-9). "Clark's Journal," 12(7-8). Draper MSS. 4 B 131; 13 S 113.

representing the county in the Virginia Assembly, was named to Bowman's former position as colonel of the one existing regiment.[16]

William Whitley stated many years later that "nothing particular happened" while Logan was away on his trip to the Holston. He must have meant only that the people living at St. Asaph's were not molested, for it was during Logan's absence that Daniel Lyon disappeared en route to the fort. With two other men, whose names were Glenn and Laird, Lyon had started from the Cumberland River to the Kentucky settlements. He had parted from his companions at the Green River, as he was going toward Logan's and they toward Harrodsburg. Glenn and Laird arrived safely, but the only trace ever found of Lyon was a piece of a leather hunting shirt which was believed to be his. It was during this same period that Barney Stagner was killed and beheaded near Harrodsburg, and that Clark's spies, Linn and Moore, returned from the Illinois country.

The long-awaited reinforcements came through the Cumberland Gap in July with the new county lieutenant, John Bowman, in command. They were met by Captain James Harrod, whose earlier trip for that purpose had been premature. The two officers traveled together as far as the Hazel Patch. Here the Wilderness Trail forked, one branch going to Boonesborough and the other to Harrodsburg by way of St. Asaph's. Bowman took the former and he and his men reached Boonesborough on August 1, and Harrod returned to his own fort. The county lieutenant had brought two companies totaling about one hundred men and commanded by Captains Henry Pawling and John Duncan. Shortly after their arrival Duncan resigned his commission and was replaced by Isaac Ruddle. Kentucky County's new colonel, Richard Calloway, returned from Williamsburg about this time, reaching Boonesborough on August 10.[17]

---

[16] Draper MSS. 4 B 108, 134; 60 J 356, 393; 13 S 101.
[17] "Cowan's Journal," 32(7-9). "Clark's Journal," 12(7,9). "Whitley's Narrative," 24. Draper MSS. 4 B 132; 31 C 55; 17 J 5(1-2); 1 OO 154-55.

These reinforcements did not arrive before they were needed. Indians appeared at Harrodsburg on August 5, but there were not more than twelve and they were driven off by the local garrison. Later in the month a larger body of savages surrounded Logan's Fort, and the second siege of that station began. The ground in the immediate vicinity had been cleared, and there was little chance for an enemy to take cover close to the fort. On the other side of St. Asaph's Branch, however, the trees were still standing, and it was from there that most of the shots came. Fortunately, the distance was so great that these were not very effective. Some of the cattle belonging to the residents of the fort were killed on the cleared ground, and one of these served as a breastwork for an Indian who crept up behind it and fired several shots at the loopholes. A member of the garrison finally killed him as he raised his head to take aim.[18]

From time to time other Indians found sufficient cover to approach the fort. On one occasion John King and another of the younger members of the garrison, bored with life inside the stockade, arranged a bet on the question of which could climb higher in a tree, feet first. A small tree just inside one of the gates was selected. King's opponent made the first attempt, only to be wounded in the heel when his feet appeared above the stockade. Logan had known nothing of this foolhardy contest until too late to prevent it.[19]

Not long after this an Indian who had hidden behind one of the trees within rifle range of the fort decided to prove that red men could be as daring as white men. Several times he stepped from behind the tree, leaped into the air, and struck his feet together. Each time he took cover again before anyone had a chance to draw a bead on him. Unfortunately for him,

[18] "Cowan's Journal," 32(9-10). "Clark's Journal," 12(9). Draper MSS. 29 S 105-106.

[19] This was the opinion of one of Logan's daughters who was told of the incident by her mother. See Mary Logan Smith to Lyman C. Draper, December 16, 1844 and April 25, 1845, Draper MSS. 12 C 44(1), 45(2). See also Draper MSS. 18 S 152-53.

he always moved out about the same distance from the tree and in the same direction. Noticing this, one of the men in the fort took aim at the spot where the warrior could be expected to do his act and fired at the proper moment to bring this affair to a sudden conclusion.[20]

By the morning of August 25 the Indians seemed to have withdrawn, and several men ventured out to get a supply of corn. But the trail to Boonesborough still was being watched by the savages. Six of Colonel John Bowman's militiamen who were approaching Logan's far in advance of a larger party were fired upon. One member of the group, Ambrose Grayson, was killed, and the Indians found time to remove his scalp before taking flight. Two others, Jonas Manifee and Samuel Ingram, were wounded.[21]

It was at this time that the Kentuckians received some tangible evidence of the connection between the Indian warfare and the British attempt to put down the revolt in America. On the body of Grayson the red men left some copies of a British proclamation. It was signed by Lieutenant Colonel Henry Hamilton, lieutenant governor of Quebec, who was stationed at Detroit. In June, 1777, Hamilton had received orders from his government to employ Indians against the colonists, and by July he had sent out fifteen war parties. Prior to receiving these instructions he had, according to his own statement, tried to discourage the savages from taking an active part in the war. The proclamation offered food, lodging, and humane treatment to all who deserted the American cause and presented themselves at any British post. Those who would take up arms against the Americans and continue in His Majesty's service "until the extinction of this rebellion" were promised "pay adequate to their former stations in the rebel service, and all common men who shall serve during that

[20] Smith to Draper, April 25, 1845, Draper MSS. 12 C 45(2).
[21] "Cowan's Journal," 32(10). "Whitley's Narrative," 24. Draper MSS. 4 B 133; 31 C 55. Draper's copy of "Cowan's Journal" has the news of this attack reaching Harrodsburg on July 28, but it is evident that August 28 was intended, as the entry appears between those for August 5 and September 2.

period shall receive his Majesty's bounty of two hundred acres of land."[22]

The copies of Hamilton's proclamation were brought to Logan, who would not risk the effect which they might have if allowed to circulate. He is said to have hidden them, and there is no reason to believe that they were ever produced as evidence. The experiences of that summer may have caused some to consider desertion, but it is doubtful if a promise of "two hundred acres of land" would have been a sufficient inducement in a country where people had reason to believe that the mere act of settlement would entitle them to a larger amount.[23]

On the day after Grayson was killed John Bowman reached Logan's with a considerable detachment. That afternoon, the enemy apparently having left the country, the men of the fort and Bowman's men engaged in a shooting match. The prize was nothing more than the bullets of all the contestants extracted from the target and given to the winner, but the scarcity of lead made even this of considerable interest. While the contest was in progress William Whitley, returning from scouting or hunting, handed his gun to his wife Esther and urged her to enter the match. Her first shot beat the best that had been made, and the men continued until dark without being able to equal her record.[24]

About the first of September, Bowman, with a company of militia, moved on to Harrodsburg. The last court for Fincastle County had met on September 3, 1776, and the division into Montgomery, Washington, and Kentucky had taken place in the following December, but as yet no court for Kentucky

[22] "Whitley's Narrative," 24. Henry Hamilton to Lords of Treasury, July 30, 1784, Draper MSS. 45 J 68. "Hamilton's Proclamation of June 24, 1777," Draper MSS. 45 J 62. There is a copy of this proclamation in Draper MSS. 14 S 124.

[23] Draper MSS. 4 B 133; 31 C 55; 18 S 152. On June 24, 1776, the Virginia Assembly had passed a bill to the effect that persons who settled on ungranted lands on the Western Waters should have "the pre-emption or preference to a grant of such lands." See Hening (ed.), *Statutes*, IX, 355.

[24] Related by William Whitley, Jr. to Lyman C. Draper, Draper MSS. 12 C 62(1). See also "Clark's Journal," 12(9).

County had been held. This had been prevented by the late arrival of the civil commissions, the failure of some of the justices to remove to Kentucky, making necessary several new appointments, and by the Indian menace which kept the question of self-preservation uppermost in the minds of the settlers. The militia officers, who had been acting in that capacity since March, had not even had the oath of officer administered to them, and the same was true of Logan in the position of sheriff. Finally on September 2 Bowman, Logan, and several other magistrates met at Harrodsburg, selected Levi Todd, a younger brother of John and Robert Todd, as clerk, declared court in session, and began to transact the county business.[25]

Although the presence in Kentucky of additional militia companies may have helped to deter the Indians, the amount of protection which they provided was limited by the fact that the period of time for which they were called up was partially consumed by the long trip through the wilderness. On September 8 the fighting strength of the county was reduced by the departure of twenty-seven militiamen for the Holston and their discharge from active duty. There probably was no connection between the two events, but three days later Indians attacked thirty-seven militiamen who had gone with John Bowman to a tract of land claimed by his brother, Joseph Bowman, about five miles southeast of Harrodsburg. The trip was made to obtain corn, and the men were in the process of shelling it when they were fired upon. They were able to make a stand, and the Indians withdrew after losing two of their warriors. The white men lost Eli Gerrard, who was killed instantly, and Daniel Bryan, one of six who were wounded, died on the following day.[26]

Additional shifting of militia personnel brought a company of forty-eight men under Captain William Bailey Smith and

[25] "Cowan's Journal," 32(10). "Clark's Journal," 12(10). Draper MSS. 4 B 133-34; 60 J 356; 13 S 101; 32 S 69.
[26] "Clark's Journal," 12(10). "Cowan's Journal," 32(10-11). Draper MSS. 4 B 134-35; 12 C 41(28); 31 C 55.

Lieutenant John Holder to Boonesborough, while Captain Henry Pawling and his company of fifty men left Kentucky. Along with Pawling went George Rogers Clark, carrying both information and a suggestion to the governor and his council. This party spent the night of October 2 at Logan's. On that same day Captain John Montgomery and thirty-eight men arrived from the Holston to assist in the defense of Kentucky.[27]

Logan began to fear that his supply of powder and lead would not be sufficient if his fort should be subjected to a prolonged siege. Near the end of October he left his family again and journeyed on horseback to the Holston. With four packhorses loaded with ammunition and with a guard of twelve men he returned to St. Asaph's without incident.[28]

So long as horses were available the obtaining of meat was an easier task. Although the advance of settlement had pushed the game farther into the woods, a man on horseback could reach it and could bring back a sufficient load to make the trip worthwhile. The provisioning of the militia companies on duty in Kentucky was handled by Joseph Lindsay, who, in his capacity as commissary for the county, was stationed at Harrodsburg. These supplies for the most part had to be obtained in Kentucky, so that the situation was only slightly different from that which would have existed if each fort had been entirely responsible for feeding its own garrison. The chief value of Lindsay's work was that of insuring a fair distribution. His accounts for the year 1777 show that Logan furnished for the use of the militia 417 pounds of beef, 314 pounds of pork, 36 bushels of corn, and an unspecified quantity of dry meat, the total being valued at £21 9s 5d.[29]

The preserving of meat was largely dependent upon the amount of salt that was available. Kentucky was fortunate in having many salt springs such as Bullitt's Lick near Salt River,

[27] "Clark's Journal," 12(12). "Clark's Memoir," 28-29. Draper MSS. 4 B 136, 138, 178, 251(1); 31 C 56; 60 J 132; 13 S 143; 1 OO 78.
[28] Draper MSS. 9 J 186-86(1). Reuben G. Thwaites, *Daniel Boone* (New York, 1919), 144.
[29] Draper MSS. 4 J 58; 17 J 7(1).

Drennon's Lick near the Kentucky, and the Blue Licks on the Licking. Logan and his men sometimes went as far as Drennon's Lick for this very essential article. With it they would cure pork, domestic beef, and buffalo beef. So long as buffaloes were plentiful, only the tongue and the hump were taken and the rest of the meat left for the wolves, but it is not likely that this wasteful practice was continued for very long.[30]

As county lieutenant, John Bowman gave considerable attention to the question of procuring salt for the settlements. Recognizing the necessity for providing adequate protection for the men who were sent to manufacture salt, he conceived the idea of erecting a fort on the Ohio for the protection of one of the salt springs, probably Drennon's. The expense of maintaining the garrison would be met by bartering salt with the settlers in the Monongahela region. Colonel Bowman obviously envisioned a favorable balance of trade. He presented his plan to the Virginia council, and on October 14, 1777, that body gave its approval. Circumstances seem to have prevented any further action, as no record of a fort having been built at that time has been found. A year later Bowman found it necessary to send James Harrod and a small detachment to the Spanish settlements across the Mississippi for salt. About the same time Virginia ordered a wagonload of large pans for the making of salt to be sent to Fort Pitt, and Joseph Bowman was authorized to take these down the river to Kentucky. The total cost to the state was about one hundred pounds.[31]

Logan and several other Kentuckians were disturbed by the fact that some of the salt springs were claimed by persons who had shown no disposition to produce salt in any appreciable quantity or to allow others to do so. In the fall of 1777 he was one of the signers of a petition to the Virginia Assembly asking that the springs be made public property if their owners had

[30] Draper MSS. 18 S 154. Thomas D. Clark, "Salt, a Factor in the Settlement of Kentucky," in *Filson Club History Quarterly*, XII (1938), 42-52.
[31] John Bowman to George Rogers Clark, October 14, 1778, Draper MSS. 48 J 42(1). Draper MSS. 18 J 84; 60 J 355; 13 S 99-100; 12 CC 65.

made no provision for the manufacture of salt. This request was considered by the assembly at its next session and refused.[32]

The year 1777 was a trying one for the people of Kentucky. It was spent under crowded and unsanitary conditions inside the stockades at Harrodsburg, Boonesborough, and St. Asaph's. War had left many widows and orphans among the 200 women and children. The Indians had destroyed a large part of the corn that had been left from the previous year, and the loss of many of the horses made it difficult to bring that which remained into the forts. Clothing too was scarce and very hard to replace.

The extent to which the British were responsible for the damage that the Shawnee and other tribes were doing on the frontier would be difficult to determine. Henry Hamilton, lieutenant governor of Quebec and superintendent of Indian affairs, had achieved among the Kentuckians an unenviable reputation as a buyer of human hair. This feeling may have arisen with the finding of copies of his proclamation on the body of Ambrose Grayson not far from Logan's Fort. In a second proclamation, which he issued at Detroit on January 5, 1778, Hamilton praised "the moderation shewn by the Indians who have gone to war from this place" and spoke of "the injunctions constantly laid upon them on their setting out . . . to spare the defenceless and aged of both sexes." He expressed regret that more persons had not taken advantage of the offers made in his previous proclamation and contended that the actions of the Indians had shown that "compassion for the unhappy is blended with the severity necessary to be exercised on the obstinate and perverse enemies of his Majesty's Crown and dignity."[33]

[32] Draper MSS. 14 S 13-15. James R. Robertson, *Petitions of the Early Inhabitants of Kentucky to the General Assembly of Virginia, 1769 to 1792*, Filson Club Publications No. 27 (Louisville, 1914), 43-44.

[33] John Bowman to Edward Hand, December 12, 1777, Draper MSS. 4 B 140-41. (General Hand was the commandant at Fort Pitt.) See also Draper MSS. 14 S 125-27.

No evidence has been found which would prove that Hamilton actually bought scalps. It is certain, however, that they were brought to him by the Indians as evidence of their diligence, that he made gifts to the savages to hold their allegiance, and that the supplies furnished to his department included "scalping knives."[34]

[34] In a letter to Sir Guy Carleton, which is undated but which was received at Montreal on March 4, 1778, Hamilton reported that the Indians had brought in seventy-three prisoners and 129 scalps. See *Michigan Pioneer Collections*, IX (Lansing, 1908), 430-33. A list signed by Hamilton on September 5, 1778, shows among the supplies for the Indian Department "150 doz. scalping knives." See "Haldimand Papers," *Michigan Pioneer Collections*, IX (Lansing, 1908), 471.

Hamilton's letter of January 26, 1779, to Sir Frederick Haldimand, British military commander for all of Canada, mentioned the need for "a supply of arms, ammunition and clothing sufficient for keeping in their present disposition such a number of Indians whom we wish to have dependent on us." (See Draper MSS. 58 J 27.)

Joseph Bowman to John Hite, July 30, 1778, quoted in Wayland, *The Bowmans*, 74, says that papers captured at Kaskaskia a few weeks earlier offered "great rewards for our scalps."

CHAPTER IV

OFFENSE AND DEFENSE

THE YEAR 1778 OPENED WITH the people who had settled around St. Asaph's still living within the walls of Logan's Fort. Although the cramped quarters and the dread of another attack must have resulted in short tempers and frayed nerves, the conditions were in some respects superior to those at the other forts. Boonesborough by March was reduced to a steady diet of meat, and even this had to be eaten without salt. At Logan's the meat was supplemented by bread, butter, and plenty of milk.

Life in the fort had its lighter moments. The young widow, Ann McDonald, lived there with the family of her father, Samuel Coburn. It is probable that she received many proposals of marriage, for women were scarce on the frontier. Ann does not appear to have made up her mind hurriedly. Her choice was not one of the young bachelors at Logan's but the militia captain at Harrodsburg, James Harrod. They were married at St. Asaph's in February, 1778, by Robert Todd, one of the justices of the peace for Kentucky County. In line with prevailing frontier custom there surely would have been a celebration, limited only by existing facilities.[1]

In March some of the men who had enlisted under George Rogers Clark, ostensibly for the defense of Kentucky, began to arrive at Logan's. Since leaving Kentucky in the preceding October, Clark had talked with several of Virginia's political leaders in regard to his conducting an expedition into the

Illinois country. This plan they carried to Governor Patrick Henry, who expressed his approval. A bill was passed by the assembly which gave the governor the necessary authority. In order to secure its passage it was so worded that only its sponsors knew what was intended. Clark at this time was transferred from the Kentucky County militia to the Virginia Line with the rank of lieutenant colonel.

It was Clark's belief that five hundred men would be sufficient to take the British posts in Illinois. He had an additional ambition which he did not communicate to Governor Henry. The Indian attacks on the frontiers were being organized by Henry Hamilton. His proclamation which his braves had left near St. Asaph's, several copies of which were now in Logan's possession, left no doubt about that. Hamilton was in command at Detroit. If the French residents of the Illinois towns and perhaps some of the Indian tribes could be won to the American cause, Detroit might be captured.[2]

Because secrecy was of the utmost importance, Clark was given two sets of instructions. Those which were made public ordered him "to enlist Seven Companies of men officered in the usual manner." They were to proceed to Kentucky and to remain under arms "for three months after their arrival at that place" and were to continue to receive pay if they should remain on duty for a longer time. His private orders mentioned in addition that he was to attack the British post at Kaskaskia, and that boats would be furnished by the commandant at Fort Pitt. As an encouragement to enlistment, Thomas Jefferson, George Wythe, and George Mason gave Clark a signed statement in which they promised to urge the assembly to grant 300 acres of land to each participant if the expedition were

[1] "Daniel Trabue's Narrative," Draper MSS. 57 J 13-14. Draper MSS. 9 J 35, 85, 202. The name of Ann Harrod's first husband is sometimes given as McDaniel, but she was awarded his land claim under the name of McDonald and this is the name she used in making application for a pension. See Draper MSS. 12 C 22-22(2), 24(2-3); 17 J 87(1).

[2] George Rogers Clark to George Mason, November 19, 1779, Draper MSS. 58 J 124-28. "George Rogers Clark's Memoir," Draper MSS. 59 J 34-36. "Trabue's Narrative," 13-14. Draper MSS. 18 J 84; 58 J 128.

successful. This, however, was overbalanced by the fact that he was forbidden to recruit east of the Blue Ridge and by the objection of some of the settlers in those regions the ownership of which was disputed with Pennsylvania to serving on a Virginia campaign. As a result Clark had to start down the Ohio with a force far smaller than the anticipated 500.[3]

Among Clark's men who were waiting at Logan's Fort for further orders were Lieutenant James Trabue and his younger brother, Daniel, then only eighteen years of age. Soon after their arrival at Logan's the younger Trabue went out with some other men to hunt for bears. He had brought with him to Kentucky a bulldog that had been trained to seize a bull by the nose but had never seen a bear. One was soon located, and the dog approached as he had been taught to do. He was knocked several yards down a hill by a swing of the animal's paw and was so badly crippled that he had to be abandoned. The hunters killed the bear and returned to the fort with the meat. Two days later the dog had recovered sufficiently to drag himself after them. He eventually became an excellent hunting dog but remained wary of the front end of a bear.

Logan had built what was referred to as a fence, probably made of brush, around part of his land, but some of the ground within had not been cleared. The Trabue brothers agreed to clear a portion and plant corn, and together they succeeded in getting an acre under cultivation.[4]

The Indians did no serious damage in the immediate vicinity of Logan's Fort that spring but were believed to be watching the various trails in the hope of waylaying travelers. Horses sometimes strayed, and if they could not be found it was assumed that the red men had taken them. When this happened to one of Daniel Trabue's horses and to several others at the same time, he and an older man, a Pennsylvania

---

[3] Patrick Henry to George Rogers Clark, January 2, 1778, Draper MSS. 48 J 14, 16-16(1). Henry to Clark, January 28, 1778, Draper MSS. 48 J 18-18(1). "Clark's Memoir," 35-37. Draper MSS. 18 J 147-147(1).
[4] "Trabue's Narrative," 8-14.

German named Lail, went out to look for them. Taking some provisions, they started toward the Holston Settlements and covered about twenty miles the first day. Fearing that a fire would attract Indians, they sacrificed this comfort, wrapped themselves in their blankets, and lay down to sleep. Next day, convinced that the horses had not been over the road which they had taken, they decided to return to Logan's by another route. Trabue was constantly on watch for Indians, but Lail insisted that he had placed a spell upon the savages' guns, and all would be well. A few miles from the fort they came back to the trail over which they had gone out, and Lail started to follow it. Trabue, fearing that it was being watched, favored going instead through the tall cane which grew so abundantly all around them. The German would not be changed and reminded his companion of the magic which was certain to save them. Hardly had he finished speaking when his own gun was discharged accidently. Lail did not realize what had happened, but it seemed obvious to him that his magic had not worked. He leaped into the cane, leaving his hat and gun lying in the trail. It was with considerable difficulty that Trabue coaxed him back to get them. When they reached the fort, Logan reported that he had discovered a trail which convinced him that the horses already were in the possession of the Indians.[5]

The Shawnee, whose villages lay to the north of the Ohio River in what is now the state of Ohio, were blamed for much of the mischief which had been visited upon the Kentucky settlements. The fact that other tribes from greater distances sometimes entered Kentucky through the Shawnee country may have caused some of the damage to be attributed unfairly to this tribe. Nevertheless, Shawnee braves had been recognized in some of the attacks, and white prisoners were known to be held in their villages. In February of 1778 Daniel Boone was captured by a Shawnee war party while he was acting as hunter for a party of salt makers at the Blue Licks on the

[5] *Ibid.*, 14-16.

Licking River. Learning that these Indians were on their way
to Boonesborough, and doubting that the fort would be able
to withstand their attack, Boone decided to bargain with their
chief, Blackfish. He would agree to lead them to the salt
makers if the chief would promise that all would be treated
as prisoners of war. If the warriors were satisfied with so
large a group of prisoners so easily obtained, Boonesborough
would be safe for the time being. Blackfish gave his promise,
and Boone and his party soon were on their way to Detroit.

One of the prisoners, Andrew Johnson, soon made his escape
and returned to Kentucky. When he came to Logan's Fort
and told of his experiences it was believed that this was an
opportunity too good to miss, as Johnson could guide a few
men to the Shawnee village from which he had escaped. Here
stolen horses might be discovered or horses that were discovered might be stolen. Because this was war, it made little
difference so long as the quality was comparable. As the only
militia captain at St. Asaph's, Logan had responsibilities at
home, so it was agreed that a party would be formed with
William Whitley in command. Harrodsburg contributed a
few recruits, and the group, consisting of Whitley, Johnson,
Nehemiah Pore, John Haggin, Samuel Pickings, John Severns,
and a few others, made its way to the Ohio, where the
crossing was made on hastily constructed rafts. Not far beyond
the river they came upon an Indian camp and secured seven
horses. Although the white men feared that they were out-
numbered by the sleeping Indians, it was believed that
surprise could make the difference, and so an attack was
discussed. Before it could be executed, they were discovered
by the Indians' dogs. After firing one volley they beat a hasty
retreat, believing that they had killed at least two of the
savages. Whitley and his men returned home with the horses
after an absence of about two weeks.[6]

---

[6] William Bailey Smith to George Rogers Clark, March 7, 1778, Draper MSS.
48 J 19. "Whitley's Narrative," Draper MSS. 9 CC 26-28. Draper MSS. 8 J
6-7. *John Bradford's Historical Notes on Kentucky* taken from the *Western
Miscellany,* compiled by G. W. Stipp in 1827 (San Francisco, 1932), 36-37.

When Clark and his men arrived in Kentucky by the Ohio River route they stopped at the mouth of the Kentucky River, where it was thought a fort should be erected. It would have been very beneficial to the three Kentucky stations, as Boonesborough and St. Asaph's lay in the basin of the Kentucky River, and Harrodsburg, though in the basin of the Salt River, was only a few miles from the divide. The site, however, had the disadvantage of being too far from the Illinois posts which Clark expected to attack, and so an island just above the Falls of the Ohio was selected instead.[7]

Those of Clark's men who had been waiting at the Kentucky forts now were sent for, a blockhouse was erected, and preparations for the coming campaign began. The men already in Kentucky were collected by Captain John Montgomery. This officer had brought a company of militiamen to Logan's Fort in October of the previous year, arriving on the same day that Clark was setting out for Williamsburg. He had remained in the Kentucky settlements since that time. In addition to the men who already had enlisted under Clark, Montgomery gained a few recruits from among the settlers themselves. Logan's Fort contributed Simon Kenton, who had been spending a part of his time there, William Whitley, and several others.[8]

Although Clark had fallen far short of the 500 men he had hoped to enlist, he realized that the Kentucky forts must not be left in a weakened state. To avoid this he sent some of the Kentuckians back to their places of residence. This group included the Trabue brothers who had come to Kentucky in response to Clark's request for men but who had taken the first step toward becoming settlers when they cleared land and planted corn at Logan's. Joseph Lindsay, who had been acting as commissary for the Kentucky militia, was sent to New Orleans to obtain supplies for Clark. His duties in

[7] "Clark's Memoir," 40-41. "Clark's Journal," Draper MSS. 58 J 128-29.
[8] John Montgomery to Virginia Western Commissioners, February 22, 1783, Draper MSS. 60 J 245-57. Clark to Mason, November 19, 1779, 128-29. "Whitley's Narrative," 28-29. Draper MSS. 31 C 56; 9 J 188(1), 203.

Kentucky were turned over to James Trabue, who was to act as commissary for the four forts, a new settlement having been started at the Falls of the Ohio by families that had come down the river with Clark. A deputy commissary was selected for each of these stations. Daniel Trabue was given this position at St. Asaph's.[9]

Clark and his little band of men started down the Ohio on June 26. Ten days earlier Boone had made his escape from his Shawnee captors and had reached Boonesborough after a four day journey. He warned the Kentuckians of an impending Indian invasion, but his action in surrending the salt makers made some people hesitant about believing him. Another prisoner, William Hancock, escaped shortly afterward. He told of hearing Boone promise Henry Hamilton that if he were present when the British and their Indian allies came with a design to capture Boonesborough he would surrender it at once. Boone admitted this but insisted that he was deceiving his captors. There is some reason for believing that he was successful. After questioning Boone, Hamilton wrote of the Kentuckians: "Their dilemma will probably induce them to trust to the savages, who have shown so much humanity to their prisoners, and come to this place before winter."[10]

Indians already had done some damage in the vicinity of St. Asaph's. Just before the detachment left to join Clark, the Samuel Coburns, whose daughter Ann had married James Harrod, decided to move from Logan's Fort to Harrodsburg. They were escorted by a party of riflemen and made the trip without incident. Shortly afterward Coburn and two companions returned to Logan's for some corn and household goods that had been left. They remained overnight and next morning prepared to depart. Logan advised against their making the

[9] "Trabue's Narrative," 16-17. "Clark's Memoir," 43-47.

[10] "Trabue's Narrative," 25. *Bradford's Notes*, 37. John Todd to ————, June 29, 1778, quoted in Temple Bodley, *History of Kentucky* (Chicago and Louisville, 1928), 153n. Henry Hamilton to Sir Guy Carleton, April 28, 1778, quoted in Wilbur H. Siebert, "Kentucky's Struggle with its Loyalist Proprietors," in *Mississippi Valley Historical Review*, VII (1920-21), 117. John Bakeless, *Daniel Boone* (New York, 1939), 229-36. "Clark's Journal," 129.

trip with so few and promised to furnish a guard for them if they would remain at his fort for another day. Coburn insisted that there was no danger, and the three started on their journey. About two hours later one of the men returned with the news that Coburn and the other man had been killed by Indians, and that he had barely escaped. The attack had taken place on the Hanging Fork of Dick's River at the mouth of Knob Lick Creek. This was only a few miles from St. Asaph's, and Logan immediately led a party of thirteen men to the site. The two bodies were found, both with the scalps removed. The signs indicated that the Indians had started toward Harrodsburg, probably thinking that the third man had gone in that direction. Following their trail, Logan and his men soon came to a place where the Indians had abandoned the pursuit, hobbled their extra horses, and hidden their plunder in a canebrake. They then appeared to have reversed their direction. Logan sent his brother-in-law, Alexander Montgomery, back to St. Asaph's to carry the news and to dispatch another group of men to the Flat Lick where it was thought the Indians might have gone in the hope of stealing more horses. This second party went out at once and lay in hiding near the Lick. It was not long before nine Indians appeared. The men agreed that no one was to fire until the braves were close enough for every shot to count. One man's gun was snapped accidently but did not go off. The others, thinking that he was seeking the honor of killing the first Indian, fired at once. It was evident that several Indians were wounded, for much blood was found, but the victims either crawled into the thick woods or were carried away by their companions. The men from the Flat Lick and Logan and his group returned to the fort at nightfall. Next morning he and eighteen of his men went to the spot where the Indians had been hit. Dogs were taken in the hope that the savages could be tracked through the cane, but this did not prove successful.[11]

[11] "Trabue's Narrative," 17-19. Draper MSS. 12 C 24(2); 9 J 203(1)-204(1); 17 CC 194.

The act establishing Kentucky County provided that the first court should be held at Harrodsburg but gave the justices the privilege of choosing a permanent county seat. The choice fell upon St. Asaph's, with the stipulation that the clerk's office would remain at Harrodsburg, the home of county clerk Levi Todd.

In July, 1778, several men from Harrodsburg were en route to St. Asaph's to attend court. They were within ten miles of their destination, and near the location of the present-day town of Danville, when they were fired upon from a canebrake. William Poage was hit, and his companions fled toward Logan's Fort without stopping to see if he were alive or dead. Although Logan was short of men after several had left for Clark's Illinois campaign, he called together a few and set out. Poage was found, badly wounded but alive. The failure of the Indians to discover him was attributed to the fact that his horse had run for quite a distance before the rider had fallen off. A litter was made, and the wounded man was carried to Harrodsburg. A few days later he died.

On the following day, as Logan and his men were returning to St. Asaph's, they were attacked near the place were Poage had been wounded. Hugh Leeper was hit in the shoulder, but the men returned the fire and the Indians fled, leaving behind a gun which was identified as Poage's. The men continued on their way, taking turns at carrying Leeper. They were caught by darkness when still five miles from the fort. Leaving the others to care for the wounded man, Logan pushed on. He reached home nearly exhausted, having carried Leeper for a mile just before parting from the others. Daniel Trabue, a Negro man, and a boy started at once with food and horses. One of the watchers, Archer McKinney, was caring for Leeper while the others slept. On seeing what he correctly assumed to be help approaching, he called to his companions to awaken them. One of them misunderstood and thought that Indians were coming. His concern alarmed the others, and all but McKinney ran for trees and cocked their guns to make a stand.

Trabue called to them and made himself known in time to prevent anyone from firing. Leeper, who had lost a large amount of blood, was held on a horse for the remainder of the journey. Although his wound was serious he eventually recovered.[12]

The attack on Boonesborough, of which Boone and Hancock had warned, had not yet materialized, but preparations for defense were continued. The fort was strengthened, and aid was sought both from the Virginia executive and from the neighboring forts. In reply to the former request, the county lieutenant of Washington County, Colonel Arthur Campbell, was authorized to send a detachment of militia, not to exceed 150 men, and a supply of powder and lead. The call for local aid brought only a few men from Harrodsburg. Logan sent fifteen out of a garrison of only forty. William Manifee, one of the first residents of St. Asaph's and a sergeant in Logan's company, was sent at their leader.[13]

This loss was partially balanced by the return of some of the men who had gone with Clark. Kaskaskia and Cahokia had been taken, and Vincennes had capitulated voluntarily. Their three month enlistment having expired, these Kentuckians must have felt that the situation at home required their attention. They returned to the Falls of the Ohio under the leadership of William Linn, and there they were discharged. Linn also carried orders for the removal of the Falls settlers from the island to the southern shore. A new fort soon was erected to protect the settlers who had come to the Falls with Clark, and this eventually became the headquarters of his Illinois Regiment.[14]

Near the end of August a scouting expedition set out from Boonesborough for the Shawnee country. Its members hoped

---

[12] Hening (ed.), *Statutes*, IX, 259. "Trabue's Narrative," 19-21. Draper MSS. 12 C 10(4), 24(7); 4 J 2, 97; 9 J 197(1)-98; 30 S 130; 11 CC 262; 12 CC 73; 13 CC 213.

[13] "Trabue's Narrative," 20-31. Draper MSS. 4 B 203-204, 253; 60 J 365; 13 S 102-103; 17 J 28.

[14] Clark to Mason, November 19, 1779, 129-36. "Clark's Memoir," 84-91. "Clark's Journal," 129-35. Draper MSS. 48 J 14.

to learn the intention of the Indians in regard to an invasion and perhaps to steal a few horses. This plan had been suggested by Boone on his return from captivity. Colonel Richard Calloway, senior officer at Boonesborough and next in rank to County Lieutenant John Bowman, had opposed the idea and for a time the matter had been dropped. Two months later, however, Boone was on his way with twenty picked men. Logan evidently raised no serious objection, because the group included several from his fort. Among these were his brother John, who had come out from the Holston Settlements, Ann Logan's brother Alexander Montgomery, who was an ensign in Logan's company, Simon Kenton, who had just returned from Clark's campaign, and the scout John Kennedy. Near a Shawnee village on Paint Creek, a tributary of the Scioto River, they engaged a small band of Indians with indecisive results. It had been their intention to penetrate more deeply into the Indian country, but discovery made this unwise. All except Kenton and Montgomery returned home at once. These two took a different route, delayed a little, and managed to bring back four of the Indians' horses.[15]

Hardly had they returned when John Bowman expressed a desire for more information about the Shawnee villages, especially the town of Chillicothe on the Little Miami River. The relative ease with which Kenton and Montgomery had captured horses on the previous trip caused them to volunteer for another attempt at combining scouting and horse stealing. George Clark and Daniel Trabue agreed to join them. Halters were fashioned from buffalo hide, leggings of deer skin were prepared, and to the usual provisions they added a quantity of salt for use in catching horses. Just before their departure from Logan's, Trabue's older brother James arrived from Boonesborough. On learning what was afoot, he persuaded

[15] Deposition of Stephen Hancock, quoted in Charles R. Staples, "History in Circuit Court Records," in *Register of the Kentucky State Historical Society*, XXXII (1934), 8. "Trabue's Narrative," 25. Edna Kenton, *Simon Kenton, His Life and Period, 1755-1836* (Garden City, N. Y., 1930), 97-99. Draper MSS. 17 J 28.

Daniel not to risk his life in this way, and so Kenton, Clark, and Montgomery made the journey without him. After spying on Chillicothe and getting the information that Bowman wanted, they selected several horses, got the halters on them, and started for the Ohio. On reaching the river the horses refused to cross. The delay which resulted from several unsuccessful attempts to get the animals into the water gave the Shawnee time to overtake them. Montgomery was killed while trying to escape, and his long blonde hair was taken as a trophy. Kenton was wounded and captured, but Clark, who had hidden under some driftwood, returned safely to Logan's Fort with news of the tragedy.[16]

On September 7, the same day that this scouting party had left Logan's, the long awaited enemy reached Boonesborough. There were ten white men and an estimated 330 Indians. Chief Blackfish was along, and in command was a French-Canadian officer in the British service, Lieutenant Antoine de Quindre. A delegation approached one of the gates under a flag of truce. They asked to see Boone, whose offers to surrender the fort evidently had been believed. After conferring with the enemy, Boone expressed the opinion that a satisfactory peace could be made if the other officers could go with him to the Indians' camp for a powwow. Colonel Calloway objected to this but finally agreed to such a meeting if held within range of the guns of the fort. After a lengthy conference which extended into a second day, the Indians pretended to be satisfied and asked to shake hands with the white representatives. This request was complied with, but the red men then insisted that each white man shake hands with two Indians at the same time. This evidently was a preliminary to taking the officers as hostages. Calloway suspected this and jerked his hands away. The other officers after a brief struggle succeeded in doing likewise and made a break for the fort, covered by rifle fire from the loopholes. Taking shelter quickly,

16 Kenton, *Simon Kenton*, 103-107. "Trabue's Narrative," 21-23. Draper MSS. 1 BB 84-85; 12 C 13(3); 9 J 188(1)-189; 5 S 130; 18 S 161.

some of the Indians were able to fire at the fleeing men. Squire Boone, brother of Daniel, was hit but managed to reach the fort. The Indians thereupon began a siege that lasted for nine days and nights. After several attempts to set fire to the fort and an effort to dig under the walls, which was discouraged by the digging of a countermine, the enemy withdrew.[17]

Ever since Boone had returned from captivity with his warning of the impending attack on Boonesborough, Logan had made every effort to prepare his own fort for a possible siege. The enclosure had been enlarged in the past year, and new cabins had been built to accommodate the increased population. Additional blockhouses had been placed in such positions that every outer structure was now of this type or a modification thereof. Provisions such as corn and pumpkins were brought inside the stockade. Daniel Trabue's public storehouse was inspected by Logan. It contained large quantities of corn, pork, buffalo, beef, and domestic beef. Logan complimented Trabue on his industry but expressed doubt as to the sufficiency of the stores if a siege should be prolonged. Desiring to bring into the fort cattle, which could be butchered in an emergency, Logan rode alone to the Flat Lick. This salt vein lay about two miles to the southeast of the fort at the foot of the range of hills known as the Knobs. As he was returning home a small band of Indians saw him and fired as he passed the point where they were hidden. One ball struck his left arm, shattering the bone and causing him to drop his gun. The Indians started after him and seemed intent upon taking him alive. He had to let go of the bridle reins to hold the injured arm, which was in danger of being torn completely off by the tall cane, but this made it difficult to control his horse. One Indian came close enough to grab the animal by the tail but was unable to maintain his hold. Logan finally placed the thumb of the wounded arm between his teeth to

[17] John Bowman to George Rogers Clark, October 14, 1778, Draper MSS. 48 J 42. "Trabue's Narrative," 25-27. "Whitley's Narrative," 29. Draper MSS. 4 B 235-38; 6 S 130-31. Charles Kerr (ed.), *History of Kentucky* (Chicago and New York, 1922) I, 181.

prevent it from dangling at his side. This left his right hand free to guide his horse. He soon outdistanced his pursuers and entered the gates of his fort, where the arm was set and treated by Ben Pettit. Particles of bone kept working their way out of the wound, and recovery was extremely slow. Logan continued to direct preparations from his cabin, and by the time the enemy arrived at Boonesborough his station was in a state of readiness. Although fifteen men had been loaned to Boonesborough, his garrison still contained twenty-four defenders.[18]

One of the residents of Boonesborough, William Patton, was away from the fort when the Indians came and returned to find himself completely cut off from his home. He remained in the woods for several days, and at times he would take a position upon a hill from which he could view some of the fighting. After about a week he watched one night an attempt of the enemy to storm the fort. When they rushed toward the walls with flaming torches the shouts and screams were terrifying. There is little reason to doubt that most of the screaming came from the savages, but Patton believed that they actually had broken into the fort and that men, women, and children were being butchered. He hastened to Logan's to tell the people there that Boonesborough had fallen.

The effect which this report produced is not difficult to imagine. Through the trying eighteen months of Indian warfare, Harrodsburg and Boonesborough had held the ends of a line which separated St. Asaph's from the Shawnee and their warlike neighbors. It is true that this line had been crossed at times, and Logan and his men had withstood two attacks in addition to raids by small parties. But so long as the larger forts stood, Indians reaching St. Asaph's from the north would have the two white garrisons at their backs and would risk being cut off from their villages. Encouraged by their supposed success at Boonesborough, the savages would be almost certain

[18] "Trabue's Narrative," 28-30. "Whitley's Narrative," 31. Draper MSS. 12 C 10(4-5), 44(2); 9 J 187-88; 17 J 9; 18 S 154-55, 168.

to try to take one of the other stations, perhaps both, so that the people at Logan's were expecting the worst. To a natural fear for their own safety and the anxiety over the fate of the people of Boonesborough there was added the belief that fifteen of their own men, who had been sent to aid in the defense of that station, had been massacred.

Although he was confined to his cabin by the serious condition of his arm, Logan still was the militia captain at St. Asaph's and acted accordingly. Insofar as it was possible for him to do so he continued to direct the preparations for withstanding a siege. The aid which Colonel Arthur Campbell had been authorized to send from the Holston had not arrived. Logan sent John Martin to explain the seriousness of the situation and to urge haste. He then called his men by turns to his cabin, where he spent considerable time in trying to raise individual morale. He did not promise success but urged that they defend the position so long as a man was left alive. He predicted that if the fort were taken the sick and wounded, if too weak to travel, would be killed. The ablebodied might be taken to Detroit as prisoners of war, but it was by no means certain that even they would be spared.

That night Indians came close enough to the fort to steal a horse and were fired upon by the sentries. Next morning it was evident from the alarm shown by the cattle that savages were around. Some cows outside the fort had arrows protruding from their bodies, but it was not considered safe to open the gates to let any of them in. The Indians might be watching for just such an opportunity. The mortality rate among cows that had worn bells was especially high because noise-makers were highly prized by the red men.

There was no attack that day, so it was assumed that the Indians were taking their time about moving their main force from Boonesborough. An all-night watch was kept with one-half of the men on duty at a time. During the next day there suddenly came warning cries from some of the men who were stationed at the loopholes that faced toward Boonesborough.

Moving figures had been seen in the distance and they were approaching the fort. Because they were in a single file, their number could not yet be determined. All of the loopholes were manned and ready. Although the danger was now at hand, the tension of the past forty-eight hours seemed to have eased. "Damn you, come on!" said one of the men, and the words were repeated all along the side of the fort that faced the enemy. Each of the defenders had picked his man and was waiting for the order to open fire when someone cried out: "It is our boys!" This was soon verified, and the gates were lifted. The men who had gone to the relief of Boonesborough had returned. Some of the people laughed for joy and some cried at being reunited with those whom they had not expected to see again. The news that Boonesborough had not fallen and that the enemy apparently had left the country was carried to Logan, who smiled for the first time since his injury.[19]

The aid from the Holston did not arrived until early in October. There was talk of taking the offensive against the enemy until it was realized that the length of time for which the Holston men had been called out was too short to permit their being used in this way. Besides, there were only eighty of them, and Kentucky County could hardly have used her full militia strength for a campaign. The three forts had to be guarded and held or the whole region would have been lost.[20]

Soon after the siege of Boonesborough, Captain Daniel Boone was tried by a court martial which sat at Logan's Fort. Four charges were brought by his superior officer, Colonel Richard Calloway. Boone was accused of surrendering the Blue Licks salt makers to the Indians. At Detroit he had told Governor Hamilton that he would surrender Boonesborough, and the inhabitants would place themselves under British protection. After his escape from the Shawnee, he had led a party across the Ohio when men might be needed at any moment for the

[19] "Trabue's Narrative," 27-32. Draper MSS. 4 B 248-53; 17 J 28; 9 J 186(1)-87. Bakeless, *Daniel Boone,* 221.
[20] John Bowman to George Rogers Clark, October 14, 1778, Draper MSS. 48 J 42(1). "Trabue's Narrative," Draper MSS. 57 J 32.

defense of the fort. When the Indians arrived at Boonesborough, Boone had favored the parley which had nearly
resulted in the capture of the officers. Calloway added that
Boone's conduct indicated that he was favorable to the British,
and that he ought at least to be deprived of his commission.

Boone had an answer to each charge. He said that the
Indians who had captured him at Blue Licks were on their way
to Boonesborough. His surrender of the salt makers, he contended, had saved the fort, which at the time was not in a
condition for defense. He admitted having agreed with Hamilton for the surrender of Boonesborough but insisted that he
was deceiving him deliberately so that Hamilton would think
that a small invasion force would be sufficient. To the third
charge he answered that his Paint Creek trip had been a
scouting expedition. It was conducted for the purpose of
obtaining information on the enemy's movements, and he
considered it to have been a success. The talks at Boonesborough he said were held for the purpose of gaining time. It
still was possible that the expected reinforcements from the
Holston would arrive in sufficient strength to distract the
Indians and perhaps to drive them off entirely.

The court was satisfied with Boone's explanations and
acquitted him of all charges. Calloway and Logan still had
some doubts and were not too well pleased with the outcome.[21]

The Indians who had wandered around Logan's Fort after
the siege of Boonesborough had stolen most of the remaining
horses. William Whitley, who had previous experience in
acquiring horses, decided to take a few men to the Shawnee
country in an attempt to replenish the supply. They painted
themselves and dressed as savages. At a camp about fifteen
miles from Chillicothe they obtained several horses and started

[21] Draper MSS. 4 B 253-56; 11 CC 14. "Trabue's Narrative," 32-33.
Bakeless, *Daniel Boone*, 229-36. Thwaites, *Daniel Boone*, 165-67.
    Daniel Trabue was present at Boone's court martial. His narrative is the
only known primary source on this event. Trabue does not name the members
of the court. Possibilities in addition to Logan would have been John Bowman,
John Todd, and James Harrod.

for home, but before reaching the Ohio they were attacked and were fortunate to escape with the loss of only one man. All of the horses were retaken by the Indians.[22]

The year 1778 had been little better than the preceding one for the Kentuckians. They had continued to live inside the stockades under very crowded conditions. The attack on Boonesborough had shown that Indians under British leadership could conduct a siege. The attacks of 1777, while sometimes given that name, had been less intensive. The appearance of Indians under white officers set a pattern which was to be followed several times in the remaining years of the Revolution.

[22] "Trabue's Narrative," 32. "Whitley's Narrative," 29-31.

CHAPTER V

BOWMAN'S EXPEDITION

INDIAN ATTACKS AND THE constant fear of being shot from ambush made the growing of crops, the production of domestic meat, and the procurement of wild meat difficult problems in Kentucky. Not only did families have to be provided for, but extra supplies had to be kept on hand for the use of the militia. A militiaman might have been an unmarried man sent from one of the counties nearest to Kentucky County for garrison duty at Boonesborough, Logan's Fort, Harrodsburg, or the Falls, but very frequently he was the head of a family living at one of these forts. He provided food for himself, his wife, and his children, and sold his surplus, if any, to the state.

Militia accounts for the year 1778 show that Captain Benjamin Logan furnished the largest amount of provisions on a list which contained the names of forty-seven settlers. His contribution was valued at £136 15s. Although they were usually on the defensive, he and his company had been on militia duty on several occasions during the year. Some drew their rations from the public storehouse, while others furnished their own and charged their expenses to the state. Logan was one of those who found his own rations for a total of fifty-two days at a cost of £12 12s. The commissary, James Trabue, made a trip across the mountains and returned in December with the money to settle his accounts. Some of the entries were marked "paid," but a line was drawn through Logan's ration account, which may indicate that he decided not to charge this to the state.[1]

The quantity of meat which could be preserved depended both upon the supply which was obtainable and upon the availability of salt. During 1778 salt was being manufactured in small quantities at Bullitt's Lick. In December the James Harrod party, which had set out from Kentucky on October 15, returned from the Spanish salt works across the Mississippi with a considerable supply. This, in the opinion of Colonel John Bowman, was the essential which would enable the Kentucky people to hold their ground. Bowman had backed Clark's expedition by promising to furnish him with 35,000 pounds of bear meat. Bears still were plentiful in the Kentucky woods, and hunters from Logan's Fort killed a great many, some weighing as much as 400 pounds dressed.[2]

In December, Henry Hamilton moved out of Detroit and down the Wabash River with 30 British regulars, 50 Frenchmen, and 400 Indians. On December 17 the officers and men of the small garrison that Clark had placed at Vincennes became Hamilton's prisoners. The British commander believed that it was too late in the season to attempt a march to Kaskaskia. Instead he ordered his Indians to watch the Ohio River for travelers and to harass the Kentucky settlements. They were to return to Vincennes in the spring.

On learning of this situation, Clark realized that his only hope lay in the possibility of surprising Hamilton. Marching across the flooded Illinois country with about 200 men, he reached Vincennes on February 23. After a brief siege and a period of negotiation, surrender terms were agreed upon near the close of the following day, and the formalities of capitulation and occupation were signed on February 25.[3]

On the day that Clark occupied the fort at Vincennes, the routine at Logan's was varied by another wedding. Benjamin

[1] Draper MSS. 17 J 12. "Daniel Trabue's Narrative," Draper MSS. 57 J 35.
[2] Bowman to Clark, October 14, 1778, Draper MSS. 48 J 42(1). Patrick Henry to Clark, December 12, 1778, Draper MSS. 60 J 8. "Trabue's Narrative," 35. Draper MSS. 18 J 84; 12 CC 65.
[3] Clark to George Mason, November 19, 1779, Draper MSS. 58 J 148-49, 157-58, 161-68. "Clark's Memoir," Draper MSS. 59 J 156-61, 210-13, 219. Clark to Benjamin Harrison, March 10, 1779, Draper MSS. 58 J 4. See also an undated letter of Henry Hamilton, Draper MSS. 58 J 116-17.

Briggs, who was a son of Logan's sister Mary and her husband Samuel Briggs, had come out from the Holston Settlements to St. Asaph's. He cleared about two acres of ground and raised a crop of corn in 1778. In the fall of that year his parents moved to St. Asaph's, bringing a family which included a grown daughter named Jane. The presence of Jane Briggs soon became known at Harrodsburg, and two of the eligible young bachelors from that fort, Levi Todd and Silas Harlan, became frequent callers. As clerk of the county court, which held its sessions at St. Asaph's, Todd had to spend a part of his time there. This could have given him an advantage over his rival. Then too, the question of parental attitudes may have been involved. Samuel Briggs is said to have considered both of the suitors good prospects, but he was impressed by Todd's education and by the position of prominence that he already had attained in county affairs. It may be that Jane was influenced by other considerations, but on February 25, 1779, she and Todd were married. The wedding took place in the Logan home, and the couple went to Harrodsburg to live.[4]

The tedious months which had been spent inside the crowded forts at St. Asaph's and at Harrodsburg came to an end for many people early in 1779. Recent damage by the Indians had been slight. The population was increasing, and there was reason to believe that additional stations could be built and maintained. This feeling of increasing strength and comparative safety must have been intensified by the news of Clark's capture of Henry Hamilton in February, and by Colonel Evan Shelby's victory over the Chickamauga, an offshoot of the Cherokee tribe, in the following April. It was believed that these were the Indians who had agreed to cooperate with Hamilton in conquering Kentucky.[5]

[4] Draper MSS. 9 J 184(1), 189(1), 202; 44 J 13(1), 20(1); 18 S 144; 12 CC 73. Levi Todd and Jane Briggs Todd were the grandparents of Mary Todd Lincoln.

[5] Thomas Jefferson to George Washington, June 23, 1779, Draper MSS. 27 S 60. "Clark's Memoir," 161. Clark to Mason, November 19, 1779, 158. John Haywood, The Civil and Political History of the State of Tennessee (Nashville, 1891), 72-73.

Among the first to leave Logan's Fort was the family of William Whitley, who had built a station of his own at the Walnut Flat five miles from Logan's in the direction of the Crab Orchard. This was occupied in January, 1779.[6]

On April 15 twenty-five militiamen under Ensign Robert Patterson were sent from Harrodsburg to establish a station at some suitable place across the Kentucky River. A spot was selected on the present site of the city of Lexington. Some corn was planted, and a blockhouse was erected and garrisoned.[7]

It was also in April that the Bryan brothers, who had established a claim on the North Fork of the Elkhorn River in 1776, returned with a party of North Carolinians and a few Virginians. They began the construction of a fort which in time became one of Kentucky's largest.[8]

Logan's Fort had been a convenient stopping place for people who came to Kentucky by the Wilderness Trail. Although it had been enlarged, it was again crowded. Three more groups of settlers moved on before the month of April had come to an end. One, led by Isaac Ruddle, went by way of Lexington. From that point to the South Fork of the Licking, Ruddle marked a trace which on several occasions was followed by Kentuckians who sought to take the offensive against the Indians. He and his people built a station on the right bank of South Licking about three miles north of the point where that stream is formed by the juncture of Hinkston and Stoner Creeks. It was a site that had been abandoned by John Hinkston in the summer of 1776. About two weeks after their arrival, these people were joined by Ruddle's brothers, James and George, who brought several other persons from Logan's Fort. John Martin, coming from Logan's with a third party of settlers, established a station on the left bank of

[6] "William Whitley's Narrative," Draper MSS. 9 CC 31. Statement of William Whitley, Jr., Draper MSS. 12 C 62(5).

[7] Deposition of Samuel Johnson, Bourbon County Complete Record Book C, 70-71. Draper MSS. 12 CC 65; 1 MM 3.

[8] Draper MSS. 60 J 382. *Bradford's Notes*, 111-12.

Stoner Creek in a large horseshoe bend. The site was about two miles upstream from the point where the two creeks came together.[9]

In addition to those who left Logan's Fort in groups, it is likely that other individuals followed the example of William Casey. This private in Logan's militia company was busily engaged in making improvements on a tract of land to which he hoped to establish a title. It lay in the valley of the Hanging Fork of Dick's River.[10]

Among the new arrivals this year were the James Allens, who had been neighbors of Logan's mother and brothers on Kerr's Creek in Augusta County. On reaching Kentucky with their four children—Sarah, Margaret, Joseph, and John—they too stopped for a time at St. Asaph's.[11]

It was also in April that Henry Hamilton, former lieutenant governor of Quebec, paid an unplanned visit to Logan's Fort. Clark had paroled many of the men whom he had captured at Vincennes, partly because of a lack of sufficient guards and provisions, but also in the hope that on returning to Detroit they would speak favorably of the Virginians. He had taken other posts by convincing the people of his friendly intentions. Even if this were unlikely in the case of Detroit, his attempt to use this method might make the task somewhat easier.

Hamilton and his officers, together with a few of his private soldiers, started to the Falls of the Ohio from Vincennes on March 8, guarded by Captain John Williams, Captain John Rogers, and twenty-five men. From the Falls, with Williams in command, the long journey to Williamsburg was continued. On April 6 they reached Harrodsburg, which Hamilton described in his journal. "The people on our first coming," he

[9] Depositions of Isaac and James Ruddle, Bourbon County Complete Record Book C, 30-31, 34-35. Deposition of Charles Gatliff, Draper MSS. 18 J 102. Draper MSS. 12 CC 66-67. J. Winston Coleman, Jr., *The British Invasion of Kentucky* (Lexington, 1951), 10-11.

[10] Draper MSS. 17 J 28; 60 J 383.

[11] Mary A. Goodson, "Captain Joseph Allen," in *Register of the Kentucky State Historical Society*, XLIII (1945), 345-46.

wrote, "looked upon us as little better than savages, which was very excusable considering how we had been represented."[12]

John Bowman sent to Logan's for horses to be used on the next lap of the journey and lent one of his own to Hamilton. Of the county lieutenant, Hamilton wrote: "Colonel Bowman acted as a person above prejudice by rendering us every service in his power." The horses arrived on April 17, and two days later the prisoners and their guards set out for Logan's Fort, which they reached in the evening of the same day.

Hamilton described the fort as being "an oblong square formed by the houses making a double street, [and] at the angles were stockaded bastions." He found the location of the fort much to his liking. "The situation," he wrote, "is romantic, among wooded hills. A stream of fine water passes at the foot of these hills which turns a small grist mill." The attitude of the residents of Logan's Fort was perhaps a little more hostile than that of the Harrodsburg settlers. "The people here," said Hamilton, "were not exceedingly well disposed to us, and we were accosted by the females especially in pretty course [sic] terms." He may have been referring to Mrs. William Manifee, who is said to have expressed interest in a tomahawk which he still had in his possession. After commenting that it must often have been used on innocent women and children, she seized the weapon and threatened the prisoner both in words and by gestures. Logan is said to have been embarrassed by this event, which took place in his own home. In referring to the Logans, Hamilton said: "The captain and his wife, who had a brother carried off by the Indians, were very civil and hospitable."

The guards and their prisoners left St. Asaph's on April 20 and marched to Whitley's Station. Here they purchased pro-

---

[12] Clark to Thomas Jefferson, April 29, 1779, Draper MSS. 27 S 65. Hamilton to Richard B. Lernoult, May 21, 1779, Draper MSS. 58 J 118-19. Clark to Mason, November 19, 1779, 169. "Clark's Memoir," 222. Draper MSS. 60 J 16. Photostatic copy of the MSS. "Journal of Lord Henry Hamilton," Filson Club, Louisville, Kentucky, pp. 151-53. The original is owned by Harvard University.

visions for the long trip through the Wilderness. The journey was then continued to Williamsburg, where Hamilton felt the wrath of state officials whose opinion of him was not greatly different from that of the frontiersmen.[13]

After consolidating his position at Vincennes, Clark began to lay his plans for the reduction of the British post at Detroit. John Bowman was urged to send all the aid that could be spared and was requested to state the number of men that he could furnish by June. Bowman promised to send 300 men when called upon if it were at all possible. Clark in his reply set June 20 as the date for a rendezvous at Vincennes.[14]

Although Bowman may have been sincere in his estimate of the aid which Kentucky County could send to Clark, he had long been considering an expedition of his own. The Shawnee were nearer at hand than any Indians with whom Clark would come in contact. They had been identified as participants in many of the attacks upon Kentucky. It was chiefly the threat of annihilation by this tribe that had forced the evacuation of the region northeast of the Kentucky River in 1776. The safe return of George Clark from the spying mission which had cost Alexander Montgomery his life and Simon Kenton his freedom had put Bowman in possession of some information about the Shawnee village of Chillicothe.[15]

Chillicothe was situated on the Little Miami River between the present-day towns of Xenia and Springfield. It was not the first town to which the Shawnee had given this name, which signifies an eternal council fire. An earlier one had been built in the valley of the Scioto, and two later ones were to be established, one on the Big Miami and the other on the Maumee. This tendency of Indians to carry the name of their old village with them when they migrated has created con-

[13] "Hamilton's Journal," 151-53. Draper MSS. 5 S 130; 18 S 155-56. Frederick Haldimand to George Washington, August 29, 1779, Draper MSS. 58 J 51-52. Draper MSS. 60 J 18-31; 18 S 155-56.
[14] Clark to Mason, November 19, 1779, 173-76. "Clark's Memoir," 221-23.
[15] Draper MSS. 5 S 130. Kenton, *Simon Kenton*, 103-107.

fusion in some of the writing bearing upon the relations between the Kentuckians and the Shawnee.[16]

Early in May, Bowman made his plans known to the other militia officers of the county and named the mouth of the Licking River as the meeting place. Although it was expected that a draft would be necessary, a sufficient number of volunteers was obtained. The largest company came up the Ohio from the Falls. It contained ninety-six men with William Harrod as captain and James Patton as lieutenant. The size of this company should not be taken as an indication that the settlement at the Falls had outgrown the others as some men from the Monongahela Valley were in that area at the time, and they had no objection to taking part in an Indian campaign on their way back to their homes.[17]

The men in and around Boonesborough were collected by Captain John Holder. Including Holder himself, they numbered fifty-eight. Logan raised forty-seven men from his own and Whitley's station. Harrodsburg sent two companies totaling seventy men commanded by Silas Harlan and Levi Todd.

Logan, with his brother John as his lieutenant, led his company across Dick's River at the mouth of Hanging Fork. They struck and crossed the Kentucky just below the mouth of Hickman's Creek. That night they camped at a spring in the valley of Clear Creek. Passing by the newly founded and almost uninhabited Lexington, they overtook the companies of Holder and Todd about twenty miles north of that point. When they made camp that night they were on the North Fork of Elkhorn River above the mouth of Little Elkhorn. Next day they crossed Dry Ridge, the divide which separates the basin of the Kentucky from that of the Licking. Another night's rest was taken on Mill Creek two miles north of Lee's Lick. This is a western branch of the South Fork of Licking

[16] Draper MSS. 4 B 186n; 8 J 248-49, 251, 299; 31 J 84-84(1).

[17] Draper MSS. 1 A 20; 17 J 14, 24-26; 48 J 89(3); 60 J 131; 12 CC 66. Deposition of James Guthrie in Ardery, Kentucky Court and Other Records, 141-42.

River. Continuing to the headwaters of Banklick Creek, they followed that stream to where it empties into the main branch of the Licking. A short march downstream brought them to the point of rendezvous.

Colonel Bowman, with Harlan's company, had traveled by way of Martin's and Ruddle's Stations. This gained him one officer, Lieutenant John Haggin, and eighteen men. On May 27 Bowman with his detachment joined the others at the mouth of the Licking. At that point the county lieutenant took command.[18]

With a total of 296 men Bowman crossed the Ohio on the following day. William Whitley and George Clark were selected as pilots, and the march up the valley of the Little Miami began. Just before dark on the night of May 29 they made a halt about ten miles from Chillicothe. No Indians had been seen, and it was assumed that their approach had not been discovered. Bowman decided to continue the march in order to surround the town before daylight and begin the attack at dawn.[19]

Just after midnight they reached an open prairie which lay to the southwest of the town. From this point Bowman and his captains moved on alone to reconnoiter. When they returned the commander regrouped his force into three companies, which were to be commanded by Logan, Holder, and Harrod. Logan then was sent to the west of the town, where he stationed his men between it and the Little Miami. Harrod led his men to the east side of the town, extending his lines until they met with Logan's. When Holder had placed his men south of the town it was completely surrounded. Bowman gave strict orders that, except in case of discovery by the enemy, no guns were to be fired until he should give the

[18] Depositions of William Whitley, Levi Todd, John Logan, Robert Patterson, James Ruddle, and Benjamin Harrison in Bourbon County Complete Record Book C, 19-20, 23, 34-35, 53-57, 73. Draper MSS. 1 A 20; 5 D 8; 8 J 150-52; 17 J 26-27; 31 J 84.
[19] Draper MSS. 1 A 20; 5 D 9; 18 J 102; 48 J 89(3)-90; 12 CC 65. Extract from *Gazette of South Carolina*, July 28, 1779, Draper MSS. 32 J 51.

signal. This would be given just as it became light enough to see clearly. All went well until the Indians' dogs became alarmed and set up a terrific clamor. A warrior came out to see what was the matter. He was within a few feet of Holder's men before he discovered them. As he shouted to give the alarm, he was shot by Hugh Ross and tomahawked by Jacob Stearns.[20]

This brought the Indians out of their cabins in short order. Some ran toward Holder's men and received a heavy fire. Others, trying to escape toward the river, got a similar reception from Logan. Near the center of the town there was a large council house, which, for defensive purposes, had been constructed as a two-story blockhouse. To this the Indians retreated and began to return the fire from the loopholes. The white men now advanced into the village from all sides and began to plunder the cabins and to set fire to them. Logan and some of his men constructed a movable breastwork which enabled them to apply the torch to cabins situated within range of the council house. Bowman made one attempt to storm this building but soon saw that without artillery it would be impossible to take it. Not wishing to sacrifice his men, he ordered a gradual withdrawal. Some of the Kentuckians kept the council house under fire from a distance, while others busied themselves at rounding up the Indians' horses. An Indian commander in the council house was heard encouraging his braves in a loud voice. This was believed at the time to be the Shawnee chief, Blackfish, who was well known in Kentucky. A white prisoner who was in the council house at the time made his escape sometime later and returned to Kentucky. The voice, he explained, had been that of one of the medicine men. Blackfish had been seriously wounded at the outset and was unable to continue in command. He died a few weeks later.

[20] Draper MSS. 1 A 20-21; 5 D 10-11; 8 J 150-52; 9 CC 31-33; 12 CC 65. John Bowman to his uncle, June 15, 1779, quoted in Bodley, *History of Kentucky*, 202-203.

During the withdrawal several men who had taken positions behind an oak log about forty yards from the council house were unintentionally left. Seven of these lost their lives in the exchange of fire with the Indians. The other eight decided to try to reach one of the cabins by running zigzag, and in this they were successful. In the cabin were some thick puncheons. Holding these behind their backs for protection, they reached the other men in safety.[21]

By this time nearly two hundred horses had been secured, and with these and a considerable amount of plunder, including furs, skins, and silver ornaments, the homeward march was begun. At least two participants, George Michael Bedinger and William Whitley, claimed many years later that the retreat had been hastened by a report that Simon Girty was bringing a party of Mingo warriors to the relief of the town. This report, they said, was brought by a Negro woman, who seemed to have escaped from the council house. Her subsequent disappearance was taken to mean that she had been sent by the Indians to circulate a false rumor. Bowman did not mention the incident in either of the two accounts that he wrote upon his return from the expedition. He explained his order to retreat in terms of the strong position held by the enemy and the very satisfactory amount of damage which already had been done to the village of Chillicothe.[22]

On the return journey the men marched in three columns with Logan's company on the right, Harrod's on the left, and Holder's in the center. They were barely fifteen miles from Chillicothe when they were overtaken. A band of Indians, which kept increasing in size, forced them to take cover and make a stand. In accordance with a prepared plan, the companies of Logan and Harrod formed the sides of a rectangle. Holder's company broke into two parts to close the ends.

[21] Bowman to his uncle, 202-203. Draper MSS. 1 A 21-24; 12 C 15(5); 5 D 13, 20; 8 J 151(1)-152, 158; 49 J 89(3)-90; 5 S 181; 18 S 156-57; 12 CC 65.
[22] Bowman to Clark, June 13, 1779, Draper MSS. 48 J 52-52(1). Bowman to his uncle, 202-203. Draper MSS. 1 A 24; 9 CC 32-33.

Within this enclosure were the horses and the plunder. Fortunately there were enough trees to afford individual protection without leaving serious gaps or greatly altering the formation. The Indians were persistent, and the battle continued for about three hours. As might have been expected, the horses became excited and some succeeded in escaping through the lines. Blackfish lay wounded at the village, and the savages now were commanded by Red Hawk, who died in this engagement. Seeing that the Indians showed no sign of withdrawing, Bowman finally ordered a charge which broke their lines and put them to flight. He had lost one man in this action and three had been wounded. Although some of the horses had escaped, the Kentuckians crossed the Ohio on June 1 with 163 mounts.

Bowman and his men camped at a spring a few miles south of the river and devoted two days to auctioning off the plunder. Horses that were believed to have been stolen from the Kentucky stations were reserved to be claimed by their owners. The others were placed on the block, along with the furs, skins, and Indian trinkets of various sorts. The total amount bid was 31,666 pounds in depreciated paper money which was the equivalent of about 1,500 pounds in specie. In accordance with the agreement under which the men had volunteered, this total was divided by the number of men to determine the average value of the plunder per man. Those who had bought more than this were given a year to pay the difference to their captains. This was to be distributed among the men who had bought less than the average. Because this was a volunteer campaign and the homes of some of the men were so far away as the Monongahela River, much of this was never collected.[23]

It is unfortunate that so many of the accounts of this expedition have been based upon the recollections of one participant,

[23] Bowman to Clark, June 13, 1779, Draper MSS. 48 J 52-52(1). Bowman to his uncle, 202-203. Draper MSS. 1 A 25-29; 12 C 15(5); 5 D 17-18; 8 J 152(1)-153(1), 278; 46 J 68; 49 J 90-90(1); 12 CC 66.

George Michael Bedinger. His version of the action, given many years afterward, built Bedinger up into a hero of considerable proportions. In the process it caused Bowman to appear as an incompetent commander and by implication a coward. The facts tell a far different story. The Kentuckians had burned more than half of the cabins in the village and had taken a large amount of plunder. It was estimated that the value of the property that was burned with the cabins was at least ten times the value of that which was carried away, and much of the Indians' supply of corn was destroyed. If the expedition failed, as some historians have contended, it is not likely that Bowman could have been solely responsible. Additional scapegoats have had to be found. The most satisfactory of these has been the party of men from along the Monongahela. The could be criticized without hurting the feelings of Kentuckians and thus they have received an undue share of blame. They are said to have been more interested in plundering than in fighting and to have refused to obey orders. These criticisms appeared in stories that were told from fifty to sixty-five years after the event. Bowman, who wrote two brief accounts as soon as he reached his home, and James Patton, the lieutenant of the company in which these men served, who wrote his account about 1792, did not blame them in any way. It has even been said that the failure was so great that Bowman was forced to resign the command of the militia of Kentucky County. This is at variance with the records. Not only was he continued as county lieutenant of Kentucky County so long as it existed, he also received the same commission in one of the counties into which it was divided. At least two contemporary newspapers, the *Virginia Gazette* and the *Gazette of South Carolina,* treated the campaign as a success.[24]

[24] Bowman to Clark, June 13, 1779, Draper MSS. 48 J 52-52(1). Bowman to his uncle, 202-203. Draper MSS. 1 A 30-31; 12 C 15(5); 5 D 17-18; 17 J 26; 49 J 89(3)-90(1); 57 J 39; 9 CC 33; 12 CC 99; 1 MM 3, 37. Extract from *Virginia Gazette,* July 10, 1779, Draper MSS. 5 D 20. Extract from *Gazette of South Carolina,* July 28, 1779, Draper MSS. 32 J 51. Lincoln County Court Order Book 1, pp. 1-3.

Not only had Bowman shown the Shawnee that Kentucky could retaliate, but he had deprived the British of about two hundred Shawnee warriors who had been collected by Captain Henry Bird to participate in a siege of Fort Laurens, an American outpost on the Tuscarawas River at the site of Bolivar, Ohio. Fearing that more of their villages would be attacked, these Shawnee left Bird and hurried to the defense of their homes. Fort Laurens for the time being was saved. Although the Americans did abandon it in July, this was not the result of an attack and the withdrawal was accomplished without loss of face.[25]

The worst that can be said of Bowman's expedition is that it may have been a factor in preventing George Rogers Clark from setting out for Detroit. On the appointed day, instead of the 300 men that Bowman had indicated he might be able to furnish, only thirty appeared at Vincennes. Men who had just returned from one campaign did not want to start out immediately on another. Clark, canceling his Detroit plans, attributed Bowman's failure to send the expected number of men to that officer's having met with "a Repulse from the Shawnees." A few more such "repulses" might have materially improved Kentucky's position.[26]

[25] Randolph C. Downes, *Council Fires on the Upper Ohio* (Pittsburgh, 1940), 218-27.

[26] Clark to Mason, November 19, 1779, 176-77. Bowman to Clark, June 13, 1779, Draper MSS. 48 J 52-52(1). Draper MSS. 4 B 128n; 1 OO 48-49.

CHAPTER VI

PREEMPTION AND PROMOTION

October 13, 1779, was a great day for the people in and around St. Asaph's. It was there that a board of commissioners appointed by the Virginia government to hear evidence regarding land claims and to award certificates of entitlement began its meetings.[1]

St. Asaph's was a logical place for the commission to start its work. It was the county seat, and, in spite of the removal of the Whitley, Martin, and Ruddle parties, it had continued to grow. Many Easterners were interested in establishing new homes west of the mountains, and Kentucky County had large tracts of unassigned land. Its southern portion, the region around St. Asaph's, still was considered safer than the part which lay near the Ohio River. Because people wanted to come to Kentucky, Richard Calloway, returning in June from the Virginia Assembly, had no difficulty in getting about forty volunteers to help him in bringing out a supply of powder and lead. When they reached Calloway's home at Boonesborough, this ammunition was divided among the Kentucky settlements. Logan sent his brother John with James Trabue and thirty other men to get his portion. One member of Calloway's party formerly had lived at St. Asaph's. Upon his return to that station with John Logan's men he expressed surprise at its growth since his departure only six months before.[2]

Among the new residents were Joseph Kennedy, Hugh Ross, Samuel Hitt, William Patton, John McKinney, Archibald Mc-

Kinney, and William Miller. Ross evidently had moved to St. Asaph's after Bowman's Shawnee campaign. At that time he had been a member of John Holder's Boonesborough company.[3]

Because all able-bodied men between the ages of sixteen and fifty served in the militia, it too was growing. John Bowman still was the county lieutenant, and Richard Calloway had been continued as colonel. George Rogers Clark, who had held the major's commission, now was a lieutenant colonel of Virginia regulars. Daniel Boone, who had been advanced to major shortly after his court martial, had gone back to his former home in North Carolina and had not yet returned. The growth in population was reflected in the filling up of what formerly had been merely skeleton militia companies and also in the formation of additional companies. The records of the commissary, James Trabue, show that by July 4, 1779, seven companies were in existence. The captains were Benjamin Logan, James Harrod, John Holder, Levi Todd, Isaac Ruddle, Richard May, and David Gass.[4]

As the senior militia captain in the St. Asaph's area, a magistrate, and Kentucky County's first sheriff, Logan was looked upon by his neighbors as their leader, both political and military. His company now contained about one hundred men, and John Logan still was serving as lieutenant. Alexander Montgomery, brother of Ann Logan, had been the ensign of this company. After he was killed by Indians, the men elected Azariah Davis as his replacement. The sergeants were Ben Pettit, William Manifee, George Clark, and Rosel Stevens.[5] The increasing population gave Kentucky County a feeling of strength. It was believed that militia garrisons at the various

---

[1] "Certificate Book of the Virginia Land Commission of 1779-80," in *Register of the Kentucky State Historical Society*, XXI (1923), 8.

[2] "Daniel Trabue's Narrative," Draper MSS. 57 J 35-39.

[3] Deposition of Hugh Ross in Charles R. Staples, "History in Circuit Court Records," in *Register of the Kentucky State Historical Society*, XXVIII (1930), 222. Lewis Collins, *History of Kentucky* (Louisville, 1924), I, 13.

[4] Draper MSS. 17 J 32.

[5] Draper MSS. 17 J 28. Collins, *History of Kentucky*, I, 12.

forts no longer were necessary, and by the end of the year they had been discontinued.

Among those who brought their families to Kentucky in the fall of 1779 were John Logan, who already had established his residence at St. Asaph's, John Floyd, by whom that settlement had been founded, and William Montgomery, the father-in-law of Benjamin Logan. The John Logans are said to have been among the first to bring cups and saucers across the mountains. In Kentucky such things were seldom seen, wooden noggins serving the same purpose. Floyd reached Harrodsburg in October with his family and his livestock. Soon he and some of his friends had established Floyd's Station on a branch of Beargrass Creek about six miles from the Falls of the Ohio.[6]

The Montgomerys came late in the season. They were met in the wilderness by Logan who took them to St. Asaph's. The family included four grown sons, William, John, Thomas, and Robert, a married daughter and her husband Joseph Russell, and several younger children.[7]

The Indians took advantage of the increased amount of traveling by watching the trails and attacking those parties that lacked sufficient protection. One such group was enroute to Kentucky in August by way of the Wilderness Trail. An attack near the Big Laurel River cost the life of the leader, James Fowler. Fortunately the attackers soon fled and the survivors were able to continue.[8]

In at least one case traveling was largely for the purpose of social diversion. George Rogers Clark had returned from the Illinois country to the Falls on August 20. He immediately notified the various Kentucky settlements of his intention of holding a celebration at the new fort which had been built on the south bank of the Ohio just above the rapids. Several people from St. Asaph's decided to attend. They set out for

[6] John Floyd to William Preston, October 30, 1779, Draper MSS. 17 CC 184-85. Draper MSS. 12 C 46(1-2); 6 J 102; 9 J 198; 49 J 89(2-3); 18 S 160.
[7] Draper MSS. 18 S 160. Collins, *History of Kentucky*, II, 471-72.
[8] "William Whitley's Narrative," Draper MSS. 9 CC 33. Draper MSS. 49 J 90(1).

Harrodsburg where they spent the night. Next day twenty men and six women, including James and Ann Harrod, Hugh McGary, and Daniel Trabue, started for the Falls. They were hardly a mile on their way when Indians were sighted in the woods. Doubting their ability to defend themselves, they hastened back to Harrodsburg. A company of men went out to investigate, but the savages had departed. Next morning the would-be celebrators, now reduced to fifteen men and three women, decided to try again. This time they had no difficulty and arrived safely at the Falls.[9]

Clark gave a ball in a large room in which a puncheon floor had been laid. James and Ann Harrod opened the festivities by dancing the first jig. A supply of rum and sugar had been brought from Illinois, so there was plenty of rum toddy to drink, and the party lasted several days.[10]

It is doubtful if Benjamin Logan was a member of the group that went to the Falls. It is even more certain that Ann Logan would not have undertaken such a trip. It was less than a month later, on September 26, that their third child and first daughter was born. Her parents decided that her name would be Jane.[11]

Although there were many reasons for the movement of people to Kentucky, such as the love of adventure and the desire to improve political or social positions, the major drawing power was land. In the May session of the Virginia Assembly an act was passed which benefited those people who already had moved to Kentucky and encouraged others to do so. It provided that those who had "settled themselves or their families" or who had borne the cost of settling others "upon any waste or unappropriated lands on the . . . western waters, to which no other person hath any legal right or claim," at any time prior to January 1, 1778, should be entitled to 400 acres of land for each family settled or any smaller amount which

[9] Clark to Mason, November 19, 1779, Draper MSS. 58 J 180. "Trabue's Narrative," 23-24.
[10] "Trabue's Narrative," 23-24.
[11] Ibid. Draper MSS. 12 C 45(4).

the individual might choose. It specified also that the tract awarded should include the particular settlement which had been made. Those settlers who desired additional land were to be allowed a preemption on any amount of adjoining land up to a maximum of 1000 acres, which might be purchased at the current state price. It must, according to the wording of the law, be land "to which no other person has any legal right or claim." There also was a clause which stipulated that "no family shall be entitled to the allowance granted to settlers by this act, unless they have made a crop of corn in that country, or resided there at least one year since the time of their settlement." An option upon a tract of Kentucky land could be obtained in still another way. All persons who prior to January 1, 1778, "had marked out or chosen for themselves any waste or unappropriated lands, and built any house or hut, or made other improvements thereon" would be allowed to preempt 1,000 acres on the same basis as those who were entitled to the 400-acre settlements. People who came to Kentucky after January 1, 1778, were not forgotten, but they were limited to the preemption "of any quantity of land, not exceeding four hundred acres."

The claims of actual settlers were to take precedence over those of officers and soldiers if the locations should happen to overlap or to coincide. In such a case the person claiming the land as a reward for military service was to make another choice. Settlement claims were to have priority over all rights of preemption.[12]

The act divided the counties on the western waters, that is, those which lay in the Mississippi Valley, into four districts, and the county of Kentucky was to constitute one of these districts. For each the governor was to appoint a four-member commission to hear evidence and to adjust claims. The commissioners were not to be residents of the district for which they were appointed. Any three of them might transact business and issue certificates "mentioning the number of acres,

12 Hening (ed.), *Statutes*, X, 39-41.

and the time of settlement, and describing as near as may be, the particular location." The certificate also was to mention "the quantity of adjacent land to which such person shall have the right of preemption." Those who appeared before this board were to pay the commissioners a fee of ten shillings for each hundred acres of land to which they were declared entitled. An additional fee of ten shillings per certificate issued would go to the clerk.

It is not surprising that there was a rapid increase in the population of Kentucky. Many people who came at this time had been in the region before January 1, 1778. They had established claims and wanted to present their evidence to the commission as soon as possible. Others came to take advantage of the preemption privilege which applied to those who came after the aforesaid date. Still others came to present the claims of their friends and relatives who were occupied with the war and were unable to make the trip. Some claims were presented by persons other than those who had established them originally, as there had been a considerable amount of buying, selling, and trading.

Although an individual could claim only one settlement for moving his own family, he might acquire additional settlement rights by moving other families at his own expense. He might also build cabins or raise patches of corn for others. This certainly was the case with the Logan brothers. Claims were established in the names of all five, but only Benjamin appears to have been in Kentucky prior to 1778.[13]

The land commissioners appointed for Kentucky County were William Fleming, Edmund Lyne, James Barbour, and Stephen Trigg. The first three were present when the commission began its sessions at St. Asaph's on October 13, 1779, and Trigg joined the others on October 28. Subsequent sessions were held at Harrodsburg, Boonesborough, Bryan's Station, and the Falls.[14]

[13] *Ibid.*, 43, 46. Draper MSS. 8 J 269. "Certificate Book," 14-15, 43.
[14] "Certificate Book," 3, 23-24.

As a result of the purchasing of the claims of others or of transporting others at their own expense, some residents established their right to much more than the 1,400 acres suggested in the law. Benjamin Logan first appeared before the commision while it was meeting at his own fort. On this occasion a certificate for 1,400 acres was issued to him in partnership with Michael Stoner and Joseph Kennedy.[15] At his next appearance, on October 19, he was not successful. A man named Charles Cameron came before the commission and presented evidence which indicated that he had purchased a settlement and preemption from Henry Pawling. Pawling had obtained this land from James Dorchester, who had settled and made an improvement on the waters of Dick's River in 1775. Logan contended that he had bought this claim from Dorchester's heir on March 23, 1779. A number of witnesses were called, some of whom testified that Dorchester had sold his claim to Pawling in 1777. The commission decided that the heir had sold to Logan that which was not legally his. Cameron's claim therefore was validated and ordered to be certified.[16]

On the following day Logan presented his claim to the tract of land on which John Floyd and his surveyors had established St. Asaph's and where Logan's Fort subsequently was erected. He was able to show that he had settled there in 1775 and had raised corn on the land in that year. The land court ordered that he be issued a certificate for 400 acres surrounding the place where he had settled and for a preemption of 1,000 acres adjacent to the 400.[17]

At the same session John Logan proved his claim to 1,400 acres of land lying at the mouth of St. Asaph's Branch. The basis for this claim was the raising of a crop of corn at that location in 1776. He proved also the claim of the youngest of the Logan brothers, Nathaniel, to an equal amount of land to be located on both sides of Logan's Creek just below the mouth of St. Asaph's Branch. This too was based upon the raising of

[15] Ibid., 10. [16] Ibid., 12. [17] Ibid., 15.

corn in 1776. Claims were established for the other two brothers, Hugh and William. A certificate for a 1,000-acre preemption was issued in Hugh's name after proof was submitted of an improvement having been made near the Little Flat Lick in 1776. William's 1,400-acre tract was to be located at some point convenient to St. Asaph's. It is likely that these crops were raised and the improvements made by Benjamin Logan, as no record of any of his brothers having been in Kentucky prior to John's arrival in 1778 has been found. The raising of corn would not have required the cutting of trees. They might have been killed by girdling and the corn planted among the dead trunks. Nor did the law say what amount of corn had to be raised to constitute a crop. "Any house or hut" was considered an improvement, and a hut in some cases was no more than a lean-to or a stack of poles laid up in the form of a square.[18]

After completing its first session at St. Asaph's the land court moved on to Harrodsburg. Here Benjamin Logan appeared in regard to a claim which he had acquired as the assignee of Robert and Thompson Sayers. The court did not reach a decision at the time, but Logan's request to have depositions taken concerning this claim was granted.[19]

Trading in land continued while the commission was holding its meetings. Logan's old neighbor from the Holston days, James Knox, had a claim to 1,400 acres on Beargrass Creek not far from the Falls of the Ohio. Although the land was poor, he succeeded in disposing of his certificate for 300 pounds. For a 1,400-acre tract of much better land in the Bluegrass region John Floyd was offered "six fine young Virginia born negroes."[20]

From Harrodsburg the commissioners moved to the Falls. They arrived on November 14 and remained until November

18 *Ibid.*, 14-15, 43. Draper MSS. 12 C 46(1-2); 9 J 198. Hening (ed.), *Statutes*, X, 40.
19 "Certificate Book," 43.
20 John Floyd to William Preston, November 26, 1779, Draper MSS. 17 CC 186-87. Floyd to Preston, October 30, 1779, Draper MSS. 17 CC 184.

25. Here Logan's claim to a settlement and preemption as the assignee of Robert and Thompson Sayers was approved. The certificate was issued to James Douglas who had become a partner of Logan in the claim. The land lay on Beargrass Creek and joined a corner of James Knox's settlement.[21]

The new year found the commission sitting at Bryan's Station. Here Logan appeared not in his own behalf but as the representative of others. On January 4 he presented the claim of the heir of William Hudson, who was killed at St. Asaph's in 1777. He was able to show that in 1776 Hudson had raised corn and built a cabin on Paint Lick Creek. A certificate then was issued covering both a 400-acre settlement and a 1,000-acre preemption.[22]

From Bryan's the commission went to Harrodsburg for another session. When Logan's turn came on January 29, he presented the claims of several of his relatives and friends. For one of his brothers-in-law, William Montgomery, Jr., he obtained 1,400 acres on Green River near Pine Lick and an additional 400 acres on Carpenter's Creek. A 1,400-acre claim on "Flat Lick Branch of Dick's River about 1½ miles below Flat Lick" was approved at the same time for John Montgomery. This could have been either Ann Logan's brother John, or Captain John Montgomery who had come to St. Asaph's with a militia company in the fall of 1777. In the following spring he had joined George Rogers Clark as a captain in the organization of Virginia regulars known as the Illinois Regiment.[23]

Logan was equally successful in obtaining 1,400 acres on Hanging Fork of Dick's River for his brother-in-law Samuel Briggs, 400 acres on the same stream for Robert Barnett, 400 for James McKinney, and 400 for Joseph Martin. His only failure was in the case of his nephew Benjamin Briggs, who

[21] "Colonel William Fleming's Journal of Travels in Kentucky, 1779-1780," in Newton D. Mereness (ed.), *Travels in the American Colonies* (New York, 1916), 621-22. "Certificate Book," 47-48.
[22] "Certificate Book," 109. Draper MSS. 4 CC 32(6).
[23] "Certificate Book," 155-57.

claimed to have made a settlement on Hanging Fork in 1777. This claim was dismissed by the court, perhaps because Briggs was still a minor.[24]

Although the land commission managed to transact its business, the winter of 1779-1780 was the most severe that the Kentuckians had experienced. The period of very low temperatures began about November 15 and lasted until the middle of February. The streams soon were frozen over, and the livestock and wild game found it difficult to obtain either food or water. It was not uncommon for the herbiverous animals of the forest to join with the cattle and horses and come up to the stations. Added to the suffering caused by the intense cold, the deep snow hampered the movement of both men and animals. One of the heaviest of the winter fell early in December. At Christmastime the Kentucky River could be crossed by walking on the ice, and by February the ice on this stream was two feet thick.[25]

When the supply of corn ran low the scarcity drove the price far above the already inflated figure which it had reached in the fall. By the end of October it was selling for thirty dollars per bushel. One month later very little could be obtained at fifty dollars per bushel. At the same time a bushel of salt cost two hundred dollars. In the spring some corn was brought to the Falls where those who could raise the money might have it at sixty dollars per bushel. These prices were a result of the decreased value of paper money as well as of the scarcity of the articles in question. At the same time a day's labor was valued at twenty dollars.[26]

Although many people had left the old forts to establish new ones, arrivals were so numerous that the cabins inside the original stockades usually were occupied. In many of the

[24] *Ibid.*

[25] Draper MSS. 4 CC 26-27; 13 CC 170. "Fleming's Journal," 623-24, 626, 630.

[26] Floyd to Preston, October 30, 1779, Draper MSS. 17 CC 185. Floyd to Preston, November 26, 1779, Draper MSS. 17 CC 186. Draper MSS. 4 CC 26-27.

forts, both old and new, the crowded conditions and lack of knowledge of even the first principles of sanitation, combined with the poorly balanced diets, produced frequent illness and sometimes death. Colonel William Fleming, who headed the Virginia Land Commission, was, in addition to being a political leader in his home county of Botetourt, a physician. He recorded in his journal a vivid description of the situation at Harrodsburg. After explaining that the spring was within the stockade and at the lowest corner of the enclosed area he remarked that "the whole dirt and filth of the Fort, putrified flesh, dead dogs, horse, cow, [and] hog excrements and human odour [ordure]" all washed into it. To these ingredients were added "the ashes and sweepings of filthy cabbins [sic]," and the situation could hardly have been improved by "steeping skins to dress and washing every sort of dirty rags and cloths in the spring." This combination, Fleming concluded, "makes the most filthy nauseous potation of the water imaginable and will certainly contribute to render the inhabitants of this place sickly." Although Fleming visited Logan's Fort on several occasions, he did not criticize the conditions there, possibly because the spring was outside of the stockade.[27]

In spite of the severity of the winter, provisions at Logan's were adequate. A little corn was brought by new settlers, and hunters were out whenever weather conditions would permit. Buffaloes were still fat in the early part of the winter, and a great many were killed. Wild turkeys could be found, but these soon became too thin to be of much value. A few bears and deer were obtained, but the supply did not last long.[28]

To procure salt for St. Asaph's a group of men went to Bullitt's Lick in the middle of the winter. It included Daniel Trabue, Jeffery Davis, William Maxey, a young man sent by George S. Smith, a Negro belonging to James Foster, and two

---

[27] "Fleming's Journal," 624-30.
[28] "Trabue's Narrative," Draper MSS. 57 J 45-49.

or three others. Smith and Foster were recent arrivals at Logan's. The journey was a difficult one, and some of the men, being inexperienced in the woods, threatened to return to the fort. One man actually did so, leaving the party with the comment: "Them that liked Kentucky might enjoy it but he would not stay in such a country."

On reaching the lick they found that some men from the Falls had arrived ahead of them and already were producing salt. Trabue knew their leader, whose name was Phelps, and a deal was arranged whereby the Falls salt makers would rent their equipment for two weeks while they took home the salt which they had made. On their return they would accept payment in salt. These pots and kettles, supplemented by those which the party from Logan's had brought, enabled them to produce about one bushel per man per week. When the Falls men returned, Trabue and his group set out for St. Asaph's and arrived safely with their salt.[29]

It was late in February or early in March that Logan left his home for the old settlements on the other side of the Wilderness. He must have remained for at least a month, because he returned to St. Asaph's on April 21. His full purpose is not clear, but the increasing interest in Kentucky land would seem to supply a part of the answer. He transacted some land business of his own and acted as a representative for others. He had taken along some land certificates for Mrs. Robert Breckinridge, a sister of Colonel William Preston, and on the return trip he brought "two military warrants of Capt. Christians of 50 acres each," which Logan seems to have purchased, and a preemption warrant for Colonel John Bowman.[30]

When it became known in the Holston Country that Logan and James Knox, both of whom were excellent woodsmen, were about to set out for Kentucky, a number of men who

[29] *Ibid.*, 41-45.
[30] Floyd to Preston, May 5, 1780, Draper MSS. 17 CC 124. Excerpt from "Journal of Virginia Land Commission," Draper MSS. 2 ZZ 75(20). "Fleming's Journal," 643-44.

were interested in going sought their aid as leaders and guides. By the time they were ready to leave the Blockhouse on the North Fork of the Holston, the party had grown to ninety-eight. They followed the usual trail through the Cumberland Gap. About eighty miles northwest of that point a lone rider was seen approaching. Logan pulled his hat low enough to hide much of his face and proceeded. When the horseman came opposite him on the narrow trail, Logan seized the bridle, whereupon the man leaped off the horse and ran into the woods. Logan recognized the horse as having been stolen from his own station. He also knew the rider, who was one of the biggest rogues in Kentucky.[31]

Two brothers named Finley, tiring of the rigid discipline which Logan and Knox considered necessary for safety, decided to move on at a faster rate. They returned on the same day, badly frightened, and reported that they had reached a point near the Raccoon Spring where they had heard screaming and the firing of guns. On the following day, when the entire party reached the site, it was found that five men had been killed by Indians. Signs indicated that these men had been members of a larger party which was traveling toward the Holston and that their companions had returned to the Kentucky settlements.[32]

With so large a company, Logan and Knox saw no objection to camping for the night at the Raccoon Spring. Although a watch must have been kept, the horses of two of the travelers, John Redd and Mordecai Hoard, were stolen or strayed away during the night. On the assumption that it was the latter, Logan loaned them the horse which he had taken from the thief. Redd and Hoard proceeded to search the surrounding woods, while the remainder of the company moved on. The horses eventually were found, and the two men rejoined the other travelers. When they reached Logan's Fort on April 21,

[31] John Redd, "Reminiscences of Western Virginia, 1770-1790," in *Virginia Magazine of History and Biography*, VII (1899-1900), 6, 245-46. Redd's original manuscript is owned by the Virginia Historical Society.
[32] *Ibid.*, 246.

the company was disbanded, its members continuing to their various destinations.[33]

Settlements had been started on the Cumberland River at the present location of the city of Nashville. One group of settlers, led by James Robertson, had followed the Wilderness Trail as far as Whitley's Station. From there Robertson had guided them to the Green River and eventually to the Cumberland, missing Logan's Fort by only a few miles.

Although these new settlements to the southwest may have given the Kentuckians a feeling of greater security, it is likely that their first effect was to provoke the southern Indians to renew their attacks along the frontier. In June, 1780, Governor Thomas Jefferson ordered William Campbell, colonel of the Washington County militia, to raise 500 men to punish the Chickamauga for their frequent raids into the southern parts of Virginia. Campbell advanced as far as the Nolichucky River, where he turned back because of the failure of North Carolina to provide the expected support.[34]

The Indians did little actual damage during the "hard winter" of 1779-1780, but the threat remained. The capture of Henry Hamilton, who, in addition to his duties as lieutenant governor of Quebec, had acted as Indian agent in the West, had shaken the faith of the red men in their British comrades. This had followed the news of the American alliance with France. Many of the Indians had been friendly with the French, and the two events combined to create confusion in their minds. The effect was partially nullified by the action of the Americans in executing two British soldiers, Lieutenant Henry Hare and Sergeant Newberry, and a civilian who was found to be carrying British dispatches. Writing of these occurrences to General Sir Henry Clinton on August 29, 1779, the British commander for Canada, General Frederick Haldi-

[33] Ibid., 247-48. "Fleming's Journal," 643.
[34] "Trabue's Narrative," 41. John D. Barnhart, Valley of Democracy (Bloomington, Ind., 1953), 41-42. Albigence W. Putnam, History of Middle Tennessee (Nashville, 1859), 66. Samuel C. Williams, Tennessee During the Revolutionary War (Nashville, 1944), 107, 136.

mand, said: "The Indians are so exasperated . . . that I fear it will not be in the power of those who have the direction of them, to restrain them from retaliating severely." This letter may not have reached Clinton by September 9 when he wrote to Haldimand expressing the hope that "the Indians from your quarter will be prevailed on to threaten the frontiers of Virginia in great force, which will operate in favor of . . . the reduction of South Carolina." Before Haldimand replied in the following January either he or the Indians had undergone a change of mind. He now doubted that they could be counted upon to give the desired assistance. Haldimand spoke of the "immense sums lavished to secure their affections" and at the same time bemoaned the effect of Hamilton's capture and of the French alliance.[35]

Before the severe winter began there was a desire among the men in and around St. Asaph's to undertake another expedition against the Shawnee. This feeling was noted by Robert Todd when he came to Logan's to buy supplies for the Illinois Regiment. It was communicated to Clark in a letter written on October 16, 1779, and on the following day Logan, acting upon the advice of three members of the land commission—Fleming, Barbour, and Lyne—also wrote to Clark asking his intentions in regard to a fall campaign and offering any assistance that he might be able to give. Both writers mentioned the defeat and massacre of David Rogers and a part of his company as one reason for the intensity of the feeling in the Kentucky settlements. Rogers had gone to New Orleans for supplies for Virginia's western troops and was returning with several boatloads. He was attacked above the mouth of the Licking River on October 4, and only thirteen members of his detachment escaped death or capture. The greatly increased population at this time might have contributed to the success of the suggested campaign, but, in

---

[35] General Frederick Haldimand to General Sir Henry Clinton, August 29, 1779, Draper MSS. 58 J 54. Clinton to Haldimand, September 9, 1779, Draper MSS. 58 J 39. Haldimand To Clinton, January —, 1780, Draper MSS. 58 J 113-14. See also a report of Major John Butler to Haldimand, Draper MSS. 58 J 54-55.

view of the severity of the winter and of its unusually early arrival, it is well that it was not undertaken.[36]

Benjamin Logan, who was one of the four original captains in the militia of Kentucky County, had by this time been advanced to the rank of colonel. This may have been due to an increase in the number of regiments, which should have resulted from the growth in population, or to the resignation of the former colonel, Richard Calloway. The tone of Logan's letter of October 17 to Clark makes the latter seem more probable. "As Col. Bowman is not in the county," he wrote, "it apears [sic] at present I have the command." He added: "I have not heard of Col. Bowman on his way out or I should not have wrote." Although Calloway was at the fall session of the Virginia Assembly at this time, there is no mention of his absence as an additional factor which would place Logan in temporary command. Thus it seems probable that Calloway's duties as a representative at Williamsburg had caused him to resign his commission as colonel. This would have created a vacancy for which Logan would have been a logical choice. Clark had severed his connection with the militia and had accepted a commission as lieutenant colonel of Virginia regulars. John Todd was in the Illinois country, and Boone had been in North Carolina for a year. James Harrod seems to have been advanced to major about the same time. Colonel William Fleming, whose journal shows him to have been very careful about the use of military titles, referred to Harrod as a major on April 11, 1780, and to Logan as a colonel on April 21. Logan's old company was given to John Logan, who had served as his brother's lieutenant.[37]

[36] Draper MSS. 60 J 428-29, 434; 64 J 238. Todd to Clark, October 16, 1779, and Logan to Clark, October 17, 1779, in James A. James (ed.), *George Rogers Clark Papers, 1771-1781*, Collections of the Illinois State Historical Library, VIII (Springfield, 1912), 371-72.

[37] Logan to Clark, October 17, 1779, in James, *Clark Papers, 1771-1781*, 371-72. "Fleming's Journal," 643-44. Clark to Mason, November 19, 1779, quoted in Bodley, *History of Kentucky*, 148. Draper MSS. 17 J 41(1); 57 J 38. Thwaites, *Daniel Boone*, 174. *Journal of the House of Delegates of the Commonwealth of Virginia* [October session], *1779* (Richmond, 1827), 4.

CHAPTER VII

INVASION AND RETALIATION

RUMORS OF AN INTENDED British-Indian invasion were abroad in Kentucky as the year 1780 opened. There were reports from the various posts in the Illinois country which indicated that the British were meeting with success in their attempt to recover the allegiance of the western Indians. If this were true, Virginia was in danger of losing not only Illinois but Kentucky as well.

By March small parties of savages were murdering travelers and hunters almost in sight of the Kentucky stations. Two separate blows fell on March 9. Near Boonesborough, Richard Calloway, who had served the county both in a civil and a military capacity, and his companion, Pemberton Rawlings, were killed. One of the residents of Bryan's Station, William Bryan, fell a victim to the Indians while he and some friends were returning from a hunting trip. Bryan's scalp was taken, and two horses belonging to the party were stolen. On the following day Ruddle's Station on the South Fork of Licking River was attacked. The firing continued from early morning until nightfall. Two of the defenders were wounded, most of the cattle were killed, and the only horses that remained were a few inside the stockade.

These events caused the people of Bryan's Station to favor an immediate expedition against the enemy. On March 13 they wrote to George Rogers Clark asking him to take command and expressing the hope that he and his regulars could bring along a few pieces of artillery. "We . . . will send as many men as we can possibly spare," they added, "and we believe every Station will do the like." When this letter had traveled as far as Lexington the residents of that settlement held a meeting to "consult on the contents" and decided to add a plea of their own. They too wanted Clark to "head our men against those Savage robbers who are again plundering our country," and promised to furnish "all the assistance the strength of this garrison can possibly spare."[1]

Indians sometimes were seen in the vicinity of Logan's Fort, and signs of their presence were found frequently. On one occasion a few hunters went to Paint Lick Creek to watch for game. A buffalo was killed and the meat was suspended from a limb while the men continued to hunt. Eventually they crossed their own trail and saw the tracks of Indians. The tracks led toward the place where the meat had been left. Knowing that the savages frequently lay in ambush at any spot to which white men might be expected to return, they decided to let the meat remain where it was. Before they could move on, two buffaloes came running from the direction in which the Indians had gone. Over the protests of the other members of the party, two of the hunters fired at one of the animals and brought it down. With one man on watch and with the additional protection of their dogs, which could be counted upon to give warning if Indians approached, the buffalo was skinned and the meat was cut up. By the time this was finished it was too dark to travel. They decided to wait for the moon, which would rise just after midnight. It was just becoming light enough to start when their horses became frightened and broke away. This convinced the men that Indians were approaching. Keeping close together, they

---

[1] George Rogers Clark to John Todd, March ——, 1780, Draper MSS. 60 J 33-34. Inhabitants of Bryan's Station to Clark, March 13, 1780, Draper MSS. 50 J 20(2-3). Inhabitants of Lexington to Clark, March 13, 1780, Draper MSS. 50 J 20(3-5). Draper MSS. 31 C 98. "Colonel William Fleming's Journal of Travels in Kentucky, 1779-1780," in Newton D. Mereness (ed.), *Travels in the American Colonies* (New York, 1916), 634.

pursued the horses and succeeded in catching them. While
this was in progress a few Indians were seen. They probably
were uncertain as to the strength of the party of hunters.
In any event they did not attack. The meat was loaded on the
horses, and the hunters set out for Logan's. They traveled
mostly through canebrakes and reached the fort safely. One
member of the party remarked that he "would not run the
same risk again for a hansom [sic] sum."

It was shortly after this that a group of men from Amelia
County who had been staying at St. Asaph's expressed a
desire to go to the Falls of the Ohio. They wanted to see the
land in that part of Kentucky and to purchase some supplies
for the return trip to their homes. Daniel Trabue, who was
a nephew of one of the men, was selected as their guide, and
a few packhorses were taken along. The party visited John
Floyd at his station on Beargrass Creek. Here they learned
that settlers were being killed and horses stolen in that region
as well. On the return journey they had an encounter with
some Indians near Linn's Station, but they stood their ground
and, when the savages withdrew, continued on their way to
Logan's Fort.[2]

About the first of May a small company left the fort on a
scouting trip. On their return they fired their guns to announce
their arrival. This frightened some boys who were working in
a field not far away. Thinking that the fort was under attack,
they fled to the nearby woods. One of the boys, who must
have been even more alarmed than the others, traveled a long
distance and succeeded in losing himself. He was so badly
torn by briars that wolves were attracted by the scent of blood
and began to follow him. At night he slept in hollow logs,
after filling the openings with chunks of wood. After about
two weeks of wandering, subsisting largely upon roots, he
struck the Wilderness Trail near Rockcastle River. Here he
was discovered by a company of travelers and brought to

2 "Daniel Trabue's Narrative," Draper MSS. 57 J 49-51.

Whitley's Station. From this point he was returned to his home at Logan's Fort.[3]

Colonel William Fleming, the chairman of the Virginia Land Commission, was a guest in Logan's home several times during his stay in Kentucky. He was there in April, 1780, just after Logan's return from across the mountains. His three horses strayed away from the station, and Fleming offered thirty dollars reward for each. This offer would certainly bring them back if they were not in the hands of the Indians. Word soon came that two of them had been seen. Logan went after them and recovered both not far from Whitley's Station. To have accepted money for this would have been completely out of character, and it is not likely that he did so.

At this time it was not considered wise for people to travel on the Wilderness Trail unless in a large company. On May 11 a party assembled, some at Logan's and the others at Whitley's. Next day this party, which included some of the members of the land commission, started on its way. A few weeks after the land commissioners left another party of travelers began to form at the Crab Orchard. Four men went from Logan's to join it. They were James Knox, an experienced wilderness traveler, Thomas Marshall, colonel in the continental army and veteran of Trenton and Brandywine, George Smith, and Daniel Trabue. This company reached the Holston Settlements just as men were being raised for an expedition which culminated in the defeat of an army of Tories at King's Mountain.[4]

The dangers often encountered along the Wilderness Trail

[3] Draper MSS. 29 S 107-108. This was related many years after the event by James Givens, who was a resident of Logan's Fort at the time. Givens thought that it happened in the spring of 1780. It bears a resemblance to an entry which Colonel William Fleming made in his journal on May 13. Fleming called the subject a "young man" and said that he had been lost for twelve days. Givens remembered it as having been eighteen. They agreed upon such points as his having lived upon herbs and having been in a weakened condition when rescued. See "Fleming's Journal," 647.

[4] Draper MSS. 2 ZZ 75(20,23). "Fleming's Journal," 647. "Trabue's Narrative," 53.

came both from the Shawnee and the Chickamauga. The latter, a branch of the Cherokee tribe, had seceded after the Cherokee leaders had made peace with the white man in 1776. Under their own leader, Dragging Canoe, they moved farther down the Tennessee River to the vicinity of Lookout Mountain. From this location they continued to harass the white settlers in every way possible. In 1780 they established their Five Lower Towns near Muscle Shoals.[5]

To the several voices that had advocated a campaign against the Indians, particularly the Shawnee, there now was added that of Daniel Brodhead, military commander at Fort Pitt. Writing to George Rogers Clark on May 20, Brodhead declared that he long had hoped to lead an expedition into the Shawnee country but had lacked the men and supplies that would be necessary. He expressed the hope that Clark was in a position to conduct such a campaign and added: "I am persuaded that they are the most hostile of any Savage Tribe and could they receive a severe chastisement it would probably put an end to the Indian War."

The counties that lay in the Valley of Virginia, between the Blue Ridge and the Alleghenies, also had been considering a campaign against the Shawnee. In acquainting Clark with this fact, Governor Thomas Jefferson had asked him to assist in any way possible. He recognized at the same time Clark's distance from the scene and his responsibility for the defense of Kentucky. "I therefore leave to your Discretion and zeal for the good of the country," said Jefferson, "to determine in what manner to concur in this expedition."[6]

The freedom to use his own judgment which was granted to Clark was wise but wasted. Clark did not see the letter until July 11. He had left the fort at the Falls to carry out a project that Virginia's leaders had been considering for more

[5] Robert S. Cotterill, *The Southern Indians* (Norman, Okla., 1954), 44-45, 55.

[6] Daniel Brodhead to George Rogers Clark, May 20, 1780, Draper MSS. 50 J 39. Jefferson to Clark, April 19, 1780, Draper MSS. 50 J 32-32(1). This letter is endorsed: "Recd. at Falls of Ohio, July 11, 1780."

than two years. It was thought that a fort on the Mississippi River below the mouth of the Ohio would provide protection for commerce on both streams and would make the escape of deserters more difficult. By the fall of 1779 Clark had selected a site twelve miles downstream from the Ohio and had written to Jefferson seeking his approval. He expressed the belief that the fort should be garrisoned with at least two hundred men and hoped that families could be persuaded to settle in the vicinity. Construction was started in the spring of 1780 by men who accompanied Clark from the Falls. The location had been changed from that originally intended to a point near the mouth of Mayfield Creek, which empties into the Mississippi only five miles below the mouth of the Ohio. This new outpost was named Fort Jefferson.[7]

Toward the end of April, Abraham Chaplin, who had been captured in the preceding fall, and George Hendricks, who had been taken with Boone and the salt makers, escaped from the Wyandot Indians and made their way back to Kentucky, arriving early in May. They brought information that the British had gathered a band of warriors from various tribes. With these and a considerable number of white troops, they were "preparing to attack the garrison at the Falls of Ohio with Cannon." The British plan actually envisioned more than this. The aim was to clear the West of Americans and to strike a blow at the Spanish enemy as well. Kaskaskia, Cahokia, and St. Louis were to be immediate objectives, and the ultimate objective was New Orleans. If Clark could be kept occupied at the Falls, where the British believed him to be, he could give no assistance to the Illinois posts or to St. Louis. If the fort at the Falls were taken, it was the British opinion that the remainder of Kentucky could be laid waste at leisure.

Receiving a message from Colonel John Montgomery at

[7] Patrick Henry to Bernardo de Gálvez, January 14, 1778, Draper MSS. 58 J 103-108. Clark to Jefferson, September 23, 1779, Draper MSS. 58 J 99-101. Clark to Mason, November 19, 1779, Draper MSS. 58 J 180. Jefferson to Clark, April 19, 1780, Draper MSS. 50 J 32-32(1). Cotterill, *The Southern Indians*, 51n.

Cahokia, Clark and his men had hurried northward from Fort Jefferson. He assisted in the defense of Cahokia and St. Louis, and the British drive down the Mississippi, weakened by Indian desertions, was turned back. Clark then returned to Fort Jefferson.[8]

Kentucky was in more danger from the other prong of the British attack. Colonel George Slaughter had come to the Falls with nearly one hundred Virginia regulars, and there were rumors of additional reinforcements from the Holston. This should have put the region in a position to defend itself, but the severity of the previous winter and the increase in population had created such a serious shortage of provisions that it was doubtful if any more troops could be fed if they did come. Added to the other difficulties, an epidemic of flux had struck the Kentucky settlements. There were several deaths and much of the population was left in a weakened condition.

It was generally believed that the attack on the post at the Falls would materialize in June. Colonel Slaughter either did not take this threat seriously or was expecting to repulse the enemy quickly and launch a counteroffensive of his own. He had demanded that Kentucky County furnish him with 1,400 militiamen for a July campaign. Even if the expected invaders had been turned back and other conditions had improved, it is not certain that Colonel John Bowman could have raised so many men. Every day people were leaving his county for what they considered to be the safer parts of the state.[9]

It soon became clear that Kentucky could expect no immediate aid from the Virginia government. There was talk of sending out one regiment under Colonel Joseph Crockett, but there was little chance that these troops would arrive in time to help in the current crisis. The inability of Virginia to give more attention to her frontiers was due in part to the fact that the war in the East had shifted from the northern to the

[8] John Bowman to Daniel Brodhead, May 27, 1780, Draper MSS. 16 S 5-8. John Bakeless, *Background to Glory* (Philadelphia, 1957), 245-52.

[9] John Floyd to William Preston, June —, 1780, Draper MSS. 17 CC 182-83. Daniel Brodhead to George Rogers Clark, May 20, 1780, Draper MSS. 50 J 39.

southern states. Two thousand men were being sent to the relief of Charleston, South Carolina, and Virginia was raising about five thousand more for the defense of her own southern border. Nevertheless, plans were being made for a campaign against the Indians in the coming year, probably with Clark in command. With men like Patrick Henry, George Mason, and Richard Henry Lee in the House of Delegates there was little doubt that these plans would be given careful attention.[10]

By the end of May an army of about 150 white men and 100 Indians was moving from Detroit in the direction of Kentucky, following the Maumee and the Big Miami rivers. The army was led by Captain Henry Bird, and the Indians were under the immediate supervision of the very capable Loyalist, Captain Alexander McKee. Additional Indians who joined on the way brought the total strength of the invaders up to 850. Bird believed that men were being concentrated at the Falls to meet him and heard that Clark was being summoned from Fort Jefferson to take command. He hoped to reach this fort before these efforts could go far enough to make it impregnable. "Col. Clarke's arrival," said Bird in a letter to his superior, Major Arent S. De Peyster, "will add considerably to their numbers, and to their confidence. Therefore, the Rebels should be attacked before his arrival." The British commander believed that if the fort at the Falls were taken first the remainder of Kentucky would give him little trouble. If, on the other hand, he were to attack the forts in central Kentucky first, he would arrive at the Falls short of ammunition, with a tired army, and with his ranks thinned by Indian desertions. "Difficulties," he predicted, "will increase as we advance & Col Clarke will be at the Falls with all his People collected to fight us at the close." Bird left to McKee the task of convincing the Indians that the Falls should be the first objective. "If this plan is not followed," he added

---

[10] John Todd to Clark, June 4, 1780, Draper MSS. 50 J 41. Todd and Stephen Trigg were representing Kentucky County in the Virginia Assembly. See Draper MSS. 13 S 183-85 and *Journal of the House of Delegates of the Commonwealth of Virginia* [May Session], *1780* (Richmond, 1827), 36-37.

prophetically, "it will be owing to the Indians who may adopt theirs."[11]

Bird's Indians did not like the idea of facing the artillery which Clark was known to have brought to the Falls from Vincennes. They believed also that opportunities for plundering would be greater in central Kentucky. With this in view, they insisted upon the boats being headed up the Ohio from the mouth of the Miami, where the matter had been discussed, and then up the Licking. This route would lead the British-Indian army into the heart of the Bluegrass region. Aboard Bird's boats were two cannon, a six-pounder and a three-pounder. At the forks of the Licking the boats were left for the return journey, and the party proceeded by land. The general course followed was that of the South Fork.

It was in the valley of this stream that Ruddle's and Martin's stations had been established in the spring of the preceding year. The weather at the time of Bird's approach was extremely wet, and the common pioneer practice of keeping scouts out had been neglected. This enabled McKee with an advance party to arrive undetected and to surround Ruddle's Station. There was firing on both sides from shortly after dawn on June 24 until noon when Bird arrived with the remainder of the force and the two cannon. The three-pounder was fired twice without doing serious damage. The six-pounder then was brought into position, and the situation took on a different aspect. Before firing this weapon, Bird demanded the surrender of the station. Although there was some disagreement among the residents, Captain Isaac Ruddle felt that he had no choice but to capitulate, as the heavier cannon could batter down his stockade. The surrender terms were put into writing by James Trabue, who had come over from Logan's Fort on commissary business and had arrived just in time to be

---

[11] Captain Henry Bird to Major Arent De Peyster, June 3, 1780, "Haldimand Papers," in *Michigan Pioneer and Historical Collections,* XIX (Lansing, 1911), 527-29. Milo Quaife, "When Detroit Invaded Kentucky," in *Filson Club History Quarterly,* I (1927), 53-57. J. Winston Coleman, Jr., *The British Invasion of Kentucky* (Lexington, 1951), 6-21.

numbered among the prisoners. It was agreed that the people would be protected from the Indians and taken to Detroit as prisoners of war. While Bird and McKee were inside the fort arranging the terms, the savages, who had been told not to enter until the next day, forced their way in, "tore the poor children from their mother's Breasts, killed a wounded man and every one of the cattle, leaving the whole to stink." Two days later Martin's Station on Stoner Creek was taken with equal ease.

Inability to control his Indians and a shortage of provisions caused Bird to decide against pushing deeper into Kentucky. He started for Detroit with about 350 prisoners. One of these, John Hinkston, escaped and reached Lexington on June 30 with the news of the twin disasters.[12]

[12] Bird to De Peyster, June 11, 1780, and July 1, 1780, quoted in Quaife, "When Detroit Invaded Kentucky," 60-62. "Trabue's Narrative," 51-52, 62-63. Draper MSS. 8 J 158(1); 60 J 375; 12 CC 66-67. *Bradford's Notes*, 81-87. Coleman, *The British Invasion of Kentucky*, 6-21.

Various figures have been given for the number of prisoners taken. A memorandum book belonging to John Duncan, who was captured at Ruddle's, says 129. (See Draper MSS. 29 J 25.) Duncan evidently was referring to his own station and did not include those taken at Martin's. The figure used here is that given by De Peyster at Detroit. (See Bodley, *History of Kentucky*, 284, 288-89.)

A few of the prisoners did not survive the trip, but most of them reached Detroit. Many of the children were adopted by the Indians. More than two years later Logan, then county lieutenant of Lincoln County, in a letter to Virginia's governor, Benjamin Harrison, asked the governor to investigate the status of these prisoners and to see if they could be exchanged. Harrison wrote to General Washington and expressed the opinion that these people came under the terms of an agreement which General Nathanael Green had made with the British commander at Charleston. This provided for the release by both belligerents of all prisoners taken in the southern states prior to June 19, 1781. By the end of November, 1782, the governor was able to report that the people from Ruddle's and Martin's were to be delivered to Washington's army. He asked that their friends and relatives be notified. On December 7 the Virginia Assembly made an appropriation to help defray the expenses of their homeward journey. Most of those who were held by the Indian tribes were released after the signing of the Treaty of Greenville in 1795. (See Logan to Harrison, August 31, 1782, in Palmer, McRae, and Flounoy (eds.), *Calendar of Virginia State Papers* (Richmond, 1875-93), III, 280-83. Harrison to Washington, October 25, 1782, copies in Virginia Executive Letter Book, Number 6, pp. 82-86 and in Draper MSS. 10 S 81-83. Harrison to Western Commissioners, November 29, 1782, Draper MSS. 10 S 90-91. Draper MSS. 10 S 93.)

Clark, having been warned about the threat to Kentucky, had left Fort Jefferson with Silas Harlan as his companion. Traveling overland, they reached Wilson's Station near Harrodsburg shortly after the fall of the Licking forts. The county surveyor's office had been opened at Wilson's on May 1, and in spite of the tragic news, there were many who seemed more interested in locating their land than in going out on a campaign. Assuming powers which he did not actually possess, Clark closed the surveyor's office. He also placed a small guard on the Wilderness Trail with orders to stop anyone who tried to leave Kentucky County.[13]

In preparing for a retaliatory expedition, Clark acted in conjunction with John Bowman and with Benjamin Logan, who now ranked second in the county militia organization. Bowman was not going along on the campaign, and so Logan became second-in-command to Clark. On July 17 Logan issued orders to the militia captains to select four-fifths of the men in each company for active duty. It was important to leave enough behind to act as guards and to do enough hunting to keep the stations supplied with meat. In at least one case he ordered a man who had been drafted for the campaign to accept the role of a hunter instead.

Like Bowman the year before, Clark named the mouth of the Licking as a meeting place. More than one hundred of the militiamen from the Harrodsburg region were told to report first to the Falls. Here boats had been constructed which were

---

13 Draper MSS. 8 J 36-37; 57 J 51. *Bradford's Notes*, 70-71, 79-80. Willard R. Jillson, *The Kentucky Land Grants*, Filson Club Publications No. 33 (Louisville, 1925), 5. The ban on leaving Kentucky would not have applied to a party which stopped at Logan's on July 11 and remained until July 13. Two companies of surveyors, one under Thomas Walker and the other under Richard Henderson, had been extending the boundary line between Virginia and North Carolina westward toward the Tennessee River. Locating this line was of particular interest to Henderson, who wanted to know just what property remained to him now that Virginia had confiscated that part of the Transylvania Company's claim that lay within her borders. Henderson's company was returning home by traveling up the Ohio to the Falls and taking the Wilderness Trail by Harrodsburg and St. Asaph's. (See John Floyd to William Preston, June ——, 1780, Draper MSS. 17 CC 182; Draper MSS. 46 J 18(11); and Williams, *Tennessee During the Revolutionary War*, 119-20.)

to be taken up the Ohio and used in ferrying the remaining men and the supplies across the river. These boats were under the immediate command of Colonel George Slaughter. The most important piece of equipment that they carried was a brass cannon, a six-pounder, which had been captured at Vincennes.

Thirteen men from Squire Boone's Station, near the present site of Shelbyville, marched to the mouth of the Kentucky River. With Boone as their captain, they joined Clark at that point. Between the Kentucky and the Licking men from one of the boats were set ashore on the north side of the river to hunt. These men, led by Hugh McGary, were fired upon by Indians. The attackers fled, leaving nine of the Kentuckians dead and several more wounded.

The remaining Central Kentucky militiamen, mostly men from Logan's, Whitley's, and Boonesborough, were told to proceed as far as Bryan's Station, where Logan would take command. Daniel Trabue, who had served for two years as Logan's commissary, expected to go along. He was persuaded instead to exchange places with his brother John, who had been a trader among the Indians and who knew some of their languages. It was hoped that he might be able to ransom their brother James, who had been captured at Ruddle's.[14]

Before Logan and his men left Bryan's Station a man who had been living there disappeared. It was supposed at the time that he had departed for North Carolina. Logan led his men northward to Buffalo Lick or Lee's Lick. It was located on Mill Creek, a branch of the South Fork of the Licking. Here they camped for a few days to hunt and cure meat for the campaign. They were joined at this place by additional men who had left Lexington on July 28. When Logan and his men resumed their march they picked up the trail that Henry Bird and his invaders had followed a month earlier. Horse tracks only a few days old were seen frequently, and near the mouth

[14] Draper MSS. 31 J 84(1-2); 60 J 105, 111-12, 114, 187; 9 CC 34; 1 OO 50, 81-82; 8 J 37, 142(1), 156, 240; 9 J 21-22. "Trabue's Narrative," 52-53. *Bradford's Notes,* 87-90.

of the Licking the animal was found. It was identified as one
which had disappeared from Bryan's Station along with the
missing man. Some believed that the rider had been captured
by the enemy, but others, knowing that Loyalist sentiments
had been expressed by a few of the people at Bryan's, suspected
the truth. He had gone to warn the Indians of the army's
approach.[15]

The force which gathered at the mouth of the Licking,
although small by modern standards, was the largest that
Kentucky ever had sent against its enemies. The regiment
under Logan's command contained 328 men from eight different companies. As was often the case with the militia, these
truncated companies varied greatly in size. Robert Patterson's
company contained 91 men, John Holder's had 44, and those
led by John Kennedy, John Doherty, Samuel Scott, William
Whitley, John Logan, and Levi Todd averaged 32. Clark
brought two militia regiments from the Falls. One, containing
just over 200 men, was commanded by John Floyd. The other,
which had 233 men, was led by William Linn. The 124 man
detachment brought from Harrodsburg by James Harrod was
no more than a battalion, but it was treated as a regiment, and
Harrod ranked as a colonel during the campaign. About eighty
Virginia regulars under George Slaughter completed the group.
The total strength of the army, excluding officers of the rank
of captain or above, was 970 men. Harrod's captains were
Hugh McGary, John Ellison, William McAfee, and Joseph
McMurtry. Serving under Floyd were Captains William Old-

<hr/>

[15] Deposition of John Napper in Breckinridge MSS., Vol. 19, pp. 3320-22,
Library of Congress. Draper MSS. 9 J 24; 4 CC 72. Lucien Beckner (ed.),
"Reverend John D. Shane's Interview with Pioneer William Clinkenbeard," in
Filson Club History Quarterly, II (1928), 127. *Bradford's Notes*, 89. John
Bradford served as a private in the company of Captain Robert Patterson during
this campaign. (See Draper MSS. 60 J 122).

A British account identifies the informer as John Clairy, also known as John
Clarke, and states that he started with the men from Logan's Fort. This
conclusion, however, may stem from the fact that even if he lived at Bryan's
Station he would have been under Logan's command. See "Haldimand
Papers," in *Michigan Pioneer and Historical Collections*, XIX, 554. A man
whom Daniel Trabue called "John Clarry" had lived at Logan's in 1778. (See
Draper MSS. 57 J 36).

ham and John Askins and, under Linn, Captains James Patton, John Swan, and James Asturgis.[16]

Logan's men had brought some provisions with them but not enough for a prolonged expedition. Their efforts to obtain game on the way had not been very successful. Most militiamen had assumed that Clark would bring plenty of food in his boats. Unfortunately the small quantity that he could procure, when divided among so many men, meant short rations for all. Thomas Vickroy, who was acting as Clark's commissary, was cautioned to be especially careful with the flour, issuing it only when specifically ordered to do so. Meat was very scarce, but the supply of corn was supplemented by the impressment of a boatload that was destined for the Falls.

The Ohio was crossed on August 1, and the army camped on the site of the future city of Cincinnati. That evening some of the men made hominy blocks or mortars by cutting trees and squaring off the stumps. A piece of heavy leather tied around each stump and extending several inches above it made a retaining wall. In these mortars corn was pounded with rough wooden pestles. If one had the patience, it could be reduced to any desired size, even down to a coarse meal. It then could be made into bread or boiled until it became a thick soup. When the march continued enough corn was parched each morning to suffice for the noon meal. In this state it could be eaten without stopping.

On August 2 the army began to move toward Chillicothe. It was broken into two divisions with Clark in command of the first and Logan in command of the second. The men marched in four lines with forty-yard intervals between. They were protected against surprise by small front and rear guards and a row of flankers on either side of the main body. The cannon, the military stores, and the provisions were kept between the two divisions. Practically all of the men were on foot, as there were only enough horses to carry the supplies

[16] Logan to Benjamin Harrison, August 31, 1782, Draper MSS. 11 S 14. Draper MSS. 12 C 22(1); 8 J 154; 9 J 21; 60 J 187-88; 49 J 89(3), 90(2); 60 J 123, 125, 140.

and to pull the cannon. In case of an attack the vanguard was to stand fast while the four columns shifted, two to the right and two to the left. They were to form a line perpendicular to the direction of march with the van at its center. The same plan was to operate in reverse if they should be attacked from the rear. In the event of an attack on either flank the two columns on the side in question were to face the enemy and hold their positions. The next column would hurry to the right to extend these lines while the last column would execute the same movement to its left.[17]

Progress was slow because of the frequent necessity of cutting a road for the cannon. It was drawn by four horses which were changed every half day. When the army was within five miles of Chillicothe, Clark's spies returned and reported that the village was being evacuated. They pushed forward more rapidly but arrived too late to bring on an engagement. The town, which had been rebuilt since Bowman's expedition, had been abandoned, and most of the movable property had been carried away. The corn was in the roasting-ear stage, and a good crop of beans was found. After feasting for a while, the Kentuckians destroyed the buildings and most of the crops, leaving only enough corn for use on the return trip.

Just before nightfall the army crossed the Little Miami River and made camp on the opposite shore. Clark intended to start early the next morning for the Shawnee village of Piqua, which lay about twelve miles away on the north bank of Mad River. The camp was arranged in a square with the horses turned loose inside the enclosure formed by the men. During the night there was a heavy rain which soaked men, guns and supplies. Just before daylight, when preparations were being made for the march, the men were ordered to test their guns to see if they would fire. Many were wet, and the loads had to be drawn, but enough fired to frighten the horses. Most of them broke through the surrounding barrier of men and rushed

[17] Draper MSS. 8 J 136, 139-40, 209; 9 J 21-23; 26 J 101; 60 J 266. *Bradford's Notes*, 89-90. Beckner (ed.), "William Clinkenbeard," 127.

across the Little Miami. Fortunately they stopped in the cornfields, where they were captured without much difficulty. Immediately the advance toward Piqua was started. It was now the morning of August 8.

About two-thirty in the afternoon Clark and Logan halted their men on a slight elevation from which they could see the village only a half mile away. Piqua was on a low hill just north of Mad River, a tributary of the Big Miami. A narrow strip of prairie lay between the town and the stream. Behind the town were cliffs through which very few passes were visible. To the west a swamp, well-filled with willow trees, made approach from that direction difficult. East of the village a bend brought the river closer to the cliffs, and the narrow space between was heavily wooded.

No sooner had the advanced guard crossed the river than it was fired upon by Indians who were hidden in the weeds. Clark ordered Logan to take his regiment up the river, cross some distance above the town, and block the enemy's retreat through the narrow passes in the cliffs. The other militia regiments under Floyd, Linn, and Harrod crossed the river and shifted slightly to the left. Clark and Slaughter, with the Virginia regulars and the cannon, crossed and advanced straight toward the town.

The Indians came out in considerable strength, and for a time they fought fiercely. After being flanked, they were forced to give ground and retreated into their village. Like the Kentucky settlements this Shawnee town was surrounded by a stockade. Now the labor of bringing the six-pounder so far began to pay dividends. It was wheeled into position, and each time it was fired a log in the stockade was splintered. Seeing that their position was hopeless, the Indians began to leave the enclosure through a back gate and to escape by way of a gap in the cliff behind the town. Logan, who was expected to prevent such a move, had struck some very difficult terrain. As a result he and his men did not reach the scene in time to accomplish their objective.

The Kentuckians had lost fourteen men in the action, and thirteen more had been wounded. It was believed that the Shawnee losses were greater, but since they carried some of their dead with them on their retreat an accurate count could not be made. One tragic occurrence saddened Clark in particular. His cousin Joseph Rogers had been a prisoner of the Shawnee for more than three years. While the fighting was in progress he tried to make his escape. Dressed as an Indian, he was not recognized and was shot down by his own people.

After destroying the village and more than 800 acres of corn, the army started its homeward march. Clark had hoped to penetrate the Indian country more deeply, but provisions had been scarce from the start. Roasting ears, although plentiful at both villages, were too bulky to carry in large quantities, and would not have been very satisfactory as a steady diet.[18]

Logan and Harrod, who were placed in charge of the sale of plunder, were still trying to collect from some of the participants more than eight years later. Fortunately for those who had bought less than the average and who therefore were entitled to a cash settlement, the amounts involved were small.[19]

In congratulating Clark upon his success, Governor Jefferson expressed regret that lack of provisions had prevented him from capitalizing upon his gains. "I hope those Savages will be taught to fear," he wrote, "since they cannot be taught to keep faith." He mentioned the detachment of Virginia regulars which was coming to Kentucky under the command of Colonel Joseph Crockett. "Crockett's reinforcement," he added, "will perhaps enable you with the occasional aid of volunteers to give them so little rest as to induce them to remove beyond our mutual interference."[20]

[18] Clark to Thomas Jefferson, August 22, 1780, Draper MSS. 26 J 101-101(2). Beckner (ed.), "William Clinkenbeard," 127-28. Draper MSS. 8 J 139-40, 142(1), 144, 145(1), 156(1), 157(1), 210, 241, 265; 9 J 24, 124-27.

[19] *Kentucky Gazette*, August 9, 1788. Lincoln County Court Order Book 3, pp. 427, 431, 573, 576-77. Lincoln County Circuit Court, Order Book, 1786-1792, pp. 79-81.

[20] Jefferson to Clark, September 29, 1780, Draper MSS. 50 J 61.

CHAPTER VIII

NEW COUNTIES WITH OLD PROBLEMS

WHILE CLARK AND LOGAN were occupied with the Shawnee, Kentucky's nearest southern neighbors, the Cherokee, took advantage of the situation and stole several horses from the residents of Harrodsburg, Boonesborough, Logan's Fort, Wilson's Station, and Whitley's Station. When Logan's regiment returned, Whitley, who was not without experience in such matters, took one companion and started for the Cherokee country along the Tennessee River. They crossed the Cumberland and followed one of its tributaries, Yellow Creek, to its source. From there they crossed over into the valley of the upper Tennessee. The two Kentuckians succeeded in capturing four of the Indians' horses, and with these they returned safely to their homes.[1]

Insofar as Logan's Fort was concerned, another casualty had to be added to the total for the Shawnee campaign. John Trabue had come out to Kentucky in the spring of 1780 as one of the deputies of the county surveyor, John May. His employment had been chiefly in the St. Asaph's region, and Trabue had joined the expedition as the commissary for Logan's regiment. On his return he became ill and died before his younger brother Daniel could return from their home east of the mountains. He was buried by Logan and the people of the fort.[2]

The severe winter had nearly exhausted the food supply in Kentucky, and the effect was felt on the August campaign, which, but for lack of provisions, might have been more extensive. Fortunately 1780 was a good crop year, and in the fall there was a surplus of corn, pumpkins, and potatoes. Milk and butter again were plentiful at Logan's, and the wild game had grown fat.[3]

Clark and Logan had left the Indians short of food but with their fighting strength virtually intact. As early as November there were rumors of an impending counter invasion. Some of the militia captains northeast of the Kentucky River were ordered to hold their companies in readiness. Reports arrived from the garrison at Vincennes that toward the end of October a large body of British and Indians had been seen at the destroyed villages of Piqua and Chillicothe, and it was assumed that they were planning to descend upon Kentucky as soon as the waters should rise. It was understood that Captain Thomas Quirk was bringing thirty or forty Virginia regulars, and Colonel Joseph Crockett, who was expected to bring a much larger force, had not been heard from.[4]

The expected invasion did not come, but in January a small band of Shawnee stole some horses near Bryan's Station. A white prisoner, who may have been brought along as a guide, escaped to the settlements. He reported that the Shawnee had erected four blockhouses at one of their villages. This seemed to indicate that they had no intention of yielding any of their territory to the white man. The fort provided them with a base from which to attack Kentucky whenever they chose to do so. This news, combined with the fact that Colonel Crockett had not yet arrived, caused many of the settlers to talk of moving to the southwest of the Kentucky River for greater safety. As a precautionary measure, Kentucky's military leaders decided to station a garrison of 150 men at the mouth of the

1 Draper MSS. 9 J 40.

2 "Daniel Trabue's Narrative," Draper MSS. 57 J 51-53, 61.

3 *Ibid.*, 61.

4 Draper MSS. 60 J 111. John Todd to Thomas Jefferson, November 30, 1780, in William B. Palmer, Sherwin McRae, and W. H. Flounoy (eds.), *Calendar of Virginia State Papers* (Richmond, 1875-1893), I, 393.

Licking River and to keep that point garrisoned until Crockett arrived. Also, by April a fort had been completed at Lexington.[5]

Before the end of the winter James Trabue, who had been taken by the Indians at Ruddle's Station and who had escaped from his captors in November, arrived at St. Asaph's. He brought news of some of the other captives. Many of these were people who first had settled at Logan's Fort. Later they had gone with the Ruddles or with John Martin to establish the stations on the Licking. Trabue also had news of prisoners who had been taken on other occasions. One man, because of the circumstances surrounding an attack on his party of hunters, had been presumed dead. The Indians had surprised the hunters and fired on them. As this member of the group started to run from the scene, another shot was fired in his direction. At the same instant he caught his foot on a grapevine and fell to the ground. Some warriors seized him before he could rise, and he was led away as a prisoner. One of his companions, who had seen him fall, escaped and reported him killed. When Logan heard this story from Trabue, he hurriedly left his fort to carry the news to the man's wife, who was planning to remarry on the following day. On hearing the report from Logan, the prospective bride canceled the arrangements. Eventually her husband was able to return to his family.[6]

By 1780 the population of Kentucky County had increased to such an extent that both civil and military administration were becoming difficult. The difficulty resulted more from the increased size of the settled area than from the increase in the number of people. After Clark had started a settlement at the Falls, a number of stations, such as Floyd's and Linn's, had sprung up in that region. The same was true of the area

[5] Todd to Jefferson, January 24, 1781, *Calendar of Virginia State Papers*, I, 460-61. Todd to Jefferson, February 1, 1781, Draper MSS. 11 S 34. Todd to Jefferson, April 15, 1781, Draper MSS. 11 S 201-202. Draper MSS. 60 J 140. The cost of the Lexington fort was $3,400.

[6] "Trabue's Narrative," 62, 68-69, 145.

northeast of the Kentucky River where Lexington and Bryan's were located. An unsettled strip of wilderness separated the Falls region from the office of the county clerk at Harrodsburg and from St. Asaph's where court was held. In the case of Lexington and Bryan's the Kentucky River sometimes constituted a serious barrier between the people and their seat of government.

These objections were set forth in two petitions, one from residents of each of the above sections, sent to the Virginia Assembly in May. The attention of the lawmakers was directed to the fact that in the northeastern section of Kentucky County the settlement nearest to the county seat was forty miles away and the farthest was at a distance of seventy miles. It was suggested that, if a division should be made, no settlement should be left more than fifteen miles from its county seat.[7]

The assembly considered the situation in Kentucky County and passed an act which provided for its division into three counties, effective November 1, 1780. All of that portion of the existing county which would be cut off by a line running up the Kentucky River from its mouth to the headwaters of its middle fork and continuing in a southeasterly direction to the Washington County line was to be the new county of Fayette. The region cut off by a line running up the Kentucky to the mouth of Benson's Creek, up that stream to its source, directly south from that point to Hammond's Creek, down that creek to where it joins the Town Fork of Salt River, then south to the Green River and down the Green to its junction with the Ohio was to constitute another new county, which was to be named in honor of Governor Jefferson. The remainder of Kentucky County, which would include the early settlements of Harrodsburg, Boonesborough, and St. Asaph's, was to be the county of Lincoln.

The act stipulated that the court of Lincoln County should meet on the third Tuesday of each month, with the first meeting to be held at Harrodsburg. At this meeting the justices were

[7] Draper MSS. 14 S 42.

to select a permanent county seat and to provide for the erection of public buildings.[8]

The first court for Lincoln County convened at Harrodsburg on January 16, 1781. On this day Benjamin Logan took the oath as a justice of the peace and also as a commissioner of "Oyer and Terminer for the trial of slaves." Other members of the county court were John Bowman, John Cowan, John Kennedy, John Logan, Hugh McGary, William Craig, Stephen Trigg, Abraham Bowman, Isaac Hite, William McBride, William McAfee, and James Estill. Two of these, Kennedy and McAfee, already had died at the hands of the Indians.

John Bowman, whose position of leadership in Kentucky County would have made him difficult to overlook, presented commissions from Governor Jefferson appointing him as both county lieutenant and sheriff of Lincoln. Stephen Trigg produced the colonel's commission. John Logan, Hugh McGary, William McBride, John Cowan, Samuel Scott, and John Allison qualified as captains.[9]

The question of a permanent county seat was not decided at the January court. At the next session, on February 21, Logan offered ten acres of land around the Buffalo Spring as a site for a courthouse and other public buildings. He offered also a tract of fifty acres located one mile southeast of this spring, which would remain the property of Lincoln County so long as the county seat were in or near St. Asaph's. This settlement was nearer both to the geographic center and to the center of population of Lincoln County than were Harrodsburg and Boonesborough. With these factors added to the offer of land, the court decided that its future sessions would be held at St. Asaph's.[10]

[8] Hening (ed.), *Statutes*, X, 315-16.
[9] Lincoln County Court Order Book 1, pp. 1-3. Draper MSS. 17 J 44. Wayland, *The Bowmans*, 106.
[10] Lincoln County Court Order Book 1, p. 5. The Buffalo Spring does not seem to have been identical with St. Asaph's Spring from which Logan's Fort obtained its water. It may have been the same as the Cave Spring, which was about three hundred yards away and much larger. See Draper MSS. 18 S 146.

There was no meeting of the court in March. At the April meeting, which opened at St. Asaph's on the seventeenth, the question of completing the roster of officers for the county militia was raised. Benjamin Logan and James Harrod were known to have received commissions from the governor making them lieutenant colonel and major, respectively. Neither had presented his commision to the court or taken the oath of office. When questioned, both men replied that they did not intend to accept the appointments, as they did not believe that they had received the ranks to which they were entitled. The court then recommended to the governor that the lieutenant colonel's commission be given to John Logan and the major's to Hugh McGary.[11]

Both men had justification for their complaints. Logan had served as colonel of the militia of Kentucky County. He deserved at least the equivalent in Lincoln, which constituted little more than one-third of the original county. Instead, the colonel's commission had been given to Stephen Trigg. The new colonel had arrived in 1779 as a member of the Virginia Land Commission and had decided to make Kentucky his home. Harrod had served as a major in the Kentucky County militia. On Clark's 1780 expedition he had ranked as an acting colonel. The major's commission in a smaller county would have been a demotion for him as well.[12]

The Virginia executive accepted the recommendations of the county court and eventually issued the necessary commissions. McGary presented his on July 18, 1781, and took the oath of office. John Logan was sworn in as lieutenant colonel on January 16, 1782.[13]

By April, 1781, the other counties were well along with

[11] Lincoln County Court Order Book 1, pp. 5-7. Lucien Beckner, "History of the County Court of Lincoln County, Va.," in *Register of the Kentucky State Historical Society*, XX (1922), 171.

[12] Draper MSS. 12 C 22(1); 60 J 187-88. "Certificate Book of the Virginia Land Commission of 1779-80," in *Register of the Kentucky State Historical Society*, XXI (1923), 23-24.

[13] Lincoln County Court Order Book 1, pp. 11, 15.

the organization of their militia regiments. Colonel William Christian had been named as county lieutenant of Jefferson. When he decided to postpone his removal to Kentucky he was replaced by John Floyd. In Fayette the county lieutenant's commission went to John Todd.[14]

Since their arrival in Kentucky in March, 1776, the Logans had witnessed the death of many of their friends at the hands of the Indians. During this time the only blow that had fallen upon their immediate families had been the loss of Ann Logan's brother, Alexander Montgomery. In the fall of 1780 the other members of her family, who had been living at St. Asaph's for about a year, started their own station just over the Knobs, on the headwaters of the Green River. Four cabins were built, and because there had been no recent sign of Indians in that vicinity, they were not given the usual protection of a stockade.[15]

About Christmastime the Montgomerys moved to the new location. One cabin was taken by William Montgomery, Sr., his wife, their grown sons Thomas and Robert, their daughters Jane and Elizabeth, and two smaller children, James and Flora. A second cabin was occupied by William Montgomery, Jr., his wife, and their small son Thomas, and a third by his brother John Montgomery with his wife and a Negro girl. The fourth cabin became the home of Joseph Russell, his wife, who was Ann Logan's sister, and their three children.

Just after daybreak on February 27 Indians quietly approached the Montgomery cabins. The elder William Montgomery and a Negro man who may have lived in Montgomery's house, not suspecting that anything was wrong, went out to get some wood. They were shot and killed just outside the door. Thomas and Robert were away from home on militia duty, and Mrs. Montgomery and Flora were visiting the Logans. This left the two girls, Jane and Elizabeth, and the

14 Draper MSS. 51 J 104; 11 S 48. James (ed.), *Clark Papers, 1771-1781*, clx, note 4.
15 Draper MSS. 5 S 130. "Trabue's Narrative," 145.

boy, James, alone in the cabin. Risking her own life, Jane dragged the body of her father inside and hastily barred the door.

By this time the Indians, a small group of Cherokee, had broken into the cabins of John Montgomery and Joseph Russell. John Montgomery was killed as he arose from his bed, and his wife and the Negro girl were made prisoners. Joseph Russell managed to escape, but the other members of his family were captured.

The fourth cabin was more strongly defended. William Montgomery, Jr., placed a heavy water trough against the door and began to fire through a crevice. In this way he gave one of the Indians a mortal wound and broke the thigh of another.

Elizabeth Montgomery took advantage of the savages' concentration on the other cabins and fled. One Indian saw her and gave chase but was not able to overtake her. On his return he happened to stop within range of William's gun and was killed on the spot. Elizabeth succeeded in reaching Ben Pettit's station with news of the attack. From there William Casey hurried to Logan's for help. Logan set out for Montgomery's Station with about twenty-five men. The Indians had departed, taking with them Russell's wife and children, the wife of John Montgomery, and the Negro girl. Because they were carrying their wounded on litters, their progress was slow, and the trail which they left was not hard for Logan and his men to follow. The pursuers came first to the Negro, who had been scalped and tomahawked but was still alive. Two of the men were ordered to take her back to Pettit's.

Within fifteen miles of the scene of the disaster the main body was overtaken. Flora Russell, eight-year-old niece of Ann Logan, looked back and saw the rescue party coming. "There is Uncle Ben!" she cried. The Indian who had her in his charge took time to kill her before fleeing.

All of the uninjured Indians made their escape through the thick cane, leaving their prisoners behind. One of the wounded braves had died on the journey. The other, who had been deserted by his fellows, was dispatched by the white men. The Russell girl was buried where she was slain. On the return trip William Montgomery, his son John, and the Negro man were buried at the ill-fated station. The survivors were taken to Ben Pettit's for the night and then on to Logan's Fort.[16]

After this unfortunate event the spring of 1781 was fairly quiet in Kentucky. There were, however, occasional rumors of impending Indian invasions. These disturbed the people of Jefferson and Fayette more than they did the residents of Lincoln County, who were farther away from the more warlike tribes. The county lieutenants of the two northern counties complained at times about the long frontiers which they had to defend. They felt that Lincoln, which had their counties for buffer regions, should be willing to assist in their defense. The situation was made more irksome by the fact that some residents of Fayette and Jefferson were moving to Lincoln for safety, and this reduced the militia strength of these counties when it was most needed. Fifty Lincoln County militiamen with John Logan in command did spend a month at Bryan's Station, acting as rangers in that vicinity. Fayette's county lieutenant, John Todd, charged that when their help was most needed they were withdrawn "on account of a few scattering Cherokees."[17]

Since the appearance of Henry Bird's cannon at Ruddle's Station in the preceding June there had been a constant fear of the same method being used with success at other forts. The effect of Clark's six-pounder on the Shawnee stockade at Piqua had been witnessed by many Kentuckians. Although it must have been an encouraging sight at the time, its lesson would not have been wasted upon men who depended upon com-

[16] Interview with Jane Montgomery Casey in Collins, *History of Kentucky*, II, 471-73. "Trabue's Narrative," 145-48. Draper MSS. 9 J 190(1)-191(1); 18 S 160-61, 169; 30 S 140-41; 9 CC 38.

[17] John Todd to George Rogers Clark, April 13, 1781, Draper MSS. 51 J 37. John Floyd to Thomas Jefferson, January 15, 1781, Draper MSS. 11 S 48. Draper MSS. 9 J 198; 51 J 104.

parable structures for their own protection and the protection
of their families. John Todd had tried to ease the tension
in his county by constructing at Lexington a fort which he
believed would be "proof against Swivels & small Artillery
which so terrify our people."[18]

One blow to Jefferson County and, indirectly to all of
Kentucky fell in March. Colonel William Linn, who had
commanded one of Clark's regiments at Piqua in August, 1780,
was killed by Indians near his station on Beargrass Creek. He
was shot from ambush.

About the same time other parties of savages killed militia
captains Chapman and Tipton in the same area. One of these
groups was followed by Captain Aquilla Whitaker and fifteen
men. At a point on the Ohio not far below the Falls these
Indians were attacked and defeated with a few casualties on
each side.

Two months later McAfee's Station on Salt River was
attacked and kept under fire for three hours. Shortly after the
Indians had withdrawn, a small force was gathered from the
neighboring stations to go in pursuit. The enemy was overtaken and six warriors were killed. The pursuers had one man
killed, and one of their wounded died a few days later.[19]

Clark and Logan hardly had returned from their Shawnee
campaign before the idea of an attempt on Detroit was revived.
Governor Jefferson wrote to General Washington about the
matter. He asked that Virginia be excused, for the time being,
from furnishing aid to the Continental army, as it was Jefferson's opinion that the regulars already under Clark's command
plus the volunteers that he could obtain would be sufficient
for a successful campaign in the West. He believed that
Virginia could furnish everything that would be needed with
the possible exception of powder.[20]

By January, 1781, Washington had expressed himself favor-

[18] Todd to Jefferson, April 15, 1781, Draper MSS. 11 S 201-202.
[19] Bradford's Notes, 102-104.
[20] Jefferson to Clark, September 29, 1780, Draper MSS. 50 J 61.

ably on the plan. Jefferson then suggested that Clark come to Richmond to begin his preparations. The governor made his own feeling toward the expedition clear by his action on January 22, 1781, when he advanced Clark to the rank of brigadier general.[21] While Clark was trying to raise men farther east, the three county lieutenants in Kentucky were gathering provisions and drafting militiamen as they had been ordered to do.[22]

Some of the troops who were called out for the proposed Detroit campaign were not dependable. Greenbriar County sent a detachment to Kentucky by way of the Wilderness Trail. This was part of a contingent which was to be commanded by Major Thomas Quirk. These men "behaved in a very disorderly manner, frequently taking and riding the public Horses . . . without leave, much to the prejudice of the said Horses." They were accused of stealing lead and whisky from the quartermaster and of losing many horses enroute due to failure to guard them properly, especially at night. The outfit finally arrived at Logan's Fort, where forty of its members deserted. While at Logan's some of the Greenbriar men even stole pads out of the packsaddles. These happened to be made of linen and could be used in various ways.

At Logan's, Major Quirk relieved his quartermaster of all ammunition except a single bar of lead, seeking to prevent its loss. He acted wisely but did not go far enough, as the bar of

[21] Jefferson to Clark, January 13, 1781, Draper MSS. 51 J 7. See also Clark's commission, Draper MSS. 51 J 18(1).

The three counties were to furnish a total of 500 men divided in proportion to their militia strength. They were to be at the Falls by March 15. See Jefferson to Clark, December 25, 1780, Virginia Executive Letter Book, December 24, 1780 to April 27, 1781, pp. 10-14, Virginia State Library.

[22] An account of the activities of the county lieutenants, Bowman, Floyd, and Todd, revealing a certain amount of friction among the counties which should not have existed in view of their exposed locations and common problems, may be found in Todd to Clark, April 13, 1781, Draper MSS. 51 J 37; Todd to Jefferson, April 15, 1781, Draper MSS. 11 S 37-38; Floyd to Jefferson, April 16, 1781, *Calendar of Virginia State Papers*, III, 47-49; Floyd to Clark, April 16, 1781, Draper MSS. 51 J 39; Floyd to Clark, April 26, 1781, Draper MSS. 51 J 44-44(1); Floyd to Clark, April 29, 1781, Draper MSS. 51 J 44(2); and Todd to Clark, April 21, 1781, Draper MSS. 51 J 42.

lead was stolen in short order. It was not likely that this detachment would be of much help to Clark.[23]

Militiamen of Berkeley and Frederick counties refused to go to the West, and Jefferson hesitated to force them to do so at a time when British troops were actually on Virginia soil. These two counties had been expected to furnish a total of 560 men. Many Kentuckians, however, realized that such an expedition might be the best way of defending their homes. Jefferson expressed the hope that the loses could be partly balanced by the appearance of more of the men of Kentucky than had been expected.[24]

Clark's commissaries were traveling through Kentucky trying to supplement the public stores by purchases from individuals. Corn was plentiful, and in Lincoln County some cattle were available. Prices were inflated, and purchases made on credit, as most of them were, cost the state at least twice the cash price. All three of the county lieutenants had difficulty in forcing some of their militiamen to cooperate. John Floyd blamed this upon the "want of Officers Authorized to sit on a Court Martial." He asked Clark to try to prevail upon the government to send him some blank commissions.

Bowman too was handicapped by a shortage of officers. The recommended replacements for Logan and James Harrod still were awaiting approval. He did succeed in keeping Captain Samuel Kirkham's company on active duty during June and July. This company's job was to protect the men who were constructing canoes at Leestown on the Kentucky River.[25]

Although Benjamin Logan now held no militia commission,

[23] These accusations were made by Captain George Davidson before the Board of Western Commissioners on December 24, 1782. Captain Davidson had commanded one of the Greenbriar Companies. See James A. James (ed.), *George Rogers Clark Papers, 1781-1784,* Collections of the Illinois State Library, XIX (Springfield, 1926), 172-73.

[24] Jefferson to Clark, February 19, 1781, Virginia Executive Letter Book, December 24, 1780, to April 27, 1781, pp. 124-25.

[25] William Shannon to George Rogers Clark, May 21, 1781, Draper MSS. 60 J 62. Floyd to Clark, May 22, 1781, Draper MSS. 51 J 53-53(2). Lincoln County Court Order Book 1, pp. 7, 11, 15, Draper MSS. 61 J 115.

he soon was able to serve Lincoln County in another capacity. In the spring of 1781 he decided to seek a seat in the Virginia Assembly. His opponent was Jacob Myers, who operated a small distillery on Dick's River. Myers is said to have been very liberal with his whisky when he was soliciting votes. Logan, however, had an appeal which weighed heavily in his favor. He was known throughout the county as a leader in Kentucky's struggle for survival, and when the voting had ended he was well in the lead.[26]

Late in April, Logan set out for Richmond, which had been the capital since the fall of 1779. In the party were Daniel Boone, who was a Fayette County delegate to the assembly, Charles Gatliff, and a few others.

The assembly that spring was forced to spend a part of its time in traveling to safer locations. The session opened at Richmond on May 7, but three days later the advance of a British army under Lord Cornwallis forced an adjournment to Charlottesville. The delegates reconvened on May 24, but it was not long before their security again was threatened. Cornwallis had detached Colonel Banastre Tarleton and his regiment of light horse for the purpose of making a rapid penetration into the interior of the state. It was hoped that this detachment could capture Governor Jefferson and some of the members of the assembly. On learning the British intentions John Jouett, better known as Jack, made a rapid ride to Charlottesville to carry the news.

Some of the members of the assembly, including the speaker, Benjamin Harrison, doubted if the danger were so great as Jouett seemed to think. A few of the members, including Patrick Henry, felt that it was better to play safe and proposed a removal across the Blue Ridge to Staunton. This suggestion finally was accepted.

Once decided upon, the movement got under way immediately. Logan, one of the strongest men in the assembly, picked up a bag containing the state's sadly depleted supply of gold

[26] Draper MSS. 9 J 34.

and silver and carried it to safety. Other members, including
Boone, remained behind to load the public records into a
wagon. They were just leaving on foot when the first of
Tarleton's men arrived. The British soldiers evidently were
not impressed by this group's appearance. They were allowing
them to continue unmolested until Jack Jouett made the
mistake of addressing Boone as "captain." Boone was seized
and sent back to the headquarters of Cornwallis. Here he was
detained overnight and was questioned on the following day.
Boone was as successful in his attempt to mislead Cornwallis as
he had been with Henry Hamilton. Shortly after his inter-
rogation he was released and rejoined the assembly at Staunton.

Some of the state's military stores had been removed to a
place of greater safety, but about three hundred guns were
lost when the British destroyed the public magazine at Charlottesville. Fortunately Tarleton followed the fleeing lawmakers for only a short distance. After reaching Staunton
they continued the session without interruption.

In spite of the difficulties which had been encountered, a
considerable body of legislation was enacted. Martial law was
established in a zone of twenty miles radius surrounding
any army. The executive was given absolute power to call
out the militia and to impress supplies. Persons who were
thought to favor the enemy were to be sent to the British army.
They would have twenty days in which to settle their affairs.
Those who should bear arms against the state, however, were
to be declared legally dead, and their property was to go to
their nearest relatives.

Logan's constituents had asked him to bring to the attention
of the assembly some difficulties peculiar to the frontier counties. People who were constantly at war with the Indians
were in most cases limited to subsistence farming, and it was
impossible to meet state obligations, such as payment of taxes,
on time. Also there were many poor people in Kentucky who
had acquired no land at all because of inability to make even
the small payment required.

Logan, who was described by one of his contemporaries as "a plain blunt man, & not particularly nice in his choice of words," had some difficulty in getting the floor. When he finally succeeded he reminded one, or so one of the members said later, of "an enraged and wounded buffalo." Even so, his obvious sincerity and the justice of his cause made quite an impression. Laws were passed granting a tax extension and making it possible for the poor to acquire land. The courts of Lincoln, Fayette, and Jefferson were to order the county surveyors to mark off for such persons tracts not to exceed four hundred acres. They were to be given two and one-half years to pay at the rate of twenty shillings per hundred acres. Although this appears higher than the fees that had to be paid to obtain a four hundred acre settlement under the act of 1779, the progress of inflation in the intervening years actually made it less.[27]

[27] William Preston to John Floyd, June 17, 1781, Draper MSS. 13 C 21. William Christian to William Preston, June 30, 1781, Draper MSS. 13 C 23-23(1). Mary Logan Smith to Lyman C. Draper, April 25, 1845, Draper MSS. 12 C 45(3). Draper MSS. 13 C 16, 24(1-2), 185; 9 J 38-40; 18 J 103; 6 S 149-50; 13 S 185. Hening (ed.), *Statutes*, X, 431-32, 435. *Journal of the House of Delegates of the Commonwealth of Virginia* [May Session], *1781* (Richmond, 1828), pp. 3-4, 10, 19.

CHAPTER IX

COUNTY LIEUTENANT

COLONEL JOHN BOWMAN HAD commanded the militia of Kentucky County and served Lincoln County in the same capacity during the first six months of its existence. On July 18, 1781, he was replaced by Benjamin Logan, who may have brought his commission with him when he returned from the spring session of the assembly, which ended on June 23.[1] It was poor health which had caused Bowman to seek relief from duty with the militia. Although there was some criticism of his failure to completely destroy Chillicothe in 1779, this does not seem to have been a factor in his replacement more than two years later.[2]

Most of the men who were being raised for Clark's Detroit campaign were to meet at Wheeling. On the appointed day no more than 250 appeared, and some of these deserted as soon as they had drawn their arms and an issue of clothing.[3] Several factors had combined to produce this disappointing result. Colonel Daniel Brodhead, commandant at Fort Pitt, was not as helpful as Clark had expected him to be. Contemplating a Detroit expedition of his own, Brodhead withheld both men and supplies.

The worst blow to Clark's plans was an act passed by the assembly empowering the governor to stop the campaign preparations. Although the executive did not take this action, the damage had been done. The Greenbriar militiamen who were already in Kentucky returned to their homes when this news arrived. The Lincoln, Fayette, and Jefferson militia drafts disbanded. Many of the men from Monongahela County who were to report at Wheeling found in the assembly's action an excuse for remaining at home. These men were influenced also by the boundary dispute between Virginia and Pennsylvania. Those who considered themselves Pennsylvanians felt no obligation to serve under a Virginia officer on a Virginia campaign.[4]

It is understandable that a state which was being invaded and whose assembly twice was forced to flee would lose interest in attacking an objective several hundred miles away. Clark, who still had the defense of Kentucky and the Illinois country to consider, descended the Ohio with the small force that he had been able to raise and arrived at the Falls on August 23.[5]

John Floyd, who had heard that the campaign had been abandoned, had written to Clark urging him to hasten his return. He complained of the loss of manpower in his county due to the tendency of the people to move to parts of the state which they considered safer. "The reason that the country is not now left waste," said Floyd, "is the inability of the Settlers to remove having already lost most of their Horses, and the Ohio only runs one way." About the same time Major George Slaughter, writing to Virginia's new governor Thomas Nelson, warned that the fort and settlement at the Falls might have to be abandoned unless help came quickly.[6]

Soon after his arrival Clark sought the advice of Kentucky's

[1] Lincoln County Court Order Book 1, p. 11. William Christian to William Preston, June 30, 1781, Draper MSS. 13 C 23-23(1).

[2] Wayland, The Bowmans, 102, 108-109. Bowman died on May 4, 1784.

[3] Joseph Crockett to Governor of Virginia, undated, Draper MSS. 60 J 79-81.

[4] Clark to Governor Thomas Nelson, October 6, 1781, Draper MSS. 14 J 73. James A. James, The Life of George Rogers Clark (Chicago, 1928), 230-41.

[5] Extract from Clark to Washington, May 20, 1781, Calendar of Virginia State Papers, III, 108-109. Draper MSS. 60 J 142-44, 267.

[6] Floyd to Clark, August 10, 1781, Draper MSS. 51 J 80. Slaughter to Nelson, August 9, 1781, quoted in Bodley, History of Kentucky, I, 294. Although Slaughter was an acting colonel on the 1780 Shawnee campaign, his permanent rank was major. See Draper MSS. 50 J 39; 51 J 87; 60 J 188.

militia leaders. He named September 5 as the date for a
meeting at the Falls to which all of the field officers were
invited. Although the term field officer included all those
having the rank of major or above, not all of these were able
to leave their counties at so critical a time. Logan went from
Lincoln accompanied by his colonel, Stephen Trigg. Fayette
sent only her county lieutenant, John Todd. Jefferson County
was represented by her county lieutenant, John Floyd, her
colonel, Isaac Cox, and her lieutenant colonel, William Pope.
Clark, who was not a militia officer but a brigadier general of
Virginia regulars, did not participate directly in the deliberations of these officers. Their meetings, which covered a period
of three days, were presided over by John Todd, the senior of
the county lieutenants.[7]

On the second day an address that Clark had prepared was
read and given full consideration. He sought to show the
militia officers the seriousness of the situation in the West. Fort
Jefferson had been abandoned, and it was not certain that the
garrison at Vincennes could be maintained. These things,
Clark believed, would be taken by the Indians as signs of
weakness, and as a result thousands more would join the
British and eventually would descend upon Kentucky. He
asked the militia leaders to consider the possibility of some
immediate stroke against the enemy.

Clark thought that before he could take any offensive action
the Indians would have gathered their corn and hidden it.
Success would be measured, not in terms of the destruction
of food supplies, but by the number of warriors killed. He
felt that more Indians would be encountered along the Wabash
than along the Miami. "Some stroke of this Sort," he continued,
"might . . . save your country another Season." Clark insisted
that the decision should be made by the militia officers.
"I wait as a Spectator," he added, "to see what a country is

---

[7] John Todd to Thomas Nelson, October 21, 1781, Draper MSS. 60 J 63.
"Clark's Orderly Book," September 5, 1781, Draper MSS. 63 J 49. Draper
MSS. 51 J 85.

determined to do for itself when reduced to a state of despera-
tion." The general did not mean that he would remain on the
sidelines while the militia officers conducted a campaign.
"I am ready to lead you on," he continued, "to any action that
. . . has the most distant prospect of advantage however daring
it may appear to be."

After studying this message from Clark, the militia officers
began a lengthy discussion. The first question centered around
the measures which should be adopted if no expedition were
undertaken. It was believed that a fuller knowledge of the
extent of Clark's authority and of his attitude toward the
garrisoning of the Ohio at points above the Falls would help
the council to make a wiser decision. In the hope of obtaining
this information the council delegated Floyd and Logan to
"wait upon the general." Clark replied that the state of
Virginia had placed him in full command of its western military
department, and that he was free to adopt any measures which
he considered to be appropriate. He insisted, however, that
to disclose his intentions would not be consistent with his
instructions.

This information was not very helpful, but, when Floyd and
Logan returned, the questions of attempting an expedition that
fall was presented without further delay. There were such
differences of opinion among the six officers present that they
decided to have two separate reports entered in the minutes.
Logan and Todd, believing that the wiser policy would be
to concentrate upon defense, favored the erection of a fort
at the mouth of the Kentucky River from which raiding
parties could harass the Indians even in the winter. In this
way some of the tribes might even be persuaded to sue for
peace. Such a fort also would provide a convenient storage
place for provisions if a major expedition should be undertaken
in the spring.

The other officers—Floyd, Trigg, Cox, and Pope—urged an
immediate campaign against the Shawnee. It was their belief
that if this tribe could be forced to ask for peace other tribes

would follow its example. All of the officers agreed that a
campaign against the Wabash Indians would be unpopular
because the Kentuckians considered the Shawnee to be their
most dangerous enemy. They believed also that the Wabash
route would be more difficult and too long for a successful
campaign so late in the season. The militia officers concluded
by offering to Clark any desired number of militiamen up to
two-thirds of their total strength, "trusting to his Experience
and proved attattchment [sic] to the Kentucky Interest to
manage them to the best advantage."[8]

After receiving the report of the council of militia officers,
Clark called together the field officers and captains of his
Illinois Regiment of Virginia regulars. This group included
Lieutenant Colonel Joseph Crockett, who presided, Lieutenant
Colonel John Montgomery, veteran of the Northwest campaign
of 1778-1779, Major George Slaughter, Major George Walls,
and eleven captains. Clark offered for their consideration his
instructions of January 19, 1781, from Governor Jefferson, his
address of September 5 to the county lieutenants, the reply
of the militia officers, and other information prepared especially
for the regular officers.

When these men learned that the total number of men
available for a campaign did not exceed seven hundred, they
put the question to an immediate vote. Montgomery, Slaughter,
and four of the captains were in favor of making the attempt.
The other nine thought it unwise. The officers then resolved
unanimously that "the Importance of the Kentucky Country
to the state is such as to make it our duty to defend it if
possible." In line with this resolution they recommended to
Clark that he maintain the fort at the Falls, now renamed
"Louisville," and that another be built at the mouth of the
Kentucky. A third fort, if it could be supported, they proposed
to locate opposite the mouth of the Miami. It was suggested
that Clark instruct the county lieutenants to provide militiamen

[8] Draper MSS. 51 J 84(1)-85(1).

for the work of erecting the forts and for garrison duty. The line officers hoped that some of their regulars, when their terms of service expired, could be reenlisted to supplement the militia garrisons. The board closed its session with the recommendation that the state be asked to send out enough regulars in the spring to capture Detroit and to maintain it as a Virginia outpost.

Before they left Louisville, Todd, Floyd, and Logan wrote a joint letter to Clark offering to supply him with corn and buffalo meat insofar as they were able to do so. They made it clear, however, that their people would expect to be paid for these provisions. They might either be purchased by Clark's commissary or, as an alternative, the county lieutenants were willing to "appoint a commissary who shall furnish the provisions and whose accounts shall be subject to our inspection." The three officers knew, or thought they knew, what decisions had been reached regarding the defense of Kentucky, for they concluded: "We wish the General Success in his plan which is quite agreeable to our wishes."[9]

Although the meetings ended upon notes of optimism and general agreement, harmony did not continue for long. Within a month Clark called upon Logan and Todd to supply militiamen for the erection of a fort at the mouth of the Kentucky. Todd went to St. Asaph's to discuss the matter with Logan, and on October 13 the two officers prepared their reply. They admitted that they had been in favor of such a fort, but they believed that the plan which was proposed in the meetings at Louisville had been so changed that they no longer could support it. By way of explanation they added that they had expected the forts on the Ohio to be built and garrisoned chiefly by regulars. The two county lieutenants offered as excuses for their refusal to comply with Clark's request the pleas that they had no tools for digging trenches and constructing earthworks, their militia forces were small and widely

[9] *Ibid.,* 86-88.

scattered, and the men were busy with their crops and would not finish harvesting before November.

When they pledged men to Clark a month earlier, Logan and Todd probably were sincere. They may have been thinking of a short campaign such as the other militia officers had suggested. However, the arduous task of constructing fortifications and the boresome duty of garrisoning them would not have appealed to the men of their commands, and in military organizations such as theirs, in which a private might consider himself the equal of his colonel, such objections had to be considered.

As an additional reason for their refusal, the two officers told of rumors that the Cherokee and Chickamauga were planning an attack on Lincoln County. It could be taken for granted, they believed, that the Shawnee would continue to plague Fayette. Another possible explanation can be found in a later paragraph. Logan and Todd had learned that Jefferson County was not being asked to furnish men either for building or for defending the new fort. "As it is solely intended for our Defense," they wrote, "on calculating the cost we concluded that we are willing to forgoe [sic] the many advantages . . . for this season and think it better to defend ourselves near home." The only concession which Logan and Todd did make was a promise to forward provisions if possible. At the same time they made it clear that they would expect them to be received "at Lees Town or somewhere on [the] Kentucky."[10]

Eight days later Todd wrote to Governor Nelson, explaining the position that he and Logan had taken. "On parting with General Clark," he said, "we expected to furnish assistance in building the garrison at the mouth of Kentucky . . . but expected it to be built principally by the regulars, & wholly garrisoned by them." He then told of the request that he and Logan had received from Clark to send militiamen and tools

---

[10] Logan and Todd to Clark, October 13, 1781, Draper MSS. 51 J 93-93(1).

for erecting the fort, and to "defend it by men drawn from the body of our militia, until he should have leisure to relieve them, which we are satisfied would not happen in any short time."

Todd told the governor that he and Logan had discussed this request and had been forced to refuse because they "had no entrenching tools, no professed engineers, no money, & we conceive it to belong to men who draw constant pay to garrison it." Todd said that both he and Logan objected to the practice of keeping regular troops "in the most interior and secure posts," and at the same time "putting the militia on duty at a place distant from 60 to 120 miles from home."

Both officers thought that if only one fort were to be maintained it should be located at the mouth of the Kentucky. If additional troops and money were available, they would favor another post "at the mouth of the Licking, opposite the mouth of Big Miami, at Laurence's Creek or Limestone Run." Todd was especially critical of Clark's belief that the Falls was "the Key of the Country." He believed that the mouth of the Kentucky was a better place for regulars to be stationed because it was nearer to the route which Indians would be likely to follow if they were invading Kentucky, and most of the provisions for a new garrison would have to be furnished by Fayette and Lincoln Counties. These could be floated down the Kentucky to the fort. "To say that the Falls is the Key to this Country seems to me unintelligible," he continued. "It is a strong rapid which may, in an age of commerce, be a considerable obstruction to the navigation; but, as we have no trade, we neither need nor have any keys to trade."[11]

After considering the cost of a Detroit expedition, a committee of the Virginia House of Delegates made a report to the effect that the inhabitants of Kentucky might be able to defend themselves if a chain of forts was constructed along the Ohio. It was suggested that the fort at Louisville be maintained and that others be constructed at the mouths of the

[11] Todd to Nelson, October 21, 1781, Draper MSS. 60 J 63-67.

Kentucky, the Licking, and Limestone Creek. From six to seven hundred men, thought the committee, would be enough to garrison the four posts. Each should be supported by two gunboats, the crews of which would be drawn from the garrisons. The committee then proposed two resolutions. One advocated postponement of the proposed Detroit campaign, and the other urged the executive to take steps to defend Kentucky. The committee's report was approved by the House on December 11 and by the Senate on December 15.

Logan attended only a part of this fall session of the assembly. It opened on October 1, and on October 3 the members agreed to adjourn until November 5. Logan was present by November 8. On November 24 he and the other Lincoln county delegate, John Edwards, were listed among the absentees. By December 18 he was back at St. Asaph's.[12]

While the discussions regarding the defense of Kentucky were in progress the Indians were not idle. Squire Boone's Station in Jefferson County suffered several attacks, and the settlers there decided to move to one of the stations on Beargrass Creek for greater safety. While the move was in progress on September 13, the savages attacked again, killing several of Boone's men. John Floyd's company which was raised to pursue the savages was ambushed and defeated on the following day with additional losses.[13]

Kentucky's southern settlements were more fortunate, but even there some losses were sustained. Early in the fall three scouts from Wilson's Station—Henry Wilson, Thomas Wilson, and James Ledgerwood—discovered an Indian camp near the forks of the Kentucky River. After securing a few of the Indians' horses, they hurried back to the settlements. Their first stop was at St. Asaph's, where Logan gave Henry Wilson the temporary rank of captain with authority to raise a volun-

[12] Draper MSS. 51 J 15, 93-93(1), 100-100(3); 11 S 9; 13 S 185. *Journal of the House of Delegates of the Commonwealth of Virginia* [October Session], *1781* (Richmond, 1828), 1-4, 14, 35.
[13] Floyd to Clark, September 14, 1781, Draper MSS. 51 J 89. *Bradford's Notes*, 102-103.

teer company and attack the savages. With about twenty-five men, Wilson set out for the Kentucky. The camp which had been seen earlier was deserted. Wilson and his men, being mounted, decided to follow the Indians and overtook them near the Cumberland River. The savages, more numerous than had been expected, divided themselves into two parties and tried to surround the whites. Wilson's men dismounted in order to shield themselves behind trees, but it soon was evident that they had encountered a force which they could not defeat. With three of his men dead and the remainder in danger of being surrounded, Wilson ordered his men to remount and make their escape. The Indians, being on foot, were quickly outdistanced.[14]

In the latter part of the summer Clark had scattered some of his Virginia regulars among the various Kentucky settlements. About twenty were stationed at Logan's Fort under the command of Lieutenant William Meriwether. Five years after Meriwether's death one of his grandsons prepared a memoir in which he told the following story. The people at Logan's Fort were glad to have this addition to their strength, but as winter approached their attitude changed. There had been no recent sign of Indians and the settlers grew tired of furnishing provisions for the regulars. Logan, upon his return from Richmond, asked Meriwether to remove his men. The lieutenant refused to comply, reminding Logan that Clark had sent him there. No one but Clark, he said, could order him to leave. The residents countered by refusing to feed the regulars. Meriwether then sent messengers to Clark asking for instructions. While he awaited their return, he declared his intention of shooting some cattle to provide meat for his men. Logan is said to have replied that if this happened he would shoot Meriwether. The memoir continued with a rather dubious account of the regulars and some of the local militiamen being drawn up in battle array on opposite sides of one of Logan's steers. Orders from Clark arrived before any blood

14 Draper MSS. 9 J 2, 40-44, 106(1); 1 OO 51.

was shed, and Meriwether's sworn pension statement shows that he returned to Louisville in December.[15] Although there are numerous instances in his career which indicate that Logan had a high temper, it is not likely that this event took place exactly as related. Logan was described by one who knew him as having been "somewhat arbitrary and overbearing," and another of his acquaintances said that he was "a large raw-boned man, fully six feet [tall, who] sometimes fought at fisticuffs," but he hardly would have threatened to shoot a man who, while awaiting orders, was merely trying to feed his troops.[16]

Furthermore, the idea that he considered protection no longer necessary is erroneous, as is evident from his letter to the governor, dated December 18. "As to the present distresst situation of this County," he wrote, "I shall say but little about it, as it apears the conducting the war in this Western Country is invested in General Clarck." After this implied criticism, he continued: "If some method is not fell upon Early the ensueing Spring to repel the Enemy, I hope your Excellency . . . will Grant me the liberty . . . to raise two companies of Light Horse for the defence of this County."[17]

Two days later two letters were written at the capital. One of these affected Logan directly and the other indirectly. The first was a circular from Virginia's Commissioner of War, William Davies, to the county lieutenants of Jefferson, Fayette, and Lincoln. "I am directed by his Excellency," said Davies, "to desire you will from time to time send to General Clark such numbers of your militia as he may require for garrison duty or to defend your frontiers." Here was an indication that the new governor, Benjamin Harrison, who had taken office on

[15] Draper MSS. 8 J 92-93; 18 J 96-97.
[16] Draper MSS. 13 CC 172; 29 S 103.
[17] Logan to Thomas Nelson, December 18, 1781, *Calendar of Virginia State Papers*, II, 665. There is an edited copy of this letter in Draper MSS. 11 S 9. The spelling used here, however, is Logan's own. Logan obviously did not know that Nelson had resigned. (See Hening (ed.), *Statutes*, X, v.) This would indicate that he left Richmond before November 30.

November 30, was going to give some attention to the defense of Kentucky and might tackle the problem of divided authority.[18] Although Clark was the supreme military commander in Virginia's western military department, his direct authority extended only to the regulars. When dealing with the militia he could merely make requests. Only upon the direct authority of the governor or when conducting a campaign could he command.

The second letter was from Harrison to Clark. It included a copy of the assembly's decision against offensive operations and outlined some plans for defense. Clark was authorized "to call upon the counties of Jefferson, Fayette, and Lincoln in proportion to their number of militia for as many men as will make up with the regulars . . . three hundred and four." One hundred of these were to be stationed at the Falls and sixty-eight each at the mouths of the Kentucky, the Licking, and Limestone Creek. Additional authority was granted to Clark to increase these numbers whenever he felt that the situation required it.

Harrison liked the idea of gunboats, which had been mentioned by the assembly, and ordered Clark to build three or four. He added that cannon, if none could be spared from the fort at Louisville, might be sent to Fort Pitt in the spring for shipment to Kentucky. The governor admitted that the work of building forts and gunboats would have to be done on credit. "We have nothing to depend on for the present," he added, "but the virtue of the people."[19]

Replying to this letter on February 18, 1782, Clark began, "The repeated disappointments I have met with from Government occasion me to Enter on the business you propose with some Regret, But shall lay aside every Reflection and commence anew." He denied having either money or credit and

18 William Davies to County Lieutenants, December 20, 1781, Draper MSS. 13 S 157. Hening (ed.), *Statutes*, X, v.
19 Harrison to Clark, December 20, 1781, Executive Letter Book 5, pp. 13-15. Draper MSS. 51 J 100-101(2); 10 S 16-20.

feared to convert any public property into cash with no certainty of getting it replaced. He favored the gunboat proposal, but insisted that the necessary cannon and rigging would have to be sent to him. "The Post of Licking," said Clark, "will be Immediately Established, and the others as soon as circumstances will admit."[20]

Early in February, Logan had occasion to meet with Clark and at least one of his officers, Thomas Quirk. Exactly what took place is not clear. Quirk, although only a major, may have felt that a line commission put him on a plane above Logan, who was a county lieutenant with the rank of colonel of militia. He may have made uncomplimentary remarks about Logan's dress or his manner of speaking. Whatever the reason, Logan felt that he had been insulted. On the day after the encounter he wrote the following note to Clark: "Honoured Sir from the treatment I received last night from Magor Thomas Quirck whom I beleave to be an Officer in Ileanoy Regiment under your Command & the said treatment hapened in your presence I do request & demand the satisfaction for that treatment that the Law Martial derects & that Law to be put in force as soon as may be."[21] What action, if any, was taken by Clark has not been determined.

There was a certain amount of friction between the militia and the regulars in the matter of the distribution of provisions. Joseph Lindsay had acted as commissary for Kentucky County under John Bowman. He was given the same duty in the two counties of Lincoln and Fayette under Logan and John Todd. In February, 1782, Clark named Lindsay as his commissary general. In this capacity he was to procure supplies for the forts which were to be built along the Ohio. On the same day that Clark made this appointment Logan wrote a letter to Lindsay. He inquired about some horses that Lindsay had in

[20] Clark to Harrison, February 18, 1782, *Calendar of Virginia State Papers*, III, 68-69. Draper MSS. 60 J 144. Clark was referring to the fact that the expenses of his campaigns had not yet been met by the state.
[21] Logan to Clark, February 12, 1782, Draper MSS. 52 J 5. Draper MSS. 52 J 3; 60 J 100.

his charge, which were intended for the use of the militia. Logan was sending some of his militiamen to the southern border of Lincoln County. He needed these horses and requested also some provisions and ammunition.[22] Lindsay may have complied on this occasion, but, after receiving his new appointment from Clark, he did not always cooperate with the militia officers. This was mentioned by Logan and by his colonel, Stephen Trigg, in letters to Lindsay. Logan implied that Lindsay had militia provisions in his possession which he had failed to report. He believed that Fayette County still was being furnished supplies from this source, and that some supplies which belonged to Lincoln County had been forwarded to Clark.[23]

It was unfortunate that such dissension came at a time when Kentucky was in danger. The chiefs of many of the northern tribes had been summoned to Detroit in the preceding November and asked to have their warriors ready to attack Kentucky in the spring. The British plan, as learned by the Americans, was to capture Fort Nelson at Louisville and then to lay waste the other settlements. Fort Nelson, named for Virginia's third governor, had been erected by Clark on the bank of the Ohio about one-half mile upstream from his 1779 fort. The Indians were urged to take prisoners whenever possible and to bring them to Detroit. From these prisoners information concerning the state of Kentucky's defenses might be obtained.[24]

When news of the British intentions reached Kentucky, Clark made some changes in his plans. Since it would take several months to build the proposed forts along the Ohio, he would strengthen Fort Nelson and build gunboats to patrol the

[22] Clark to Lindsay, February 18, 1782, Draper MSS. 29 J 54-54(1). Logan to Lindsay, February 18, 1782, Draper MSS. 32 J 5. Logan to Lindsay, March 11, 1782, Draper MSS. 29 J 57-57(1).

[23] Trigg to [Lindsay], February 21, 1782, Draper MSS. 29 J 53-54. Logan to Lindsay, March 11, 1782, Draper MSS. 29 J 57-57(1).

[24] William Irvine to George Washington, February 7, 1782, Draper MSS. 11 J 11. Clark to Lindsay, March 5, 1782, Draper MSS. 11 J 17. Clark to Benjamin Harrison, March 7, 1782, Calendar of Virginia State Papers, III, 87-88.

river. This was mentioned in a letter to Governor Harrison in
which Clark urged that equipment for the boats be sent as
soon as possible. "This intelligence," he explained, "hath occasion'd us to alter our former plan of opperation [sic] and
strengthen ourselves by water as much as possible." Although
this could have been clearer, it should have been taken to
mean that the building of the forts would be postponed and
the building of boats would be pushed. "No vessels they can
bring across the portages from the Lakes," Clark continued,
"will be able to face such as we can navigate the Ohio with,
could we get furniture for them."[25]

To assist with his new plan Clark asked Logan to have a
detachment of the Lincoln militia ready to march to Louisville
by March 15. He ordered the commissary general to be
prepared to furnish that post with "three hundred Rations of
Beef pr day." Lindsay was asked also to be on the lookout for
experienced carpenters and boatbuilders. They were to receive
"good wages in hard money" if they would come to Louisville
at once. Clark evidently had been supplied with some "hard
money" very recently. "We are going to Build armed Boats to
Station at the mouth of Miami," he explained to Lindsay, "to
dispute the navigation of the Ohio either up or down."[26]

The residents of Jefferson County, who stood to benefit most
from the proposed strengthening of Fort Nelson, were called
upon to contribute their proportionate number of militiamen
for the work. John Floyd informed Clark that these men would
be ready on the appointed day, but he added: "It will I find
be a great mortification to the Inhabitants in general, if no
post is erected on the Ohio above the Falls."[27]

The first detachment of Lincoln militia was brought to
Louisville in March by Lieutenant Colonel John Logan. To
him Clark gave the command of all the militia units which
were employed in strengthening the fortifications. The super-

25 Clark to Harrison, March 7, 1782, *Calendar of Virginia State Papers,* III,
87-88.
26 Clark to Lindsay, March 5, 1782, Draper MSS. 11 J 17 or 29 J 55-55(1).
27 Floyd to Clark, March 8, 1782, Draper MSS. 52 J 9-9(1).

intending of the construction work was assigned to Major John Crittenden, who had been Clark's aide-de-camp.[28]

In April these Lincoln men were replaced by another Lincoln company under Captain William McBride. This time Benjamin Logan came along, probably to see for himself just what was being accomplished. Soon after his arrival he turned the men over to his second-in-command, Colonel Stephen Trigg, who remained throughout the one month tour of duty.[29]

[28] Draper MSS. 60 J 134; 63 J 106; 1 OO 109-110. Lincoln County Court Order Book 1, p. 15.
[29] Pension statement of Abraham Estis, Draper MSS. 1 OO 110.

CHAPTER X

BRYAN'S STATION AND
BLUE LICKS

ALTHOUGH THE FIGHTING in the East seemed to have ended with the surrender of Cornwallis at Yorktown, the British-Indian menace in the West still was present. While Logan was furnishing men for the strengthening of Fort Nelson at Louisville, he also had to guard the frontiers of the largest of the three counties. It was impossible to prevent the penetration of so lengthy a border, but once Indian signs were seen or damage was done within its limits, immediate pursuit by mounted men had to be arranged. This was the case on March 15, 1782, when Logan placed Captain James Estill and his company on active duty. Indians had attacked Strode's Station across the Kentucky in Fayette County, killing two men, wounding a third, and capturing several Negroes. There were indications that the invaders then had crossed the river into Lincoln County. Captain Estill, after a few days of scouting, picked up their trail and followed them back into Fayette. On March 22 they made a stand on a hill known as Little Mountain, overlooking Hinkston Creek. The opposing parties had about twenty-five men each, but the Indians had the better position. Captain Estill, Lieutenant John South, and six other men were lost before the remainder could make their escape. The Indians were able to remove their dead, and so their losses could not be determined.[1]

With rumors of a bigger invasion still in the air, Clark began to fear that the fighting strength of Kentucky would be seriously depleted by the return of unattached males to the other side of the mountains. He asked Logan to place a guard on the Wilderness Trail with instructions to order parties traveling eastward to turn back. It would be difficult to determine just how effective this measure was. A member of one departing group afterward claimed that his party was too strong to be stopped, but that at Logan's request they had given him their names for transmision to Clark. If this were the case, it is likely that the list which Logan obtained had an extraordinary number of John Does. On top of the difficulty of stopping groups which were bent upon leaving, there must also have been considerable risk of losing small parties which avoided the usual trail until the guard had been passed.[2]

John Floyd viewed the frequent Indian incursions as being related to a British plan to capture Fort Nelson and then to overwhelm all of Kentucky. The capture of the settlers' horses would make flight difficult and effective pursuit of the enemy impossible. The increasing tendency of militiamen to fail to appear when called up for duty he blamed upon the current talk of a separation of Kentucky from Virginia. Some of the militia delinquents may have believed that this would occur soon enough to prevent their being brought to justice. The idea of separation was being pushed by several Pennsylvania land speculators and by two Virginians, Arthur Campbell and John Donelson. In May, however, Clark reported to the governor that "by the exertions of many of the principal officers of the country . . . we are like to reduce the people to subordination." He went on to explain that the Kentuckians had begun to suspect that they were being misled. "In a short time," he continued, "it will be dangerous . . . to speak of new

---

[1] Draper MSS. 13 C 57; 60 J 106-109, 376; 12 CC 62. The town of Mount Sterling is located at the site of this battle. Kentucky has named a county in Captain Estill's honor. Two days after the Battle of Little Mountain or Estill's Defeat Governor Harrison penned his answer to Clark's request for cannon for his gunboats. He promised to supply what he could and to deliver them to Fort Pitt. See Harrison to Clark, March 24, 1782, in Draper MSS. 52 J 11-11(1) or in Executive Letter Book 5, pp. 82-83.

[2] Draper MSS. 4 J 8, 38, 49.

government in this quarter. . . . The body of the people now seem to be alarmed for fear Virginia will give up their interest."[3]

In the meantime Logan was wrestling with the problems of defending his county and sending aid to Clark at Louisville. His difficulties were increased by the lack of a commissary under his direct control. Clark, in line with an amendment to the militia law, had moved Joseph Lindsay from the position of militia commissary to that of commissary general for the Western Department. Such a step toward military unification might have been an advantage in a country where distances were shorter and communications better. In Kentucky, however, it was a great disadvantage. It meant that Logan had to obtain his militia supplies from Lindsay by sending a request to Clark. The material needed might be much closer to Logan than to either Lindsay or Clark. On April 8 Clark notified Lindsay that Logan had reported that he was "much distressed for the want of Beef and Salt for the support of those militia that may be thought necessary to guard the upper part of Lincoln." Clark suggested that some of the public beef at Lexington be made available to Logan. At the same time he asked Lindsay to purchase 500 pounds of hemp for the gunboats that he was building at Louisville. Later in the month Logan sent Captain John Martin and his company to Louisville for powder and salt. They returned with these necessities on May 2.[4]

Like all militia commanders, Logan had some difficulty in enforcing the universal enrollment and service that the law required. Men living on the fringes of the settled area were hard to reach. An amendment to the militia law, passed by the assembly in the spring of 1781, authorized the arrest of

[3] John Floyd to John May, April 8, 1782, Draper MSS. 11 S 137-41. Clark to Harrison, May 2, 1782, Draper MSS. 60 J 148-49. Thomas P. Abernethy, *Western Lands and the American Revolution* (New York, 1937), 302-303. Barnhart, *Valley of Democracy*, 56. Draper MSS. 9 CC 34.

[4] Clark to Lindsay, February 18, 1782, Draper MSS. 29 J 54-54(1). Clark to Lindsay, April 8, 1782, Draper MSS. 11 J 19. Draper MSS. 29 J 56; 60 J 120.

delinquents. They were to be delivered to an officer of the Continental army who would make the rounds for that express purpose and were to serve six months in the Continental forces. Nearly a year after the law was passed no Continental officer had yet appeared in Kentucky. This causes "great neglect of duty," said Logan, in a letter to the governor, "as it is generally known by the militia [that] the[y] can not be brought to Justice in this Country." He asked the governor to try to find some solution to the problem.

Logan then made reference to another letter to Harrison's predecessor, Thomas Nelson, to which he had received no reply. It contained the county court's recommendations of five citizens for appointments as justices of the peace and a request for some blank militia commissions. The five suggested were Nathaniel Hart, a former member of the Transylvania Company, Hugh Logan, who had moved his family to Kentucky from Botetourt County, George Adams, John Edwards, and Alexander Robertson. Benjamin Logan now added the name of David Guess to the list as a replacement for James Estill. He explained that the county had only five justices remaining, the minimum number that could constitute a court. Because they lived in widely separated parts of the county, it was very difficult to get them together for the transaction of public business.[5]

It is impossible to say just which of his many problems was uppermost in Logan's mind when he circulated a notice asking the people of his county to elect one representative from each militia company "to serve as a member of [a] committee to Take into consideration matters of Public Concern." He made it clear that he was making the request as a private citizen. The committee was to meet at the courthouse on April 1, 1782, but no record of the proceedings has been found. Such a committee would likely have discussed the problems of getting provisions for the militia, of getting all men who were subject

[5] Logan to Harrison, April 29, 1782, *Calendar of Virginia State Papers,* III, 142. Summers (ed.), *Annals,* 565.

to militia duty to serve, and of getting enough justices together
to hold court. The practice of using the area covered by the
residences of the members of a militia company as a political
unit was to be followed frequently in the years ahead. If this
meeting concerned any of the matters about which Logan
wrote to the governor on April 29, it is surprising that he
allowed four weeks to elapse before writing. He may have
been occupied with his farm or perhaps with his family, which
on April 8 was increased by the arrival of a second daughter,
who was named Mary.[6]

During the months of May and June, Logan continued to
call upon one after another of his militia companies to serve
as scouts on the frontiers of his county or as construction
workers at Louisville. One group was sent to Estill's Station,
which had been weakened by the losses at Little Mountain.
These men remained for the usual thirty-day period of duty.
Captain Nathaniel Hart and his company served on the frontiers from May 24 to June 24. Captain John Boyle's company
was sent to Louisville under the command of Major Hugh
McGary. If the situation demanded, militiamen might be used
either for longer or for more frequent periods of duty. Returning from Louisville, Boyle's company had a month at home
and then patrolled the borders of Lincoln County from July 18
to August 13.[7]

Early in May, Clark reported to Governor Harrison that his
fortifications at Louisville soon would be completed. He
admitted that his greatest hope lay in the gunboats or row
galleys, one of which he expected to complete within twenty
days. Seventy-three feet long, it was to have forty-six oars
and would carry one hundred ten men. It had high gunwales
surmounted by hinged sections which in case of an attack
could be raised to make the sides even higher. According to
Clark it could "lay within pistol shot of the shore without the

6 Draper MSS. 12 C 45(4); 26 C 1; 32 J 66.
7 Pension statement of James P. Barnett, Draper MSS. 32 J 45-46. Draper
MSS. 60 J 104-105, 110-111.

least danger." He hoped that enough cannon would be available to permit the installation of a six-pounder, six four-pounders, and a two-pounder in each boat. Those cannon which had been ordered by the government had not yet arrived but were reported to be on the way. A few days later, Harrison, in a message to the assembly, confirmed this report.

Although an invasion of Kentucky with Fort Nelson as the first objective still was expected, May and June passed with no sign of the enemy's approach. By July 6 the first of the row galleys with a few guns mounted was ready to move up the Ohio to patrol the region around the mouths of the Miami and the Licking. It was agreed that regulars would take it to the mouth of the Kentucky, where they would be replaced by Fayette County militiamen. Virginia line officers were to remain in command. On June 27 John Todd had started a forty-man militia company to the meeting place with a promise to relieve these men within four weeks. Led by Captain Robert Patterson, this company proceeded to Drennon's Lick a few miles from its destination. On learning that the galley had not arrived, Patterson decided to camp at Drennon's and give his men a chance to replenish their supply of meat.[8]

Word soon came from Clark that the boat was ready to move, and Patterson was ordered to proceed down the Ohio until he met it. This row galley, which had been christened the *Miami,* was commanded by Clark's best artillery officer, Captain Robert George. The Fayette militiamen met the boat as they had been ordered to do but were not very cooperative. They demanded and received double rations of flour. Insisting that they were soldiers and not sailors, they refused to accept the duty of rowing, and Captain George had to keep his regulars at the oars. The militiamen marched along the shore until they reached Big Bone Creek in Northern Kentucky. Here

[8] Clark to Harrison, May 2, 1782, Draper MSS. 60 J 148-51 or *Calendar of Virginia State Papers,* III, 150. John Floyd to Clark, June 16, 1782, Draper MSS. 52 J 2-2(1). Todd to Patterson, June 27, 1782, Draper MSS. 1 MM 105. Draper MSS. 10 S 29; 1 MM 36; 29 J 92(1-3). Bodley, *History of Kentucky,* I, 300.

they declared their intention of returning to their homes even though their period of active duty lacked a week of being completed. Captain Patterson and his lieutenant went aboard to discuss the situation with George. Both of the militia officers were of the opinion that their men "would sooner fight than come on board." Patterson later claimed that he and his men returned home because the river was so low that the boat could go no farther, but this seems to be at variance with the facts.[9]

In spite of the difficulties which were experienced in operating it, the row galley had a beneficial effect. The British long had expected another American invasion of Canada, originating this time in the West. They were convinced that it would come not later than the summer of 1782, and that their enemies would be assisted by Frenchmen and Indians. On the day that Patterson's men took their leave of the galley Indian spies were watching from a hill on the opposite side of the Ohio. They may have been drinking, for they reported to their Tory leader, Alexander McKee, that they had seen two large boats both equipped with cannon. The boats, they said, were accompanied by the largest army of both Indians and whites that ever had approached their villages. McKee concluded that such a host could not be expected to stop with the destruction of a few Indian towns. Surely this was the prelude to the expected invasion. He notified his superiors that he and Captain William Caldwell, who had just arrived with a party of Lake Indians, would try to keep their forces between the enemy and Detroit. It seems clear that at this time there was no danger of British and Indian invaders crossing into Kentucky anywhere near the mouths of the

[9] Clark to Patterson, July 5, 1782, Draper MSS. 32 J 1. Robert George to John Todd, July 19, 1782, Draper MSS. 52 J 25-25(1). Deposition of Robert Patterson, Draper MSS. 4 J 84. Draper MSS. 4 J 19; 31 J 88(1); 32 J 34. John Bakeless, *Background to Glory, The Life of George Rogers Clark* (Philadelphia and New York, 1957), 288. Patterson's own account of duty with the galley is in part an attempt to justify his own conduct. See Robert Patterson, "Battle of the Blue Licks," 15 pp. MSS., Durrett Collection, University of Chicago.

Miami or the Licking. If a few more of these gunboats had been ready the region might have been secure. After the unsuccessful experience with the militia, the galley was placed under the command of Captain Jacob Pyeatt and was operated by men who were enlisted as marines. These men, who received ten dollars per month and an outfit of clothing, were mostly former members of Virginia line companies whose terms of enlistment had ended.[10]

By the first of August, Clark must have doubted that an attack was coming. He was involved in a correspondence with his commissary regarding the disappearance from Bullitt's Lick of some public salt pans, items which he implied that Logan might know something about. At the same time he was considering a drive into the Indian country in cooperation with General William Irvine, who hoped to make a similar move from Fort Pitt in the fall. This plan was known to the British, who already had added 200 men to their forces protecting Detroit.[11]

Caldwell and McKee must soon have realized that the reports concerning the army that was said to be with the galley had no basis, and that the expected drive on Detroit had not gotten under way. Their Indians being hard to retain in a state of inaction, they decided upon action instead. Giving the galley a wide berth, they marched to a point nearly opposite the mouth of Limestone Creek seventy miles upstream from the mouth of the Licking. From that location they crossed the Ohio into Kentucky. Their stated purpose was to draw a

[10] Extract from *Maryland Journal*, July 9, 1782, Draper MSS. 3 JJ 90. This was copied from a London newspaper of April 1, 1782, which mentioned as its source certain letters written by Sir Frederick Haldimand, British commander in Canada. Captain Alexander McKee to Major Arent S. De Peyster, July 22, 1782, "Haldimand Papers," in *Michigan Pioneer and Historical Collections*, XX, 32-33. Jacob Pyeatt to Clark, August 4, 1782, Draper MSS. 59 J 29-29(1). John Floyd to Clark, March 8, 1782, Draper MSS. 52 J 9(1).

[11] Clark to Joseph Lindsay, July 15, 1782, Draper MSS. 29 J 59. Clark to Lindsay, August 6, 1782, Draper MSS. 29 J 60. Clark to Irvine, August 10, 1782, Draper MSS. 11 J 22. Frederick Haldimand to Sir Guy Carleton, July 28, 1782, "Haldimand Papers," in *Michigan Pioneer and Historical Collections*, XX, 34.

party away from one of the forts and take some prisoners from whom they might get additional intelligence regarding Clark's intentions.[12]

A letter from "a Gentleman at Quebec to his friend at Edinburg," written on July 17, 1782, gives the impression that the British commanders in America had more in mind than the mere taking of a few prisoners. An American advance to Sandusky under Colonel William Crawford had been stopped with great loss to the invaders on June 4 and June 5. This invasion was treated by the letter writer as a forerunner of Clark's drive against Detroit. If the British command placed this interpretation upon Crawford's expedition, then it is likely that Caldwell and McKee were sent into Kentucky to draw Clark's attention from his objective. Nothing in Caldwell's report can be taken as either confirming or denying this opinion. He had expected to attack Wheeling but was diverted by the inaccurate report that Clark's army was near the mouth of the Licking with two gunboats. Caldwell had 1,100 Indians with him at the time. He may have been sorry, as he afterward claimed, that the report proved false, for many of the red men, not being prepared for a long campaign, left him as soon as it was seen that there was to be no immediate engagement. Caldwell was determined not to return to Detroit without having struck a blow at his enemies, though when he and McKee made their way into Kentucky their force was down to 300 men, including Canadian rangers as well as Indians.[13]

On August 14 a small detachment of warriors, after capturing two boys at Holder's Station on the Kentucky River, was overtaken by Captain John Holder and a party of Kentuckians at the Upper Blue Licks on the Licking River. The result was

[12] McKee to De Peyster, August 28, 1782, "Haldimand Papers," in *Michigan Pioneer and Historical Collections*, XX, 49. Temple Bodley, *George Rogers Clark, His Life and Public Services* (Boston, 1926), 212.

[13] Haldimand to Carleton, July 28, 1782, "Haldimand Papers," in *Michigan Pioneer and Historical Collections*, XX, 34. Caldwell to De Peyster, August 26, 1782, quoted in Reuben T. Durrett, *Bryant's Station*, Filson Club Publications Number 12 (Louisville, 1897), 208-209. Draper MSS. 11 J 6-9.

a complete defeat for Holder, with four of his men losing their lives.[14]

By daylight on the morning of August 16, Caldwell, McKee, and the renegade Simon Girty had brought their men to Bryan's Station, a stockaded fort about five miles northeast of Lexington. As soon as their presence was discovered two messengers slipped out of the fort undetected and hastened to Lexington for help. Colonel John Todd, the county lieutenant of Fayette, was in Lincoln County at the time. The senior officer present was his younger brother Major Levi Todd, the husband of Logan's niece.

Taking about thirty men with him, Levi Todd set out for Bryan's Station. He was joined by ten men from Boone's Station, which lay to the south of Lexington. With a force which might have been larger had not some of Boone's men gone to the rescue of Captain John Holder, Levi Todd sought to break the Indian lines now surrounding Bryan's Station. Seventeen mounted men got through and joined the defenders inside the fort. Todd and the rest of his men, some mounted and some on foot, were turned back. The attackers continued to fire upon the fort until the morning of August 17 and made several attempts to burn it. Seeing that the defenders were not to be drawn out and that the fort could not be taken without artillery, Caldwell and his Indians concentrated upon destroying the crops and the livestock. They then left, carrying two of their wounded and leaving five of their number dead.[15]

[14] Logan to Benjamin Harrison, August 31, 1782, Draper MSS. 11 S 10. Draper MSS. 60 J 373, 381, 396, 404.

[15] Levi Todd to Benjamin Harrison, September 11, 1782, *Calendar of Virginia State Papers*, III, 300-301. Levi Todd to Robert Todd, August 26, 1782, *ibid.*, 333-34. Logan to Harrison, August 31, 1782, *ibid.*, 280-83. Daniel Boone to Harrison, August 30, 1782, *ibid.*, 275-76. Andrew Steel to Harrison, August 26, 1782, *ibid.*, 269-270. Copies of the first four of these letters may also be seen in Draper MSS. 11 S 203-205; 11 S 115-18; 11 S 10; and 60 J 17 respectively. See also Caldwell to De Peyster, August 26, 1782, in Durrett, *Bryant's Station*, 208-209; McKee to De Peyster, August 28, 1782, "Haldimand Papers," in *Michigan Pioneer and Historical Collections*, XX, 49-51; Draper MSS. 52 J 36(1); and "McKee Letters," Durrett Collection, University of Chicago.

Returning to Lexington, Levi Todd quickly dispatched a message to Stephen Trigg asking for immediate aid. He requested the Lincoln County colonel to relay the information to Logan and also to John Todd. The message expressed the hope that Trigg, who lived near the Fayette-Lincoln border, would see fit to act on his own authority without waiting for orders from Logan at St. Asaph's.

Trigg received this message the same afternoon. John Todd, who was not far away, was summoned at once. Hearing that Logan was in Harrodsburg that day and assuming that he would remain for the night, Trigg wrote a note on the back of Levi Todd's message and sent it to that place. He said that already he had ordered Captains McBride, Madison, Gordon, and Overton, and Ensign Adams to be at Captain Gordon's next morning ready to march to Lexington. If the messenger found Logan at Harrodsburg he was to wait for any orders that the county lieutenant might wish to send. Logan had returned to his home that night, and the messenger brought that information back to Trigg. It was now eleven o'clock on the morning of August 17. Trigg started Levi Todd's message to St. Asaph's. With it he sent a new note explaining how far arrangements had progressed. He had ordered six captains to turn out, each with one-half of his company, but at the time of writing only sixty men had appeared. "I should not have taken this step without your orders but the case seemed urgent and [I] had no doubt but [that] you would approved what I did." Stephen Trigg was wrestling with a problem with which frontier militia officers often had to contend. When an emergency arose it took time to notify his men and even more time for the men to make their way to the designated meeting place. Should an officer set out with the first arrivals and risk not having enough men to do the job, or should he wait for all to appear and perhaps reach the trouble spot too late? Somewhere between these extremes a balance had to be struck. "We shall wait a few minutes," said Trigg, "and go on."[16]

[16] Trigg to Logan, August 17, 1782, Draper MSS. 52 J 35. Levi Todd to Trigg, August 16, 1782, Draper MSS. 52 J 36(1).

Shortly after this note was written Trigg and two other Lincoln County field officers, Majors Hugh McGary and Silas Harlan, led their men across the Kentucky. Colonel John Todd of Fayette accompanied them. By nightfall they had reached Levi Todd's Station, six miles from Lexington. Here more of the Lincoln militiamen overtook them, and they arrived at Bryan's on August 18 with 130 men. At Bryan's they were joined by Colonel Daniel Boone, Major Levi Todd, and some of the Fayette militiamen. With a total of 182 men, all mounted on good horses, they set out to follow the rather obvious trail that Caldwell, McKee, and their Indians had left. As the only county lieutenant present, John Todd had the command. They camped that night at the site of Ruddle's Station on the South Licking.

It was after nightfall on August 17 when Trigg's messages reached Logan at St. Asaph's. He immediately sent couriers to all of the inhabited portions of Lincoln County with orders for "every man to turn out." By the next morning 154 had assembled. Without waiting for more, Logan set out. By the end of the day he had reached the Kentucky at the mouth of Hickman's Creek, and the next morning they crossed into Fayette County and arrived at Lexington about noon. Logan found the residents of that town rather indifferent, the prevailing opinion being that a sufficient number of men had gone with Colonels Todd, Trigg, and Boone. He pushed on to Bryan's Station where, in spite of the recent siege, a similar feeling of confidence was in evidence. Being unable either to convince the people that the pursuit might have been rash or to raise additional men, Logan continued his march. He had covered only five miles when he met about twenty-five men. They were fleeing from pioneer Kentucky's worst disaster. He covered their retreat and pulled his own force back to the vicinity of Bryan's and Lexington.[17]

After a short night's rest at Ruddle's, John Todd and his men

[17] Logan to Harrison, August 31, 1782, Draper MSS. 11 S 10-11. Levi Todd to Robert Todd, August 26, 1782, *Calendar of Virginia State Papers*, III, 333-34. Draper MSS. 52 J 35-35(1); 63 J 129.

had continued to follow the enemy's trail. This took them to
the Licking River at a point just across from the Lower Blue
Licks. Here for the first time they could see a few of the
Indians on a ridge on the opposite side of the stream. The
Licking at this place bends into the approximate shape of a
horseshoe. The enemy was inside and the Kentuckians had
struck the shoe near its toe. Caldwell and McKee had kept
most of their Indians out of sight. The few that were seen
probably were decoys. The two British officers had extended
their lines from the point where the river first changes its
course to the point where its general course is resumed. The
water was deep in all parts of the bend with the exception of
the place to which the trail led. Here, near the middle of the
horseshoe, it could be forded easily. Thus a party meeting
defeat inside of the big bend would be in a serious predica-
ment. If the survivors could reach the ford they might, if
mounted at the time, gallop their horses across and escape.
If cut off from the ford, a place of relative safety could be
reached only by swimming, and a man on a swimming horse
makes a better target than a man on a galloping horse.

After some discussion the Kentuckians crossed the river and
proceeded in three columns. Within sixty yards of the enemy
they dismounted and tied their horses. Forming their lines
parallel to those of their opponents, they continued to advance.
Trigg commanded the right wing, McGary the center, and
Boone the left. Tradition has placed John Todd with Trigg.
It is far more likely that he would have been with McGary.
Here was the highest ground—the logical place from which to
direct the operation. Also his wings were commanded by full
colonels. McGary was a major and had gained that rank only
after James Harrod had refused to accept it. Boone's men were
the first to make contact with the enemy. With heavy firing
both delivered and received, they pushed the Indians back
nearly one hundred yards. Subsequent events seem to indicate
that at least a part of this withdrawal was planned. On the
right, Trigg's men had crossed some ravines without stopping

to search them. Indians who were hidden there were soon at their backs. Trying to escape from this trap, Trigg began to shift his men toward the center. There they became entangled with McGary's, some of whom immediately lost their effectiveness by shifting behind Boone. Within five minutes after the first shot was fired the Kentucky lines were in confusion. Todd had held no men in reserve, and reloading under fire had been difficult. The trees on the ridge were small and offered little protection. Caldwell and McKee had been able to select their position, leaving the Kentuckians to make the assault. Now that confusion reigned in the ranks of the attackers, the British officers ordered their Indians forward. Warriors from several tribes were present. The Wyandots in particular were artists with the tomahawk. Many of the Kentuckians went down as they tried to reload. Escape soon was uppermost in the minds of the survivors. As Major Levi Todd described the scene a few days later: "He that could remount a horse was well off, and he that could not saw no time for delay." Some died before they reached the river and some as they tried to swim across, either on their horses or alone. Only a few had been able to cross at the ford, and the Indians, pursuing for two miles beyond the river, cut down some of these. The losses included Colonels Todd and Trigg, Major Harlan, four captains, five lieutenants, and about sixty privates. Joseph Lindsay, the commissary general, along as a volunteer, lost his life. Major Edward Bulger of Fayette died of his wounds a few days later.[18]

News of the disaster convinced Logan that a large body of Indians was involved, and he was unwilling to run additional

[18] Levi Todd to Robert Todd, August 26, 1782, Draper MSS. 11 S 115-18. Levi Todd to Benjamin Harrison, September 11, 1782, Draper MSS. 11 S 203-205. Daniel Boone to Benjamin Harrison, August 30, 1782, Draper MSS. 60 J 70-71. Logan to Harrison, August 31, 1782, Draper MSS. 11 S 17-18. William Caldwell to Arent S. De Peyster, August 26, 1782, in Durrett, *Bryant's Station*, 208-209. Alexander McKee to De Peyster, August 28, 1782, "Haldimand Papers," in *Michigan Pioneer and Historical Collections*, XX, 49-51. Boone's commission as a colonel was dated February 7, 1781. See Draper MSS. 63 J 129.

risks. All of the Lincoln men had been ordered to turn out, which should increase his strength within a few days. Early in the morning on August 22, John Logan, lieutenant colonel of the Lincoln militia, reached Lexington with two ensigns and 134 men. Major McGary, upon his return from the battlefield, was sent to Lincoln to assist in the raising of the militia. On August 23 he returned with about 140. Late in the afternoon of that day Logan set out for Blue Licks with 470 men. Stopping for only two hours of sleep, they reached the scene of the battle at ten o'clock on the morning of August 24. All signs indicated that the enemy had not tarried long, and therefore could by now have recrossed the Ohio. The stripped and mutilated remains of forty-three men were buried in a common grave. The condition of the bodies was such that not one could be positively identified. Of those men who still were missing, it was impossible to say at the time which had been killed in the river and carried away by the current and which had been taken alive. Logan and his men returned to Lexington on August 25, and on the following day the men returned to their homes.[19]

Between thirty and sixty years after the Battle of Blue Licks many of the accounts of participants and of the friends and relatives of participants were recorded by Humphrey Marshall, John D. Shane, Lyman C. Draper, and others who were interested in history. With the passage of time these stories became more and more colored. Those who had access to Marshall's *History of Kentucky* began to confuse what they had seen with what they had read. There are numerous accounts purporting to give the conversations of the officers at councils held at Bryan's Station, at Ruddle's Station, and on the west bank of the Licking. Boone is pictured as a cautious leader who favored waiting for Logan. When this idea was rejected he is said to have proposed several alternatives to a direct crossing of the river in the face of the enemy. The

[19] Levi Todd to Robert Todd, August 26, 1782, Draper MSS. 11 S 115-18. Logan to Harrison, August 31, 1782, Draper MSS. 11 S 17-18. Draper MSS. 52 J 35(1)-36; 60 J 120-21.

usual villain in these stories is Hugh McGary. He is said to have favored waiting at Bryan's for Logan and as a result to have been accused of cowardice by Todd and Trigg. Supposedly these two officers hesitated on the bank of the Licking and McGary threw the charge back at them. Some even claimed that he broke up the officers' council at the river by calling upon all men who were not cowards to follow him. One of those who made such a charge was a private named Henry Wilson. He accused McGary of wrecking the deliberations by urging his horse into the river and leading the men across. Wilson did not seem to remember that earlier in the same account he had told how he and some of the other men had watched their officer, Silas Harlan, coming back from the council, and had wondered as he approached what the decision had been. Obviously it could not have happened both ways. McGary may have sought to influence the council, but that body seems to have made its own decision.[20]

Of far more importance are the charges and countercharges that were made soon after the battle. McGary claimed that Trigg had delayed sending his message to Logan until it was to late for Logan to gather his forces and overtake the advance party. He claimed also that Todd would have been expected to surrender the command to Logan because a majority of the men were from Lincoln County, and this Todd did not wish to do. This charge frequently has been distorted, and the claim has been made that Logan would have assumed the command because he outranked Todd. This, however, was not the case. John Todd became county lieutenant of Fayette at the time of its formation and he had been county lieutenant of Illinois County before that. Logan did not replace John Bowman as county lieutenant of Lincoln until July, 1781. If the accusation made against Todd had any basis, McGary's explanation would be the better one. McGary, however, was trying to justify himself. He may not have known that Trigg's first message

---

[20] Henry Wilson's account is in Draper MSS. 9 J 55-57. For other accounts see Draper MSS. 12 C 24(4), 62(9); 8 J 105-106; 9 J 192; 6 S 155, 158; 17 S 236; 18 S 157; 9 CC 52, 12 CC 70, 134-35; 3 DD 289; 5 XX 54.

went to Harrodsburg, where its writer had reason to believe that Logan could be found. Its return had necessitated a second attempt.

Of the many letters written soon after the battle only two have been found which have anything critical to say about McGary. Colonel Arthur Campbell, who was not within 150 miles of Blue Licks at the time of the disaster, accused him of uttering "seditious expressions." His only source seems to have been Benjamin Netherland, who participated in the battle as a private. Netherland's reliability may be judged by a comment of Governor Harrison. Replying to some Fayette officers who had suggested Netherland for a major's commission, Harrison wrote: "You certainly do not know the man, or your court could never have recommended him. You will have a blank commission which you'll please to fill up to any other person that the court shall recommend, but you have my positive orders that it be not to Netherland."

The other contemporary letter which is critical of McGary was written by McGary himself. To Benjamin Logan he said, in a somewhat ironical vein, "I suppose you have heard of my bad conduct." McGary's bad conduct, if it can be so described, seems to have consisted of an attempt to shame the other officers into ordering a crossing of the river. Here may have been spoken the words which Campbell described as "seditious." The charge that he led the men across in defiance of his superiors has never been substantiated. Clark and Logan evidently did not blame him. They took him along on their next campaign as a lieutenant colonel.[21]

The first report to the governor was written on August 26 by Andrew Steel. A private in the militia, Steel was under no obligation to make a report. He may have done so as a means of relieving the tension which such an experience is likely to have created. Steel limited himself for the most part to relating

[21] McGary to Logan, August 28, 1782, Draper MSS. 52 J 35(1)-36. Arthur Campbell to William Davies, October 3, 1782, *Calendar of Virginia State Papers*, III, 337. Harrison to Levi Todd, October 14, 1782, Draper MSS 10 S 57. Draper MSS. 5 C 51(4, 12-13); 12 C 36; 60 J 191.

the details of the battle. He did charge, without sufficient evidence, that Logan's aid had not been sought.

On August 30 Daniel Boone, now the senior officer in Fayette County, wrote his report. He asked for 500 men for the protection of Kentucky and suggested that they be placed wherever the county lieutenants thought best. "If you put them under the Direction of Genl: Clarke," he continued, "they will be Little or no Service to our Settlement, as he lies 100 miles west of us, and the Indians North East." Boone complained that the men of Fayette frequently were called to Louisville to protect the people of that region.[22]

On the following day Benjamin Logan prepared his report. "I am inclined to believe," he wrote, "that when your Excellency and Council become acquainted with the military operations in this country that you will not think them so properly conducted." He then told of attending the council of field officers at Louisville where it was decided to build forts along the Ohio instead of attempting a campaign. From that point on Logan selected his facts in such a way as to present only the militia's side of the picture. He said that he had been asked for men to build a fort at the mouth of the Licking, but that they had been used at Louisville instead. Not once did he mention that the first call had been for men to erect a fort at the mouth of the Kentucky, and that both he and John Todd had refused to comply. He criticized the row galley and accused Clark of "weakening one end [of Kentucky] to strengthen another." It was unfair to ignore the fact that the galley had not remained at Louisville, but had been sent to patrol the Ohio around the mouths of the Miami and the Licking. The refusal of militiamen to serve aboard it probably had hampered its activity.

Without accusing anyone in particular, Logan implied that there had been misapplication of funds and misuse of supplies in Clark's military department. This charge had some basis

<hr />

[22] Andrew Steel to Harrison, August 26, 1782, *Calendar of Virginia State Papers*, III, 269-70. Boone to Harrison, August 30, 1782, *ibid.*, 275-76. Durrett, *Bryant's Station*, 231.

and had been the subject of some correspondence between the governor and the general. Clark had taken it as a personal criticism, but Harrison vigorously denied that such had been intended.

Having relieved his mind of certain things, Logan suggested that General William Irvine, a Continental officer in command at Fort Pitt, might provide some protection for the Kentucky settlements if Virginia could send him supplies for that purpose. He mentioned also the lack of a militia colonel in his county due to the death of Stephen Trigg, and suggested that James Harrod, who had acted as a colonel in the 1780 campaign, be given the commission. Logan realized that such recommendations should come from the county court, but declared himself "at a loss how to proceed on the occasion, for all our magistrates have been killed except three, and there can be no court to send a recommendation." He concluded by reminding Harrison that "a defensive war cannot be carried on with Indians, and the Inhabitants remain in any kind of safety." Here again he was forgetting that at the officers' council in September, 1781, he had favored defense rather than offense. "Unless you can go to their Towns and scourge them," he continued, "they will never make a peace; but on the contrary [they will] keep parties constantly in your country to kill, and the plunder they get, answers instead of Trade."[23]

On September 12 Andrew Steel wrote his second criticism of the conduct of military affairs in the West. He objected to the emphasis placed upon Louisville, located on the northwestern

[23] Logan to Harrison, August 31, 1782, *Calendar of Virginia State Papers,* III, 280-83, or Draper MSS. 11 S 12-13. Logan occasionally received help in the writing of official letters. Lyman C. Draper, when he could not get possession of original manuscripts, made copies, and these he often edited, thus giving the impression that the writer was better educated than actually was the case. In this example, however, the style of the original letter as published in the *Calendar of Virginia State Papers* is superior to Logan's own style, and aid in its preparation is clearly indicated.

See also John Todd and Logan to Clark, October 13, 1781, Draper MSS. 51 J 93-93(1). Harrison to Clark, December 20, 1781, Draper MSS. 51 J 10(2); and Clark to Harrison, February 18, 1782, *Calendar of Virginia State Papers,* III, 68-69.

border of Kentucky, and felt that most of the money and
effort which had been expended in defending the western
country had been applied to Fort Nelson, Fort Jefferson,
Kaskaskia, and Vincennes. The amount spent upon the three
Kentucky counties, he thought, would in comparison be "less
than a Mathematical point."[24]

Levi Todd, in his personal report of September 11, had
limited himself to an account of the engagements at Bryan's
Station and Blue Licks and a request for help. On the same
day, he joined with Daniel Boone, Robert Patterson, Benjamin
Netherland, Eli Cleveland, and several other Fayette officers
in a combined criticism of Clark and a request for aid. (Netherland was not actually an officer, but was being recommended
for a commission at this time.) "Our militia," they said, "are
called on to do duty in a manner that has a tendency to protect
Jefferson County, or rather Louisville—a town without inhabitants, a fort situated in such a manner, that the enemy coming
with a design to lay waste our country would scarcely come
within one hundred miles of it, & our own frontiers open &
unguarded." They suggested that if no campaign could be
attempted at the time, the plan of erecting forts at the mouths
of the Licking and Limestone Creek be readopted and carried
out.[25]

Although Logan was unfair to Clark, an officer who had less
opportunity to know the facts was equally unfair to Logan, to
Clark, and to nearly everyone who had been connected with
the tragedy. Colonel Arthur Campbell, county lieutenant of
Washington County, whose plan for a new state in the West
had been blocked for the time being by some of these same
officers, wrote his opinion of the Blue Licks affair to Colonel
William Davies of the Virginia War Office. "Todd & Trigg,"
said Campbell, "had capacity but wanted experience. Boone,
Harlan, and Lindsay had experience, but were defective in

[24] Steel to Harrison, September 12, 1782, *Calendar of Virginia State Papers*,
III, 303-304.
[25] Militia Officers of Fayette County to Harrison, September 11, 1782,
Draper MSS. 60 J 74-77.

capacity." There is an element of truth in this much of Campbell's letter, but he continued, in a more critical and even a malicious vein: "Logan is a dull, narrow body from whom nothing clever need be expected. What a figure he exhibited at the head of near 500 men to reach the field of action six days afterwards, and hardly wait to bury the dead, and when it was plain, part of the Indians were still in the country. Genl. Clarke is in that country, but he has lost the confidence of the people, and it is said become a Sot; perhaps something worse." In addition to the fact that Logan arrived at Blue Licks five and not six days after the battle, Campbell made several other errors. The Indians, according to one of the officers who led them, were not "still in the country," but had crossed the Ohio two days after the battle. Logan, although he had received little education, should not have been described as "dull." There is no evidence to indicate that Clark at this time was anything approaching a "sot." Logan had delayed his march to Blue Licks because he was waiting for reinforcements. He did not want to risk a second disaster. There were above 300 Indians at Bryan's Station and about 100 less at Blue Licks if the British figures can be accepted. Logan, however, had only the estimates of survivors, and these ran as high as 600. In all of the criticisms of Clark one fact had been overlooked. He was responsible for the Illinois country in addition to Kentucky. His selection of the Falls of the Ohio as his head-quarters had to be made with this fact in mind.[26]

The blow at Blue Licks had fallen at a time when the war east of the mountains had virtually ceased. The loss of life not

[26] Arthur Campbell to William Davies, October 3, 1782, *Calendar of Virginia State Papers*, III, 337-38, and Draper MSS. 11 S 119-20. Caldwell to De Peyster, August 26, 1782, in Durrett, *Bryant's Station*, 209. Steel to Harrison, August 26, 1782, *Calendar of Virginia State Papers*, III, 269-70. McKee to De Peyster, August 28, 1782, "Haldimand Papers," in *Michigan Pioneer and Historical Collections*, XX, 50-51. McKee said that they waited all day for Logan because their prisoners had indicated that he was expected with 100 men. Leaving the site, they crossed the Ohio on "the second day after the battle." McKee has all of his dates for this campaign two days late, so it is fortunate that the time of crossing the Ohio was thus related to the time of the battle.

only was high, but it included a disproportionate number of officers, both military and civil, as a man who held a militia commission was often a magistrate, a sheriff, or a county clerk as well. Two factors caused the loss of officers to be out of proportion to the loss of enlisted men. One was the tendency for an officer to lead his men into battle. The other resulted from the method that had to be used in calling out the militia. A captain would be notified to call out all or part of his company, but because some of the people were now living on their own land claims instead of in the settlements, this would take time. Each captain had to decide how long he could wait for late arrivals, and in most cases he would report to his superiors with fewer men than he had been ordered to bring. Therefore when an engagement took place the number of officers participating would be out of proportion to the number of enlisted men, and it is not surprising that this was true of casualties as well.

For several weeks after the disaster at Blue Licks it appeared that the British and Indians intended to take advantage of the damage which had been done and the confusion which had resulted. Kincheloe's Station in Jefferson County was attacked and burned, and its thirty-seven inhabitants were made prisoners. Colonel Arthur Campbell expressed the fear that the British intended to drive all of the settlers from Virginia's western counties before signing peace terms. He urged that there be an immediate expedition against their Indian allies. Colonel William Christian of Montgomery County offered to lead such an expedition. Nevertheless, Governor Harrison opposed the idea of a campaign. He pointed out that no money was available to pay the expenses and that an early winter might catch the invaders in the Indian country, increasing the possibility of failure.[27]

[27] William Christian to Harrison, September 28, 1782, Draper MSS. 11 S 108-114. Harrison to Christian, October 9, 1782, Draper MSS. 10 S 53-54 or Executive Letter Book 5, pp. 3-6. Campbell to Davies, October 3, 1782, *Calendar of Virginia State Papers*, III, 337-38. Logan to Harrison, August 31, 1782, *Calendar of Virginia State Papers*, III, 282.

Logan tried to protect all of the stations in his county, but after the losses at Blue Licks their defense meant spreading his forces until no station was certain of its ability to protect itself. Nathaniel Hart, formerly of the Transylvania Company, had built his own fort in 1779 at the White Oak Spring about a mile up the Kentucky River from Boonesborough. Hart had been killed by the Indians in July, 1782, and by September the fort had only three men to defend it. This situation was made known to Logan, who sent two of his men, all that could be spared at the time, to supplement this tiny garrison. One of the residents of this same fort wrote many years later that: "It was not a very easy matter to order a married man from a fort where his family was, to defend some other—when his own was in imminent danger."[28]

The loss of life at Blue Licks hit Lincoln County harder than Fayette, numerically speaking, but Fayette had lost her county lieutenant. The Virginia Council gave early attention to this matter, and on September 25, 1782, Daniel Boone was given the commission that John Todd had held. At the same time Levi Todd was promoted from major to colonel, and Robert Patterson was advanced from captain to lieutenant colonel.[29]

As would be expected, the property loss at Blue Licks also was high. Logan reported that Lincoln County's losses included "36 horses, 26 guns, 4 shot pouches, 1 horn, 25 saddles, 19 bridles, 3 pair of saddle bags, 5 blankets . . . & 1 bell." He estimated the total value at a little over 575 pounds. Boone reported "18 horses lost, 6 guns, 12 saddles, 1 bridle, & 8 blankets." It is possible that both officers were reporting only those loses for which claims had been submitted.[30]

In October, Governor Harrison wrote his replies to the letters that he had received from Logan, Todd, Boone, and the Fayette officers. There were expressions of sympathy for

[28] Nathaniel Hart, Jr. to James T. Morehead, n.d. in James T. Morehead, *An Address in Commemoration of the First Settlement of Kentucky* (Frankfort, Ky., 1840), 147-49.

[29] Draper MSS. 60 J 369.

[30] Draper MSS. 60 J 128-30. James (ed.), *Clark Papers, 1781-1784*, 94.

the losses sustained, implied criticisms of John Todd and Stephen Trigg as commanders, and suggestions to the effect that revenge might be obtained in the future. Harrison seemed amazed to learn that the Ohio River forts had not been built. He expressed the belief that they could have prevented the disaster, because settlers could have been warned in time to collect their total strength. Logan and the other officers were censured for not keeping the executive informed as to the state of affairs in Kentucky. Harrison hinted at the possibility of an offensive in the spring. He hoped that the 200 men in the counties of Botetourt, Washington, and Montgomery whom he had made available for the defense of Kentucky would not be needed. The expense of sending them to Kentucky might make a spring campaign out of the question. The governor did not agree with Logan on the value of General William Irvine at Fort Pitt as a protector of Kentucky. Irvine's forces, he said, were very little larger than Clark's. "Kentucky," said His Excellency to the Fayette officers, "is as much the object of my care as Richmond, and I shall shew it on all occasions."[31]

Harrison wrote also to Clark condemning his failure to build the forts on the Ohio and repeating the order in positive terms. A new order for cannon for the defense of Kentucky was sent to Isaac Zane. The governor's surprise regarding the situation in Kentucky would seem to indicate that he had not read Clark's letter of March 7, 1782, very carefully. In it Clark had explained the change of plans from the building of additional forts to the strengthening of Fort Nelson and the building of gunboats, giving the expected attack upon that position as his reason.[32]

The difficulty of enforcing militia service, about which Logan

[31] Harrison to Logan, October 14, 1782, Draper MSS. 10 S 64-67. Harrison to Todd, October 14, 1782, Draper MSS. 10 S 55-57. Harrison to Boone and the Fayette Officers, October 14, 1782, Draper MSS. 10 S 57-60. Copies of these letters may be seen also in Executive Letter Book 6, pp. 7-25.

[32] Harrison to Clark, October 17, 1782, Draper MSS. 52 J 50-51(1). Clark to Harrison, March 7, 1782, *Calendar of Virginia State Papers*, III, 87-88. Executive Letter Book 6, pp. 13-19 has the former letter dated October 14, 1782.

had complained to the governor, was eased somewhat in the summer of 1782. The idea of placing delinquents in the Continental army had not worked because of the distance of Kentucky from any Continental establishment. This was replaced by an order to put them in an organization of Virginia regulars, a fairly simple procedure because Virginia troops were constantly on duty at Fort Nelson.[33]

The 1782 session of the assembly improved the militia situation still more. There had been no provision for the payment of militia except when used outside of the state or when acting in conjunction with regulars. The new act provided that "all militia called into service since the first day of January," 1780, or to be called into service in the future, should "receive the same pay and rations as the officers and soldiers of the continental army," but there was to be no pay for service of less than ten days duration. Scouts, because of the extra "fatigue and trouble," were to receive five shillings per day.[34]

Governor Harrison, in the message which he delivered to the assembly on October 21, 1782, expressed doubt as to the effectiveness of the defensive measures that were being taken for the protection of Kentucky. He suggested that the assembly consider the possibility of a campaign against the Indians.[35]

[33] Logan to Harrison, April 29, 1782, *Calendar of Virginia State Papers*, III, 142. Clark to Harrison, October 18, 1782, *Calendar of Virginia State Papers*, III, 345-47.
[34] Hening (ed.), *Statutes*, XI, 181.
[35] Draper MSS. 10 S 78-80.

CHAPTER XI

MIAMI RIVER EXPEDITION

THE CONTROVERSY WHICH followed the Battle of Blue Licks did not blind the military leaders in Kentucky to the importance of retaliation. Without waiting for permission from the Virginia government, General Clark and the three county lieutenants, Logan, Floyd, and Boone, began to plan a campaign against the Shawnee in the valley of the Miami River. Clark, whose claims for expenses incurred on past expeditions had not yet been approved, sold some of his own land to obtain money for provisions.

Leaving Major George Walls to get the Virginia regulars at Fort Nelson ready, the general went to Lincoln County. He again ordered guards placed on the Wilderness Trail and also on the trail to the Cumberland settlements to intercept men who might try to avoid the campaign by leaving Kentucky. John Floyd was made responsible for repairing and caulking twenty boats that would be needed for carrying men and supplies up the Ohio from Louisville. For this work he employed men who would not be expected to take part in the expedition. Some were not physically fit while others were past fifty, the age at which militia duty ceased to be compulsory. Major Walls was to see to the loading of the provisions, ammunition, and guns.

Some militiamen volunteered for the campaign, but others had to be drafted. Lincoln, the most populous of the three counties, furnished a regiment consisting of two battalions.

As his battalion commanders Logan selected his brother John and Hugh McGary. Although he was still a major, McGary ranked as a lieutenant colonel on the campaign. Gabriel Madison and William Hoy, who were captains, ranked as majors. These temporary promotions resulted from the fact that official replacements for those Lincoln County officers who died at Blue Licks had not yet been announced. The other captains in the Lincoln militia at the time were William Whitley, James Downing, Samuel Kirkham, Simon Kenton, Robert Barnett, George Adams, John Boyle, John Doherty, John Woods, James Ray, John Smith, John Snoddy, Lawrence Thompson, Nathaniel Houston, John Irvine, Andrew Kinkead, Thomas Moore, Samuel McAfee, and John Martin. It is not certain that all of these officers were out on this expedition. Whitley, Downing, Kirkham, Kenton, Barnett, Smith, Kinkead, and Martin definitely were. A small company of light horse was included. It was commanded by Captain William Mc-Cracken with Green Clay as his lieutenant. The Jefferson County militia furnished one battalion with both John Floyd and Colonel Isaac Cox along. The Fayette battalion was somewhat smaller than those from Jefferson and Lincoln. Daniel Boone and Robert Patterson were in command. Major George Walls led the regulars from Fort Nelson, and Major John Crittenden served as Clark's aide. William Johnston was quartermaster general for the campaign. The total strength of this little army was 1,050 men.[1]

The mouth of the Licking River was selected as the meeting place for all of the companies, and November 1 was named as the date. The men from Jefferson County and the Virginia regulars went up the Ohio by boat. Those from the other two counties traveled through the woods with orders to spread out and hunt on the way. On the second night out of Lexington

1 Draper MSS. 9 J 65, 193; 32 J 47; 52 J 53; 60 J 107-108, 111, 113, 116, 118, 131, 160-61, 171-72, 191-94, 369; 63 J 116-29; 10 S 80. "Lincoln County Militia, 1780-1783," in *Register of the Kentucky State Historical Society*, XXV (1927), 310-12. "Roll of Lincoln Militia," in *Register of the Kentucky State Historical Society*, XXIX (1931), 221.

they camped on Mill Creek where many of these same men had made a camp on the 1780 campaign. Several buffalo and deer were killed, and the meat was added to the store of provisions. Hunting cost the life of one of the Lincoln County militiamen. He was skinning a deer when his gun, which had been placed on a log, was accidently discharged, killing him instantly.

On November 2 the army crossed the Ohio. Work was started on a blockhouse opposite the mouth of the Licking. Here a captain, a lieutenant, and thirty privates were to remain to guard the boats and such provisions as would be needed for the last phase of the homeward journey. Among these men were several who were ill and believed not able to stand the long march into the Indian country. Clark ordered each battalion to make a report of the number of horses and the amount of supplies it had available. The quartermasters of the four battalions were to furnish to Major Walls a total of twenty-two horses. These, working in relays, were to pull the cannon, a six-pounder, which had been so effective against the Shawnee two years earlier. This left a pack animal for every six men. The lack of grain for the horses would of course limit their endurance, and with no forage except the amount of grass that could be obtained within the nightly encampments the time that each team could spend in pulling the cannon was very short. Each battalion was authorized to draw provisions sufficient for fifteen days. This was loaded on the packhorses with one man responsible for three animals.

Guides would be needed in the Indian country. They would be indispensable after Chillicothe and Piqua, which some of the Kentuckians had attacked in previous years, had been passed. For this duty the general chose John Soverigns and Daniel Sullivan. Both men had been prisoners of the Shawnee and knew their country and their language. Clark prepared a marching plan and gave a copy to each of the battalion commanders, whom he ordered to make every man acquainted with it. In his instructions to the entire army he stressed the importance of discipline and subordination, explaining that upon these factors the success of the campaign and the safety of all might depend. Two o'clock in the afternoon of November 3 was set as the time for the march to be resumed.

Before the Battle of Blue Licks, Clark had considered a campaign such as this and had been in correspondence with General William Irvine at Fort Pitt about the matter. The plan now was for the two officers to lead their men into the Indian country at about the same time. On October 3 Irvine wrote to Clark that his advance would be delayed and suggested that Clark postpone his march also. When this letter was delivered to Clark he was on his way to the Shawnee villages.[2]

At the appointed time the men formed in columns and the marching plan was put into operation. The guides led the way, followed by an advance guard of fifty men. Next came four groups of twenty-five men each, two a little to the right of the line of march of the advance guard and two a little to the left. These were called the advance parties. Two hundred yards behind came the main body of the army. The Jefferson and Fayette battalions were combined into a regiment under the command of Colonel Floyd. It marched in two parallel columns with a one hundred yard interval between. Two hundred yards to the left was the Lincoln regiment, advancing in the same type of formation. It was led by Benjamin Logan, who was second-in-command to Clark. Between the two regiments were the cannon and packhorses. Behind the main body marched four rear parties of twenty-five men each. Last of all came a fifty-man rear guard. The wings were protected by thin columns of flankers, who served principally as lookouts. In case of an attack en route, the advance guard and advance parties were to hold fast while the right of Floyd's two columns and the left of Logan's flanked the enemy. The other

[2] Draper MSS. 8 J 125, 149, 164(1); 9 J 65, 193-193(1); 11 J 22; 52 J 44-46; 63 J 116-18; 9 CC 42; 12 CC 71, 136-37. Deposition of John Napper, Breckinridge MSS., Vol. XIX, 3320-22, Library of Congress.

two columns were to await orders. In the event of an attack from the rear the same general plan would be followed with the rear guard and rear parties holding. If the enemy should attack the army's right, Floyd's outside column was to stand fast. The rear parties and rear guard were to execute a flanking movement to the right and the advance parties and advance guard to the left. Floyd's other column was to break into two parts which would fill the gaps between the first column and the flankers. Logan's regiment would constitute the reserve and would await orders. If an attack should come from the left this plan was to operate in reverse.[3]

The first afternoon's march took the Kentuckians up the valley of the Little Miami River. Some of the men had followed Clark along this same trail in 1780. At that time the first objective had been the Shawnee village of Chillicothe, which had been rebuilt after John Bowman's 1779 attack. In 1780 the destruction of this town had been complete. The Indians had abandoned the site and had moved westward to the waters of the Great Miami. The guides were kept busy at finding a smooth trail for the cannon. In places a road had to be cut, and by evening the army had covered only seven miles. Camp was made on the banks of the Little Miami.

The next morning Clark named Logan as president of a general court martial which was called for nine o'clock. The general's order book does not name the defendants nor does it indicate what decisions were reached. Clark may have believed that the chances for a successful campaign would be increased if some examples were made very early. The march continued to the site of Chillicothe, where the army left the Little Miami and traveled westward to Mad River, a tributary of the Great Miami. The Shawnee village of Piqua on the north bank of this stream had been the scene of a battle between the Kentuckians and the Indians two years earlier, but it too had been abandoned. Crossing Mad River, Clark led his men

[3] Draper MSS. 32 J 47; 63 J 121-26.

toward the Great Miami, which he expected to strike at the mouth of Loramie's Creek. Here the Shawnee had a village known variously as New Chillicothe, New Piqua, Upper Piqua, or the Standing Stone.[4]

When he was within a few miles of his destination, the general issued orders covering the expected battle. The officers were to see that no man left the ranks without permission, because "nothing is more dangerous than disorder." Prisoners were not to be killed but should be held for possible exchange for white people known to be in the hands of the Indians. Execution of prisoners, he pointed out, might bring some form of retaliation such as the massacre of all white people held by the Shawnee. No soldier was to take any plunder until permission was given. After that, any goods obtained must be delivered to the quartermasters for division among the battalions in proportion to their numbers.

It was now November 10. John McCasland and three other men were sent ahead as spies. They saw at a distance two Indians seated on a log, and the Indians saw them at about the same time. They ran toward their town not knowing whether a few white men had come to recover stolen horses or an army had come to destroy them. The Indian leaders sent out a few mounted warriors to investigate. It was now afternoon. The spies had reported to Clark, and Major George Walls had been sent ahead with a mounted party. The Indians who were out on horseback saw this party approaching. Being too few to give battle, they hastened back to the village to inform their people that the Long Knives were almost upon them. Evacuation of New Piqua was started immediately. Because virtually all of their property was being left behind, it proceeded rapidly.

Clark hurried his army forward, arriving in time to see the warriors disappearing. Several prisoners, chiefly women and

[4] Draper MSS. 8 J 163(1); 9 J 192(1)-193(1); 63 J 119; 9 CC 42; 11 CC 65; 1 OO 110. J. Winston Coleman, Jr., *The British Invasion of Kentucky* (Lexington, 1951), 29.

children, were taken. The gathering of plunder and the destruction of the town could wait. There were other villages that could be reached quickly. The army was divided into four groups, one of which was to remain at New Piqua in the hope that the warriors from that village would return. A second group, consisting of 500 men, was given to Hugh McGary. This officer's objective was McKee's Town, only a few miles away. This village had been named for Alexander McKee, one of the most capable Indian agents in the British service. He had commanded Indians under Henry Bird in the 1780 invasion of Kentucky that resulted in the capture of Ruddle's and Martin's stations. At Bryan's Station and also at Blue Licks, which McGary had reason to remember, he had been second-in-command to William Caldwell. The Indians of McKee's Town had been warned in time to flee. Two of their prisoners took advantage of the confusion to make their escape, and both were rescued by McGary's men. One was a Negro boy. The other, a white man named John Holly, had been captured at Boonesborough nearly five years before. The vacant village was plundered and destroyed. Daniel Boone led another detachment of 100 men to Willstown, a little more than ten miles away at the junction of the Miami and Stillwater Creek. Here the story was repeated. The Indians were gone, but their property was there. All of their goods which could be carried, including many furs and skins, were saved. The remainder was burned with the cabins.[5]

The deepest penetration of the Indian country was accomplished by a party of 150 men led by Benjamin Logan. Taking Captain McCracken and his company of light horse and stripping enough packhorses for the rest of his men, Logan set out up Loramie's Creek. Fourteen miles up this stream lay the trading post of a French Canadian, Pierre Loramie. Its position had been carefully selected, and much of the travel

[5] Draper MSS. 8 J 116, 125, 148(1)-149, 163(1)-164, 320(2)-321; 9 J 69; 63 J 26-28; 6 S 158-59; 9 CC 42; 11 CC 65; 12 CC 71; 27 CC 30, 34; 3 JJ 103.

between Lake Erie and the Ohio River passed that way. The route led from the lake up the Maumee River and then up one of its tributaries to the head of navigation. From there a portage had to be made to Loramie's Creek. Loramie's store was at the southern end of the portage. Here he traded firearms, ammunition, cloth, ornaments, and cheap trinkets for the Indians' furs and skins. He was loyal to the British cause and helped to outfit some of the expeditions against the Kentucky settlements. The Kentuckians had every reason for wanting to destroy this source of some of their trouble.

It was nearly dark when Logan and his men reached Loramie's. The trader had lighted a candle, which he extinguished upon hearing the approach of horsemen. Participants differed as to when and under what circumstances he made his escape. One thought he left by the back door before the Kentuckians entered. Another believed that he hid behind his front door, mingled with the crowd, and took his leave in the confusion. Loramie's helpers left too, although one was killed in the process and a Negro girl was captured. The trading post and the cabins surrounding it were stripped of as much plunder as could be transported—bolts of cloth, furs, skins, silver broaches, and trinkets of various kinds. All of the buildings then were burned. Logan and his men traveled a few miles downstream and camped for the night, returning to the main army next morning.[6]

The sleep of Clark and the men who remained at New Piqua had not been unbroken. The camp formed a hollow square around the town, which lay on the west bank of the Miami. During the night Indians fired several times from across the river. One man was mortally wounded. A cold rain added to the discomfort and made it difficult to keep campfires going. The sentries had the risky job of keeping the Indian snipers at a distance without getting shot themselves. One of

[6] Coleman, The British Invasion of Kentucky, 6, 29. Draper MSS. 8 J 126, 273; 9 J 69, 74, 194-94(1); 32 J 47; 6 S 159; 18 S 157; 12 CC 137; 27 CC 30; 3 JJ 103.

them, Joseph Turner, saw a figure approaching, fired, and missed. Before he could fire again he saw that it was a squaw, unarmed and old. She was taken into camp where the guide, Daniel Sullivan, recognized her. When he was a prisoner of the Indians she had befriended him and saved his life. When the army was ready to leave for home Clark offered to leave a cabin standing for her use and to have it well supplied with provisions, but she preferred to go with the other prisoners, and Sullivan gave her his horse to ride.

Before the night had ended, Clark's order to spare the lives of prisoners was disregarded by one of his men. Hugh Leeper of Lincoln County had been seriously wounded by an Indian four years earlier. Ignoring the men who were guarding the prisoners, he rushed forward and sank a tomahawk in the head of a young warrior. Although Leeper was censured by some of his comrades, no record of official action has been found.[7]

The next day collection of the goods that the Indians had abandoned at New Piqua was completed, and the destruction of the town was begun. Parties ranged over the area looking for Indian warriors who might be in hiding. Several were found, and nine were killed before the day ended. On a campaign such as this, destruction of the enemy's towns and of his stores of provisions were prime objectives. This kept the braves hunting to feed their families and left less time for annoying the white settlers. Each Indian family had its supply of corn, either in its living quarters or in a nearby cabin built for that purpose. Some had quantities of dried beans as well. Major John Crittenden estimated the amount of corn destroyed on this expedition at ten thousand bushels. General Clark stated later that "the quantity of provisions burned surpassed all idea we had of the Indian stores." One more prisoner was taken that day, a young woman who was described by one of the Kentuckians as the "most splendid looking squaw I ever saw." At the same time another white prisoner was

[7] Draper MSS. 8 J 149; 9 J 195-96; 6 S 158; 9 CC 42-44; 11 CC 54-66; 12 CC 137.

rescued. She was Mrs. John McFall, who had been captured at Ruddle's Station in 1780.[8]

On the following day Captain William McCracken went out to look for his horse, which had strayed beyond the lines. He saw a man standing at a distance and partially hidden by some bushes. Assuming that this person was white, McCracken called to him and asked if he had seen a stray horse. The man replied in acceptable English that there was a black horse near where he was standing. As McCracken approached, this stranger fired a rifle, the ball striking him near his elbow. His assailant then fled, eluding some men who went in pursuit. McCracken had only a flesh wound, and he was washing it in a stream when Logan came to investigate. Logan advised him to look after the wound carefully, because Indian rifle balls sometimes were poisoned. The captain seemed proud of his wound and was quoted by one of the men as having said that "he would not take $500 for it." There was a physician with the army, but Logan learned afterward that the doctor had given McCracken's brother only some salve and a rag to use as a bandage. The wound became infected, and McCracken's condition grew steadily worse.[9]

The plunder was divided among the four battalions and auctions were held at New Piqua. The understanding was that the proceeds would be equally divided among the men. As usual a man who bought more than his proportionate share was expected to make up the difference in cash as soon as possible. One who bought less than the average would be due a cash settlement. An Irishman named Burk contributed an almost worthless saddle to the stock of plunder. To the surprise of the other men he bought it at the auction for

[8] James R. Albach (comp.), Annals of the West (Pittsburgh, 1858), 397, 397n. Bakeless, George Rogers Clark, 296. Annie P. Coffman, "Reminiscences from the Life of Col. Cave Johnson," in Register of the Kentucky State Historical Society, XX (1922), 211. "Autobiography of Cave Johnson," 12 pp. MSS., Durrett Collection, pp. 9-10. Draper MSS. 8 J 126-27, 149, 163(1)-164; 9 JJ 196; 60 J 69; 9 CC 42-43; 11 CC 54-66; 12 CC 71, 137.

[9] Draper MSS. 8 J 127; 60 J 243-45; 18 S 251; 9 CC 43; 11 CC 65; 12 CC 71.

twenty-five shillings. Their expressions changed when he cut into the padding of the saddle and produced a far larger amount of money than he had paid. It was supposed that he had found this at Loramie's and had hidden it.

The Kentuckians now had been in the Shawnee country for four days. Fearing that the weather might change for the worse, Clark decided to withdraw. The return route was down the Miami to the mouth of Mad River and then direct to the blockhouse across the Ohio from the mouth of the Licking. This point was reached on November 17. Captain McCracken, who by now was in a serious condition, had to be carried on a litter. He died in sight of the Ohio and was buried beside the blockhouse.[10] The army was disbanded at the blockhouse, and the men were free to travel homeward by whatever routes they preferred. The prisoners were taken to Louisville by the regulars.[11]

When Governor Harrison heard that the Kentuckians were invading the Indian country, he wrote to Clark in a rather critical vein. "The desire the people have of revenging themselves on the savages for the loss of so many valuable friends, I suppose was the cause of your undertaking an expedition," he said. "Otherwise, it was certainly wrong to do it without consulting me." The governor seemed fearful of the consequences of this invasion of the Indian country. "I have some reason to apprehend," he continued, "that it will rather prolong than shorten the Indian War as my advices from the Northward tell me that the English have called in all their parties, and mean no more to act on the offensive." In the same letter the governor mentioned the Ohio River forts again and insisted that they be built.[12]

Harrison soon learned of the success of the campaign and

[10] Draper MSS. 8 J 125-27, 164, 288; 9 J 74, 196; 18 S 246; 9 CC 43; 11 CC 65-66; 12 CC 71, 137.

[11] John Floyd suggested that the survivors hold a reunion across the Ohio from the mouth of the Licking when fifty years had elapsed. When the time came cholera was raging in Cincinnati, and no meeting was held. Draper MSS. 8 J 164-64(1), 288; 9 J 196-96(1); 32 J 47; 5 S 160; 12 CC 71.

[12] Harrison to Clark, December 19, 1782, Draper MSS. 10 S 95-97.

his tone changed. He wrote both to Clark and to Logan congratulating them and praising the officers and men who had served under them. "Your expedition will be attended with good consequences," said the governor to Clark. "It will teach the Indians to dread us, and convince them that we will not tamely submit to their depredations." To Logan, the governor wrote, "Be assured Sir that the Executive entertain the highest sense of your conduct and services and I beg you to accept of our warmest acknowledgements for them, and that you will communicate both to the Officers and men under your command our thanks, and assure them we shall ever entertain a proper sense of the important services they have rendered their country in thus manfully stepping forth to revenge the Blood of their countrymen, and correcting the Insolence of a bloodthirsty and vindictive Enemy, who have so long triumphed over us, and desolated our frontiers."

Harrison explained that he always had favored offensive operations but had differed with those to whom he had to answer. This statement was consistent with his message to the assembly in the preceding October.[13]

Most of the military operations west of the mountains had been conducted on credit. The settlers who had contributed provisions or who had gone out on the various campaigns had received only promises of future payment. By 1782, with the end of the war in sight, a commission had been named to visit Kentucky, to listen to and examine evidence, and to approve or disapprove claims. In his letter of April 29, 1782, to Harrison, Logan had asked the governor to "please forward the commissioners appointed to adjust our claims and superintend our conduct in this Western Country or let us know where we are to apply with our accounts." After several prominent Virginians, including William Preston and William Christian, had asked to be excused, a board composed of William Fleming,

---

[13] Clark to Harrison, November 27, 1782, Draper MSS. 60 J 162. Harrison to Clark, January 13, 1783, Draper MSS. 52 J 73. Harrison to Logan, January 13, 1783, Executive Letter Book, January 1, 1783 to November 20, 1786, p. 18.

Samuel McDowell, Caleb Wallace, and Thomas Marshall was named. All but Marshall arrived in Kentucky on October 24, 1782.[14]

Although little could be done until Clark, Logan, and the other officers had returned from their campaign, short sessions were held at Harrodsburg and at Lexington. When the army finished its work, Clark not only submitted his accounts but asked the opinion of the board on the question of the forts along the Ohio. The commissioners replied that a fort at the mouth of the Kentucky would be highly desirable. It would lie in the path of those tribes which were most likely to attack Kentucky. It also would provide protection for Drennon's Lick, a potential source of large quantities of salt and a favorite place for Indians to kill and cure game while harassing the Kentucky settlements. Thomas Marshall, who by this time had joined the other members, differed on this point. He favored a fort at the mouth of Limestone Creek. This, he believed, was a logical landing place for people who wished to settle in Fayette, which was still the most thinly populated of the three counties.[15]

In addition to submitting his payrolls and accounts to the

[14] Logan to Harrison, April 29, 1782, *Calendar of Virginia State Papers,* III, 142. William Christian to Governor Thomas Nelson, October 10, 1781, Draper MSS. 10 S 205-206. William Fleming to Governor Benjamin Harrison, December 26, 1781, *Calendar of Virginia State Papers,* III, 672-73. Draper MSS. 60 J 371. Bodley, *History of Kentucky,* 319-20.

[15] Clark to the Western Commissioners, December 15, 1782, Draper MSS. 60 J 167-70. Thomas Marshall to Clark, January 27, 1783, Draper MSS. 52 J 74. Draper MSS. 60 J 371-72. Bodley, *History of Kentucky,* 323, 323n.

Harrison to Clark, February 27, 1783, in Executive Letter Book, January 1, 1783 to November 20, 1786, pp. 56-57, ordered Clark to proceed with the fort at the mouth of the Kentucky and to garrison it with one-half of the regulars at Louisville. Orders for forts at the Licking and at Limestone Creek were declared superseded, "unless you discover that the Indians are still determined on war, in which case you will as soon as possible take post at Limestone to cover the county of Fayette and promote its settlement, which post you must garrison altogether with militia."

Harrison to Major George Walls at Fort Nelson, August 28, 1783, *ibid.,* 195, expresses disappointment that the fort at the Kentucky had not been built but said, "You'l please to suspend the execution of the orders till you hear again from me."

commissioners, Logan exerted himself to provide military escorts for them when they traveled from place to place. Meetings were held at all of the principal settlements, and each case was decided on its merits. Sometimes reductions in the usual scale of pay were recommended for officers who had led smaller numbers of men than their ranks would entitle them to command. On April 14, 1783, the board adjourned at St. Asaph's to complete its work at the home of William Fleming in Botetourt County. Logan was paid for boarding their horses, but he seems to have looked upon the commissioners themselves as guests.[16]

In the spring of 1783 there were indications that the Indians were not yet ready to make peace. Joseph Martin, one of Virginia's Indian agents, reported to the governor and to Logan that in the preceding November twenty chiefs from four of the tribes around Detroit had come to Chickamauga. They had talked with some of the Cherokee in regard to a great campaign against Fort Pitt, Fort Nelson, and the posts in Kentucky and Illinois. They then visited the Choctaw and the Creeks, some of whom accompanied them to St. Augustine where dispatches were delivered to the British commandant from his counterpart at Detroit. Martin predicted that these emissaries would return in March and warned Logan to be on his guard from that time on.[17]

Fortunately no such dangerous union of the tribes as that which Martin had predicted was effected, but small parties of Indians continued to do damage in Kentucky. In his letter of April 9, 1783, Governor Harrison was able to report to Clark, whose request for an early retirement from the Virginia line had just been approved, that peace terms with England had been signed. The few Indians who had learned of this appar-

[16] "Journal of William Fleming, 1782-83," Draper MSS. 2 ZZ 69(10, 12, 20). Draper MSS. 60 J 373-75. James (ed.), *Clark Papers, 1781-1784,* pp. 345-87. "Lincoln County Militia, 1780-1783," in *Register of the Kentucky State Historical Society,* XXV (1927), 310-12. Accounts of Military Claims Commission in Fleming MSS. at Washington and Lee University.

[17] Martin to Logan, February 20, 1783, Draper MSS. 46 J 74-74(1). Martin to Harrison, February 2, 1783, Draper MSS. 60 J 172-75.

ently were not impressed. On April 8, John Floyd, his brother Charles, and Alexander Breckinridge were traveling from Floyd's Station on Beargrass Creek to a point on Salt River. They were attacked by Indians, and John Floyd was seriously wounded. With his death two days later, Kentucky had lost two of her three county lieutenants in less than eight months.[18]

Three days after Floyd's death Indians appeared in Logan's vicinity and attacked the home of Michael Woods at the Crab Orchard. Woods was away from home at the time. In his cabin were his wife, his grown daughter Hannah, and a Negro man who was slightly crippled. One of the Indians forced his way in, but Mrs. Woods managed to bar the door before others could enter. The Negro grappled with the intruder but was getting the worst of it when one of the women suddenly seized an ax and sank it in the Indian's head. The Negro is said to have suggested letting another in and repeating the process until the entire party had been dispatched. Fortunately help arrived before this was tried. The warning that there were Indians in the neighborhood had reached St. Asaph's, and Logan had hastened to Whitley's Station, where men were assembling. As they approached the Woods' home the five remaining Indians made a hasty departure. The one who was killed was wearing the shirt of a white man, Absalom Mounts, who had been killed a few days before.[19]

[18] Clark to Harrison, March 8, 1783, Draper MSS. 60 J 258-62. Harrison to Clark, April 9, 1783, Draper MSS. 52 J 84 or Executive Letter Book, January 1, 1783 to November 20, 1786, pp. 95-99. The governor was referring to the preliminary peace agreement of November 30, 1782. See also Draper MSS. 12 C 47(3); 6 J 104; and "Fleming's Journal, 1782-1783," in Newton D. Mereness (ed.), Travels in the American Colonies (New York, 1916), 672-73.

[19] "Fleming's Journal," Draper MSS. 2 ZZ 69(22). Draper MSS. 12 C 67(2-3); 9 J 204(1); 9 CC 36-37.

CHAPTER XII

SEPARATION MOVEMENTS

BENJAMIN LOGAN WAS PROMINENT in the civil as well as the military affairs of Lincoln County. Always a magistrate, he was in regular attendance at the meetings of the county court. Before a courthouse was erected the court met in his own home. For several months after the disaster at Blue Licks there were not enough magistrates available to hold court, as five judges were required. This defect was remedied on January 21, 1783, when George Adams, John Edwards, Hugh Logan, Gabriel Madison, and Alexander Robertson presented their commissions and were installed as justices. The January court concerned itself primarily with the settlement of the estates of those who had fallen at Blue Licks.

It was not until May that the court found time to consider the question of replacements among the officers of the militia. As the growing population made an increase in the total number of commissions desirable, the county court now made enough recommendations to fill the vacancies and to double the number of field officers. John Logan and Gabriel Madison were suggested for colonels, John Edwards and John Smith for lieutenant colonels, and George Adams and Anthony Crockett for majors. On July 22 the Virginia Council acted favorably on all of these recommendations and issued commissions accordingly. James Harrod, whom Ben Logan had named in his letter of August 31, 1782, to Governor Harrison as deserving a colonel's commission, and Hugh McGary, who already was a major and who had acted as a lieutenant colonel in the campaign of the preceding November, were not mentioned.

At the same session of the court Benjamin Logan, John Cowan, and John Logan were recommended to the governor as suitable persons for the position of sheriff. Ben Logan, who had served in this capacity under Kentucky County, was selected by the governor and his council, and his commission was started on its way to St. Asaph's. It was presented by Logan at the November court and the oath of office was administered.[1]

The court for Lincoln County, although first convened at Harrodsburg, had been meeting at St. Asaph's for two years. The records do not indicate that any public buildings had been erected. Logan still was providing space in his own home or perhaps in vacant cabins in the fort. At the May session, 1783, Logan and George Davidson were named as a committee "to employ persons to remove the Courthouse and prison . . . to such place on the Land laid off for that purpose as they shall think most convenient." Apparently this was accomplished during the ensuing summer. On August 21 the court appointed Ben and Hugh Logan "to view and receive the prison and courthouse if compleated agreeable to contract." These buildings had been erected on the ten acres around the Buffalo Spring which had been a part of Logan's original settlement, and which he had offered to the county for that purpose. If Logan was satisfied with the buildings at the time, he must later have had more prisoners to house than he had expected. On April 20 of the next year, in his capacity as sheriff, he "came into Court and objected against the Prison as insufficient."[2]

The county taxes at this time were payable in tobacco. The total budget for 1784 was 25,260 pounds of this product. The levy was made not upon property, but as a poll tax, twelve

[1] Draper MSS. 60 J 370. Lincoln County Court Order Book 1, pp. 22, 53, 56, 123.
[2] Lincoln County Court Order Book 1, pp. 56, 98-99, 163.

pounds of tobacco being contributed by each of 2,105 persons. Logan's annual salary as sheriff was 1,248 pounds of tobacco. The same amount was paid to the county clerk, Willis Green. As sheriff it was Logan's duty to collect the taxes, and at the June court of 1783 he was ordered to use a portion of the receipts for the clearing of roads from the Lincoln Courthouse to the mouth of Hickman's Creek and to John Crow's Station near the present site of Danville.

When Logan and some of the other magistrates met to hold court in August they received a recommendation from James Thompson, the county surveyor, that Daniel Boone be appointed as his deputy. Boone's position as county lieutenant of Fayette evidently left him with time on his hands and a need to supplement his income. Thomas Allen and Samuel Grant were appointed to examine Boone. They found him qualified to fill the position, and the oath of office was administered to him.

At the same meeting of the court a jury found Hugh McGary "guilty of betting and winning a mare worth four pounds." On the basis of an act of the Virginia Assembly entitled "An Act to Suppress excessive gaming," it was decided that he should "be deemed an infamous gambler" and that he should not "be elligible [sic] to any office of trust or Honour within this state." McGary was ordered to pay the cost of the trial. In the following February the court found it necessary to regulate the price of liquor. It was decided that whisky should be sold for 15s. per gallon and rum for £1 4s. The price of whisky toddy was set at 1s. 3d. per quart and that of rum toddy at 2s. 6d. At the same time Logan's youngest brother, Nathaniel, was granted a license to operate an ordinary for a period of one year.[3]

Although the county courts handled a considerable volume of business, many types of cases had to be taken to the supreme court at Richmond. This was a great inconvenience

---

[3] *Ibid.*, 72, 78-79, 98, 139, 141, 244.

for people who lived west of the mountains. On December 14, 1781, a petition explaining the difficulty was read in the Virginia Assembly. That body responded at its May session in 1782 by passing a bill creating the District of Kentucky, which was to include the three western counties—Lincoln, Jefferson, and Fayette—and would have its own supreme court consisting of one judge and two assistant judges. This court would have original jurisdiction over "all treasons, murders, felonies, crimes and misdemeanors" committed in the District of Kentucky. The act became effective on August 1, 1782. To Benjamin Logan, who had played so important a role in the affairs of Kentucky and who knew the difficulties of conducting civil affairs at so great a distance from the capital, the establishment of the district must have appeared as an important step in the direction of political maturity.[4]

In addition to county and militia business Logan had a growing family and a large amount of land to supervise. His children—David, William, Jane, Mary, and soon Elizabeth, who arrived on May 22, 1784—had been born at intervals of from two to three years. By the spring of 1782 the Logans had moved outside of the stockaded fort. Not more than three hundred yards from the walls Logan had built what one of his daughters described years afterward as the first frame house in Kentucky. On St. Asaph's Branch just below the fort he erected a mill.[5]

Within a short time after the Revolution had ended, Logan's mother and his unmarried sister, Margaret, came to Kentucky, where his sister Mary Briggs and his brothers Hugh, John, William, and Nathaniel already lived. Late in 1782 Ann Logan's sister Jane Montgomery, one of the few persons who had escaped capture at the time of the Indian attack on Montgomery's Station, was married to William Casey. Casey

[4] Draper MSS. 11 J 33; 10 S 84; 13 S 149-50; 14 S 46-48, 79. Hening (ed.), *Statutes*, XI, 85-92, 397-98, 499. Robertson, *Petitions*, 66-68.
[5] Mary Logan Smith to Draper, April 25, 1845, Draper MSS. 12 C 45(3-4). Draper MSS. 18 S 144; 29 S 109-10.

had been a member of Logan's party which rescued the prisoners taken at Montgomery's.[6]

Logan generally was careful to comply with all of the legal requirements relative to the surveying and entering of land claims, but on a few occasions circumstances interfered. This was true in the case of a 200-acre military warrant which he had purchased from another man. When he failed to enter it in time it was appropriated by the surveyor John May. Although Logan had offered to the justices of Lincoln County two tracts of land for public use, no deed to these had yet been recorded. Thus it may be said that he did not part with any of his Lincoln County land until July 20, 1784, when he sold 200 acres to John Glover. This was followed by sales of 150 acres to Jeremiah Pearce on August 2, 1784; 437 acres to Lewis Bouderie on December 22, 1784; 100 acres to Richard Jackman on February 18, 1785; and 150 acres to John Embry on September 29, 1785.[7]

Although he lacked education, Logan helped to provide for the training of the youth of Kentucky. At its May session in 1780 the Virginia Assembly passed a bill providing for an institution of higher learning in Kentucky. It would be known as the Transylvania Seminary. Among the trustees named in the act were "William Fleming, William Christian, John Todd, Stephen Trigg, Benjamin Logan, John May, Levi Todd [and] John Cowan." Because of the unsettled conditions which existed during the Revolution, the Transylvania board did not meet until March 6, 1783. At this meeting Logan was one of the signers of a petition to the Virginia Assembly asking that the board be incorporated and empowered to fill vacancies in

[6] Draper MSS. 9 J 189(1)-190; 17 J 56-64(1), 81-82(3). Lincoln County Court Order Book 1, p. 7. Augusta B. Fothergill and John M. Naugle, "Virginia Tax Payers, 1782-87, Other Than Those Published by the United States Census Bureau," 142 pp., bound typescript, Lexington (Kentucky) Public Library, p. 77. Hattie M. Scott, "The Logan Family of Lincoln County, Kentucky," in *Register of the Kentucky State Historical Society*, XXX (1932), 173.

[7] John May to Robert Patterson, December 12, 1782, Draper MSS. 1 MM 109. Lincoln County Deed Book A, pp. 34-36, 63-65, 71-72, 75-76, 142-43.

its membership. In May the assembly acted favorably upon this request, and the school soon was in operation at the home of the Reverend David Rice near Danville. Because of a lack of young men qualified for college, it was for several years little more than a grammer school.[8]

Relations with the Indians seemed to improve with the ending of the Revolution, although there were several incidents. In the summer of 1783 the Shawnee exchanged a few prisoners at Louisville, but an attempt in the following summer to complete the process ended in failure. Small parties of Indians still entered Kentucky and sometimes did considerable damage. In May, 1783, word came that some northern Indians had crossed the Ohio and were camped on the Big Sandy. There was no immediate danger, and it was not a case for calling out the militia, but a potential threat did exist. When Ben and John Logan raised a party of volunteers and went to investigate, the Indians had abandoned their camp and appeared to have left the country. A similar situation existed in the fall of 1784 when some hunters reported sighting an Indian camp on the North Fork of the Kentucky River. Ben Logan and Thomas Kennedy took about forty volunteers to the area and engaged twelve Indians, two of whom they killed.[9]

On the day after the Battle of Blue Licks representatives from the Chickasaw nation reached Kentucky with the stated intention of making peace with Virginia. This delegation consisted of a white man, Simon Burney, and two warriors. They called upon John Bowman, who transmitted their statements to the governor. Bowman mentioned John Donelson and

[8] Hening (ed.), *Statutes*, X, 287-88; XI, 282-87. Robertson, *Petitions*, 69-72. "Fleming's Journal, 1782-1783," in Mereness (ed.), *Travels in the American Colonies*, 670. Fleming Papers, McCormick Library, Washington and Lee University, pp. 266-67. "Record of the Proceedings of the Board of Trustees for the Transylvania Seminary," 179 pp. bound MSS., Library of Transylvania College.

[9] Extract from *Maryland Journal*, September 9, 1783, Draper MSS. 3 JJ 110-11. Extract from *Maryland Gazette*, October 15, 1784, Draper MSS. 3 JJ 135-36. Pension statement of James P. Barnett, Draper MSS. 32 J 48. Draper MSS. 12 C 62(17-18).

Benjamin Logan as suitable persons to conduct such negotiations. Logan, in his letter of August 31, gave the same information to the governor. He expressed the opinion that a treaty, if desired by the government, could be arranged by Donelson, "who has before served as an Agent for the State, [and who] is willing to transact any business of that kind."[10]

Both Bowman and Logan told the governor that the Chickasaw admitted doing some damage in Kentucky, but they blamed their action upon Clark's having built Fort Jefferson upon their lands without consulting them. Clark considered this a poor attempt at self-justification. He was convinced that the Chickasaw "had done a great deal of mischief for two years before, and the building [of] that post" had prevented an attack upon Kentucky "by them and their allies." When their peace talk reached him, Clark wrote a reply. Upon his own authority he sent Captain Robert George to treat with them. This action he hoped the governor would approve. It was his belief that the Chickasaw could be persuaded to exert pressure upon the other southern tribes and perhaps to force them to make peace also. The governor, hearing from Bowman and Logan before Clark's letter was written, named Donelson and Joseph Martin to negotiate with the Chickasaw.[11]

A year later it was evident that Logan was not pleased with the results of Virginia's peace talks with the southern tribes. Writing to the governor on August 11, 1783, he stated that the Indians continued to commit murders in Lincoln County and that horses were being stolen almost constantly. Although Virginia's agents were holding talks with the Chickasaw and the Chickamauga, no peace agreement had been announced. Logan felt that John Donelson had spent more of his time in representing a land company which wanted to make a purchase

[10] Bowman to Harrison, August 30, 1782, *Calendar of Virginia State Papers*, III, 277-78. Logan to Harrison, August 31, 1782, *Calendar of Virginia State Papers*, III, 280-83.

[11] Clark to Harrison, October 18, 1782, *Calendar of Virginia State Papers*, III, 345-47. Robert S. Cotterill, "The Virginia-Chickasaw Treaty of 1783," in *Journal of Southern History*, VIII (1942), 487.

in the great bend of the Tennessee River than he had devoted
to representing Virginia. He believed also that much of the
mischief in his county was the work of the Chickamauga. A
party of volunteers had been formed to march against their
towns, but Donelson, hearing of this, had asked Logan to
forbid it. Logan complied but asked the governor if it would
not be better to defeat them and bring them to terms than to
trust an agent who might forgive all of the Indians' crimes in
order to purchase some of their land at a low price. Obviously
Logan's opinion of Donelson had changed since he recommended him to the governor for this particular service.[12]

On November 12 Harrison wrote to Logan and also to
Donelson and Martin. He told Logan that the assembly had
stopped offensive operations against the Indians due to lack of
money. He had since urged that funds for this purpose be made
available and that he be given authority to send the militia out
of the state whenever he believed that the Indians were in
need of correction. The governor pointed out that Donelson
was unknown to him and had been appointed on Logan's
recommendation. In his letter to the two negotiators Harrison
reminded them that land buying and treaty making should not
be mixed.[13]

In his message to the fall session of the assembly in 1782
Governor Harrison had expressed the hope that the establishment of the district court would silence a group in Kentucky
who had petitioned the Congress to form the region into a
separate state. The principal aim of this group was to have
Virginia land titles declared invalid. It would then be possible
for these and other speculators to buy Kentucky lands cheaply
and to sell them at a profit to the occupants or to others.
Congress at the time had taken no action on the petition, but

[12] Logan to Harrison, August 11, 1783, *Calendar of Virginia State Papers,*
III, 522-23. Walker Daniel to Harrison, May 21, 1784, Draper MSS. 11 S 185.
[13] Harrison to Logan, November 12, 1783, and Harrison to Martin and
Donelson, November 12, 1783, Executive Letter Book, January 1, 1783 to
November 20, 1786, pp. 229-32, Virginia Archives.

individual members had implied that the matter would be handled as soon as the war had ended.[14]

Although the separation movement in its early stages involved mainly land speculators and people who had come to Kentucky from states other than Virginia, by 1784 it was entering a new phase. Many of those who were leaders in the district and who formerly had been stanch defenders of Virginia's title to Kentucky began to see possible advantages in creating a new state. These men believed that the distance of Kentucky from the Virginia capital constituted a barrier to effective government. They felt also that the district court was not adequately supported. It was thought that the present judges would soon resign, and many people feared that with the recompense so small no qualified men could be found to replace them. A third grievance stemmed from the fact that the inhabitants still felt themselves at the mercy of the Indians. Militia officers could lead the pursuit of war parties that actually invaded the district, but no one had the authority to order the militia to march to the Indians' villages and punish them for their misconduct, and there were many who doubted that a satisfactory peace could be obtained in any other way. The need for settling matters with the Indians probably was uppermost in the minds of many Kentuckians when they learned of the death of Walker Daniel, attorney general for the district, at the hands of savages on July 12, 1784. Daniel, who had been at the forefront of those who defended Virginia's title to Kentucky against land companies and disaffected residents, was shot from ambush while traveling between Sullivan's Station and Bullitt's Lick.[15]

Early in November of the same year the district court was in session at Danville, a town about half way from St. Asaph's

[14] Harrison's Message to the Assembly, Draper MSS. 10 S 78. Walker Daniel to William Fleming, April 14, 1783, Draper MSS. 46 J 78(1-2).

[15] Walker Daniel to Harrison, May 21, 1784, Draper MSS. 11 S 187-89. Extract from *Maryland Journal*, December 19, 1783, Draper MSS. 3 JJ 114-21. William Johnston to Harrison, August 14, 1784, Draper MSS. 11 S 193-95. Abernethy, *Western Lands and the American Revolution*, 302-303.

to Harrodsburg, which recently had been established on land donated by Walker Daniel. At the same time the board of trustees of the Transylvania Seminary was meeting there. Logan, who had just received word that the Cherokee and the Chickamauga were planning an invasion of Kentucky, called for a meeting to be held on November 7 to discuss the situation. It should be noted that this was not a council of militia officers, although some of those who attended held commissions in the militia. It was not a meeting of Danville residents, even though several of these attended. It was a meeting of leading citizens from all parts of the district. They had come to Danville, some to attend the court, some to attend the board meeting, and some at Logan's request.

Logan opened the meeting in what one witness described as "a much more parliamentary manner than I expected," and laid before those present the information that he had received. Colonel William Fleming, a former member of the Virginia Council who already had headed two commissions to Kentucky, was looked upon as the chairman, although no election took place. Because it was growing late it was decided that another session would be held on the following day.

When the group reconvened Fleming proposed the name of Isaac Shelby for chairman, and he was elected. Christopher Greenup, who like Shelby favored an immediate expedition against the Indians, was selected as clerk. Thus the advocates of action lost two votes at the outset. The more conservative faction, whose principal spokesmen were Fleming, Caleb Wallace, and George Muter, argued that there was no officer in the district who was authorized by law to raise men, impress supplies, and march the militia into another state, all of which might be necessary if Indians who resided in North Carolina were to be attacked. Although he was still the county lieutenant of Lincoln, Benjamin Logan seems to have taken no part in the discussion. He was ready to lead an army if such a course were deemed wise, but the finer points of law he was willing to leave to others.

Before the day had ended a message from Joseph Martin was delivered to Logan. Martin stated that the Cherokee were never in a more friendly mood, and that even the unruly Chickamauga were talking of peace. The information concerning the supposed warlike intentions of these Indians may have originated with land speculators who hoped to produce a temporary decline in land prices. Regardless of its origin, the more dependable information from Martin left the Kentuckians no excuse for a campaign. Nevertheless, it was evident to both factions that a situation which made it impossible for the district to defend itself except within its own borders was not a safe one. One of the members suggested that it was a good time to take steps leading toward the separation of Kentucky from Virginia, a possibility which had been recognized by the framers of Virginia's constitution. The meeting took upon itself the responsibility of calling for the election of delegates to a convention at Danville on December 27, which would determine the steps to be taken.[16]

Although the delegates were to be elected by militia companies, this did not mean that only members of the militia could vote or that only such persons were eligible for election. The term "militia company" meant not only a military unit but also a civil district covering the geographical area in which the men belonging to that unit lived. The use of such districts in the collection of taxes and in the appointment of constables was a regular procedure.[17]

It is evident also that a delegate was not required to be a

[16] District of Kentucky, Order Book 1, p. 46. Ebenezer Brooks to Arthur Campbell, November 9, 1784, Draper MSS. 11 J 37-38. Draper MSS. 11 S 135. Hening (ed.), *Statutes*, IX, 118-19. *Kentucky Gazette*, October 18, 1788. Thomas P. Abernethy, "Journal of the First Kentucky Convention," in *Journal of Southern History*, I (1935), 67. (The original journal may be seen in the Fleming Papers.) Abernethy, *Western Lands*, 303-304. William Littell, *Political Transactions in and Concerning Kentucky* (Frankfort, 1806), 15-16. "Proceedings of the Board of Trustees of the Transylvania Seminary," 3-5.

[17] Brooks to Campbell, November 9, 1784, Draper MSS. 11 J 37-38. Draper MSS. 17 J 56-64(1), 81-82(3). Lincoln County Court Order Book 1, p. 31. Levi Todd to [Robert Patterson], February 24, 1787, Draper MSS. 2 MM 2.

resident of the militia district that elected him. Benjamin Logan, who paid his taxes in Captain John Martin's district, was elected from Captain Barnett's, while Martin's district sent Isaac Shelby to the convention. William Fleming, who was elected from Captain Montgomery's militia district in Lincoln County, never moved his residence any nearer to Kentucky than Botetourt County. Although there may be some basis for the charge made several years later that some of the delegates were elected by the votes of very few men, there is no valid reason for saying, as some historians have done, that they represented the militia rather than the people.[18]

The delegates, nineteen from Lincoln County, nine from Jefferson, and seven from Fayette, were to assemble at Danville on Monday, December 27. Not all of them arrived on the appointed day, but, a quorum being present, the convention proceeded to organize. William Fleming was elected as chairman and Thomas Perkins was named as clerk. Isaac Shelby, who arrived with Ben Logan on December 29, was selected immediately as chairman of the committee of the whole.[19]

Among the several resolutions passed there was one which condemned an act of the Virginia Assembly placing a tax of five shillings per hundred acres on future land grants in excess of 1,400 acres. Ben and John Logan were among those who considered the tax to be fair and who voted against the resolution. This certainly would not put the Logans on the side of the speculators.

This convention did not go beyond the passing of resolutions. Its members realized that some of their grievances were the result of their great distance from the capital, and these, they

[18] *Kentucky Gazette*, October 18, 1788, April 25, 1789. Bodley, *History of Kentucky*, 357. Bodley (ed.), *Littell's Political Transactions*, vi n. John Mason Brown, *Political Beginnings of Kentucky*, Filson Club Publications No. 6 (Louisville, 1889), 60-62. "Journal of the First Kentucky Convention," Fleming Papers, p. 3.

[19] Extracts from *Pennsylvania Packet*, March 23, 1785, May 9, 1785, Draper MSS. 2 JJ 370-75; 3 JJ 176-82. Abernethy, "Journal of the First Kentucky Convention," 70-72.

believed, could never be redressed while Kentucky remained
a part of Virginia. Even so, they moved with caution. They
did not seem to feel certain that the people of Kentucky had
elected them with full authority to petition for separation.
Their last resolution recommended the election of delegates to
another convention which would meet in Danville on the
fourth Monday in May, 1785. The delegates would be elected
with authority to make application for statehood. After agree-
ing that representation would be in proportion to population
and that Lincoln County would have twelve delegates, Jefferson
eight, and Fayette eight, the convention adjourned on January
5, 1785.[20]

When elections were held on the various county court days
in April, 1785, Benjamin Logan won seats both in the second
convention and in the Virginia Assembly. A year earlier it
would have been impossible for one man to have done justice
to both offices. The assembly had been holding two sessions
in most years, the first opening in May, the month in which
the convention would meet. At the May session in 1784,
however, the assembly had voted to hold only one session per
year, convening on the third Monday in October. The new
law went into effect in 1785.[21]

The delegates to the Second Kentucky Convention, which
opened in Danville on May 23, reached agreement upon several
points. A petition was to be sent to the Virginia Assembly
asking for the establishment of Kentucky as a separate state,
and a resolution was passed declaring that the new state ought
to be admitted to the union with the same rights and privileges
as the original thirteen. As the members of this convention
desired yet another authorization from the people of the dis-

<hr />

[20] "Journal of the First Kentucky Convention," Fleming Papers. Hening
(ed.), Statutes, XI, 445. Abernethy, Western Lands, 305-306. John D.
Barnhart, Valley of Democracy (Bloomington, Ind., 1953), 69-70.

[21] Mann Butler, A History of the Commonwealth of Kentucky (Cincinnati,
1836), 147. Thomas M. Green, The Spanish Conspiracy (Cincinnati, 1891),
58. "Harrison of James River," in Virginia Magazine of History and Biography,
XXXII (1924), 301. Hening (ed.), Statutes, XII, 9n.

trict, they drafted an address to their constituents recommending that the petition to the assembly and all other matters that had been under consideration be referred to another convention. Its members would be elected in July and they would meet at Danville in August. It was stipulated that there should be thirty members elected according to population; ten from Lincoln County, eight from Fayette, six from Jefferson, and six from the new county of Nelson. In order that everyone might know what was being proposed, copies of the petition to the assembly and of the address to the people were sent to each county clerk with instructions to post them at the doors of the courthouses.[22]

While Logan was in Danville he attended a meeting of the Transylvania Board of Trustees. At this meeting Harry Innes, James Garrard, and James Wilkinson were chosen to fill the places of three deceased board members, John Bowman, Walker Daniel, and John Moseby.[23]

Between the second and third conventions Kentucky was subjected to another Indian alarm. Scouts reported that a large party had crossed the Ohio, and Logan quickly raised a force and advanced to meet them. When the Indians' campsite was reached, every savage had departed, and all signs seemed to indicate that their numbers had been greatly overestimated. Occurrences such as this were not uncommon, but Logan, the senior county lieutenant in the district, believed that it was far better to march and find no Indians than to risk an attack upon one of the settlements.[24]

After serving as sheriff of Lincoln County for two years, Logan relinquished the office in the spring of 1785. In June the court appointed Isaac Shelby and John Edwards to settle his accounts and to report upon the status of tax collections for the

[22] Bodley (ed.), *Littell's Political Transactions*, 13-14. *Bradford's Notes*, 150-51. Extracts from *Maryland Gazette*, July 1, 1785, and October 11, 1785, Draper MSS. 3 JJ 138-39, 156.

[23] "Proceedings of the Board," 5-8.

[24] Arthur Campbell to Governor Patrick Henry, June 15, 1785, and July 5, 1785, *Calendar of Virginia State Papers*, IV, 37-38, 40.

years 1783 and 1784. Collections from delinquents, however, were still being credited to Logan's account as late as October 21, 1788.[25]

The Third Kentucky Convention met at Danville on August 8, 1785. Samuel McDowell, who had served as president of the preceding convention, was honored with that position again. Logan and the other delegates approved a petition similar to the one drafted by the second convention. It requested that an act be passed to make the District of Kentucky a separate state. Again the principal reason given was the distance of the western settlements from the capital, about five hundred miles, and the difficulties of traveling through two hundred miles of wilderness in order to reach it. This situation made it very hard to obtain aid in the event of an invasion. George Muter and Harry Innes, who had been elected to the Virginia Assembly, were selected to present the petition to that body.[26]

In addition to Muter and Innes, the four counties in the District of Kentucky were represented in the House of Delegates by Logan, James Garrard, Christopher Greenup, Joseph Crockett, Richard Terrell, and John Fowler. These men gave some of their attention to securing ammunition for the defense of Kentucky but were present at most sessions of the assembly. On a few issues the roll was called and it is possible to tell how Logan voted. On November 3 the legality of the election of former governor Benjamin Harrison to the House of Delegates was questioned, as he had been defeated in Charles City County, where his main plantation lay. Since the invasions of Arnold and Cornwallis, Harrison had been living in the county of Surry, where he also owned land. The election there was somewhat later than in the former county. Harrison became a candidate in Surry and won. The house voted 57 to 49 to seat

[25] Lincoln County Court Order Book 2, pp. 42, 75; Order Book 3, pp. 26, 302.

[26] Extract from *Maryland Gazette*, October 11, 1785, Draper MSS. 3 JJ 72, 258-63. Abernethy, *Western Lands*, 307-308. Bodley (ed.), *Littell's Political Transactions*, x, 14, 68-70. Butler, *Kentucky*, 148-49. Robertson, *Petitions*, 79-82.

him, with Logan voting in the affirmative. On November 21 Logan was with the 50 to 48 majority in defeating a bill to postpone the collection of taxes for the year 1785.

On December 7 Logan was placed on a committee to consider a bill which would divide Lincoln County into three parts. This bill had been drawn up in answer to a petition received from some of the residents of Lincoln. A few days later he was with Greenup and James Garrard on a similar committee to consider the division of Fayette County. These two bills passed both houses of the assembly, and the District of Kentucky gained three counties—Madison, Mercer, and Bourbon.

On December 13 Logan, Garrard, and Greenup were named to a committee to consider amending an act governing land entries and surveys on the western waters. On December 16 he helped to defeat a proposed change in the preamble of the Statute for Religious Freedom. Next day he was with the majority in passing this important measure by a vote of 74 to 20. On the day before Christmas a bill to repeal "an act to authorize the manumission of slaves" failed to pass to a second reading. Logan was one of those who helped to defeat it. Although he owned a few slaves throughout his life, he believed that an owner should have the right to set his slaves free if he wished to do so. A bill was received from the senate to make Kentucky's first settlement, Harrodsburg, an incorporated town. It was passed by the house, and, although Harrodsburg would lie in the new county of Mercer and not in Lincoln, Logan was named as one of the trustees.

The most important action of this session of the assembly concerning Kentucky was that taken upon the petition for statehood. An enabling act passed by the house on January 6 made separation possible under certain conditions. One condition was that "Kentucky must become a member of the Confederation at the same time that she became a separate State." There also was a provision that "all land claims set up under Virginia law must remain equally valid under the jurisdiction of the new State." Virginia was taking no chances on a separation being effected in opposition to the will of the people of the District of Kentucky. This enabling act called for the election in August, 1786, of delegates to a fourth convention, which would meet in Danville on the fourth Monday in September. Each county was to send five delegates who would accept or reject separation on the terms laid down in the act. In the event of acceptance, the convention was empowered to name a day after September 1, 1787, on which Virginia's authority over Kentucky should come to an end. There was an additional stipulation that before June 1, 1787, Congress must have agreed to the separation and to the admission of Kentucky as a new state. The enabling act was passed by the Senate on January 10.

At this time it must have appeared to Kentucky's delegates at Richmond that statehood soon would be a reality. Three conventions had favored it, and it was not likely that a fourth would do otherwise. But Congress and the Indians still were factors to be reckoned with.[27]

[27] *Journal of the House of Delegates of the Commonwealth of Virginia, 1785* (Richmond, 1828), 21, 46, 75, 89-90, 94-96, 110, 115, 130. Logan, Crockett, Terrell, and Fowler to Edmund Randolph, January 5, 1786, *Calendar of Virginia State Papers,* IV, 79 (Original is in Executive Papers, Patrick Henry, Jan.-Apr., 1786). Hening (ed.), *Statutes,* XII, 37-40, 223-25. Abernethy, *Western Lands,* 308-309. "Harrison of James River," 300-301. *Bradford's Notes,* 160-61. Butler, *Kentucky,* 149-50.

CHAPTER XIII

MORE INDIAN TROUBLES

AFTER LOGAN HAD STARTED to Richmond, the Indians struck two blows in quick succession at travelers on the Wilderness Trail. The first party, consisting chiefly of the McClure family, was attacked just before dawn at their camp on Skaggs' Creek. Six of the travelers, including the three McClure children, were killed instantly. McClure made his escape, but Mrs. McClure and a Negro woman were captured. The news was carried to Whitley's Station, and a party of twenty-two men raised by John Logan and William Whitley went in pursuit. The savages were overtaken, two of them were killed, and the two prisoners were rescued. A large quantity of plunder was recovered. Ten days later another company of travelers led by a man named Moore was defeated near Raccoon Creek with the loss of nine of their number. Again Whitley led the pursuit, recovering eight scalps and all of the horses and other loot and killing three of the Indians.[1]

Congress now was making an attempt to negotiate with both the northern and the southern Indians. On January 31, 1786, George Rogers Clark concluded a treaty with the Shawnee at the mouth of the Miami. This should have relieved the minds of the Kentuckians, who considered these Indians to be among their most dangerous enemies. Nevertheless, the fact that other tribes which were expected had failed to appear was sufficient reason for apprehension. In addition there were many who doubted the sincerity of the Shawnee themselves.[2]

In the spring and summer of 1786 the Indian situation grew steadily worse. Most of the raids seemed to come from the Wabash region, and thus Jefferson County was hardest hit. One of these incursions cost the life of Colonel William Christian, who, with Captain Isaac Keller, died at the head of a company of pursuers. Christian, a former member of the Virginia Council and a brother-in-law of Patrick Henry, had been a civil and military leader in Fincastle County and later in Montgomery. Because he owned land in Jefferson County and was expected to move there, he was named as county lieutenant when the county was formed. He declined the appointment, however, and it was not until the fall of 1785 that he moved his residence to Kentucky.

Conditions in Jefferson County grew so bad that the county lieutenant, William Pope, and fifty-three other residents sent an appeal for aid to the people of Lincoln, Fayette, and Nelson Counties. They used the same argument which earlier had been employed by Kentucky County in making requests for aid from her eastern neighbors. Jefferson, they pointed out, was a barrier against the Indians of the Northwest. If it had to be abandoned the other counties would find themselves on the frontier.[3]

This appeal and the atrocities which were committed brought a series of letters from leading Kentuckians to Governor Patrick Henry. Benjamin Logan enclosed a copy of the Jefferson County request and spoke of the deaths of Christian and Keller. He reported also that Colonel John Donelson, who had represented Virginia in negotiations with the southern Indians, had been killed in the southern part of Lincoln County on April 11. It was Logan's opinion that the southern and the northwestern

[1] Draper MSS. 12 C 62(28-31); 9 CC 7-8, 10, 45-48. *Bradford's Notes,* 155-56.

[2] Draper MSS. 11 J 36, 40. Abernethy, *Western Lands,* 316. Bodley (ed.), *Littell's Political Transactions,* 14.

[3] Arthur Campbell to Patrick Henry, June 15, 1785, *Calendar of Virginia State Papers,* IV, 37-38. Draper MSS. 11 S 48, 53, 153, 201. John May to Patrick Henry, April 19, 1786, Draper MSS. 12 S 41-43. Draper MSS. 12 S 48-51. *Calendar of Virginia State Papers,* IV, 160-61.

Indians had agreed to cooperate in the subjugation of Kentucky. He informed the governor that several settlements already had been abandoned. Before closing his letter, Logan hinted at the need for a campaign by reminding Henry that "General Clark is in the County of Jefferson . . . is recovered from a low state of health, & is likely to be able to serve the public." He made no specific suggestions but concluded: "I hope your Excellency & the Honorable Council will fall on such measures & give us such directions for our Safety as you in your wisdom may think best."[4]

Judge Samuel McDowell gave about the same information to the governor but was more direct in his suggestions regarding a campaign. He realized, however, that under the existing law this would have to be authorized by the Virginia government. George Rogers Clark estimated that the tribes along the Wabash had at least fifteen hundred warriors, and he believed that they were being encouraged by British traders. He predicted that help from the assembly or from Congress could not arrive in time. Nothing, in Clark's opinion, but an immediate volunteer campaign would save the situation.

When Governor Henry learned of the death of his brother-in-law at the hands of the Indians and of the serious situation which existed in Kentucky, he wrote immediately to the president of Congress. He predicted that "the necessity of the case will enforce the people, for the purpose of self-preservation, to go against the offending towns." This was the climax of a controversy in which the governor already had questioned the willingness and ability of Congress to defend the frontier.

On the same day the governor wrote to Logan authorizing him to call a meeting of the militia commanders of all counties in the district to adopt measures for defense. Since the Kentuckians had never been denied the right to defend themselves within their borders, it was assumed that this message referred

---

[4] Logan to Henry, April 19, 1786, *Calendar of Virginia State Papers*, IV, 120 and Draper MSS. 12 S 46-47. The quotation is from the latter source. Draper, when copying a letter, did not hesitate to correct spelling and punctuation.

to defense wherever it might be required by the existing situation. Logan named Harrodsburg as the place for the meeting of the county lieutenants and set August 2 as the date.[5]

Before the appointed day some opinions were expressed upon the legality of such a campaign, upon what its objective should be, and upon the question of who should lead it. Abraham Chaplin, a Kentucky lawyer, warned George Rogers Clark, who was being mentioned as a suitable commander, that no one in the District of Kentucky had the authority to order militiamen to go beyond the borders of the state of Virginia without their consent. Clark was troubled about the change of plans from a volunteer campaign, which he had advocated, and on which each man would furnish his own equipment and provisions, to a militia campaign for which supplies might have to be obtained by impressment.[6]

There was little doubt at the time that the more dangerous Indians were along the Wabash. The raids usually came from that direction. The settlers at Vincennes had suffered several attacks and had appealed to Clark and the Kentuckians for aid.[7]

The question of a commander for the campaign caused little controversy. Clark had resigned his brigadier general's commission at the close of the Revolution, but he remained in the minds of most Kentuckians the outstanding military man to have served in the West. Stories of his addiction to alcohol and of his resulting incompetence were being circulated in the East, but the people of Kentucky attached little significance to them. "I have been with him frequently," wrote one of the

[5] McDowell to Henry, April 18, 1786, Draper MSS. 12 S 39-41. Clark to Henry, April ——, 1786, Draper MSS. 12 S 44-46. Draper MSS. 14 S 138. Bodley, *Kentucky*, 373-74. Greene, *The Spanish Conspiracy*, 53. Governor Henry's authorization was based on an Order in Council of the preceding day.

[6] Chaplin to Clark, July 26, 1786, Draper MSS. 53 J 40. Draper MSS. 12 C 49(9). Temple Bodley, *George Rogers Clark, His Life and Public Services* (Boston, 1926), 282.

[7] Daniel Sullivan to Clark, June 23, 1786, Draper MSS. 53 J 35. John Small to Patrick Henry, June 23, 1786, Draper MSS. 53 J 36. John Small to Clark, July 22, 1786, Draper MSS. 11 J 81(1-2).

governor's correspondents, "and find him as capable of Business as ever, and should an Expedition be carried against the Indians I think his name alone would be worth Half a regiment of men." Benjamin Logan, to whom the writer showed this letter, agreed with the sentiments expressed and asked that his own recommendation of Clark be conveyed to Governor Henry.[8]

The meeting that Logan called to order at Harrodsburg on August 2 included not only the county lieutenants, but a majority of the field officers of the seven counties in the District of Kentucky. It was agreed that an expedition against the Wabash Indians was necessary and that half of the militia, except in the region east of the Licking River, should be drafted for that purpose. Clark would be asked to take command, but, if he should refuse, that duty would fall to Logan. The troops were to be at Clarksville, across the Ohio from Louisville, by September 10.[9]

The militia officers were uncertain about their power to impress supplies and sought the opinions of the attorney general and the judges of the district court. These officials replied that it was their belief that the military powers of the Virginia Executive under the state's militia laws and under the Articles of Confederation had been delegated to the field officers of the district by the Order in Council of May 15, 1786, which authorized them to take the necessary steps for defense. Thus it was their opinion that impressment was legal.[10]

It then was agreed that each county lieutenant should secure enough provisions and ammunition for fifty days and a packhorse for every four men. If these things had to be obtained by impressment they were to be appraised and receipts given to the owners. John May was named as

---

[8] John May to Patrick Henry, July 14, 1786, *Calendar of Virginia State Papers*, IV, 156-57. Draper MSS. 18 S 157.

[9] Levi Todd to Patrick Henry, August 29, 1786, *Calendar of Virginia State Papers*, IV, 166. Draper MSS. 53 J 42; 10 S 125, 128-29; 12 S 71-73.

[10] Draper MSS. 12 S 123-24. *Calendar of Virginia State Papers*, IV, 195.

commissary for the expedition, and Christopher Greenup was to act as quartermaster. Some of the needed supplies were surrendered willingly, but at times impressment was required. Even when this was necessary there was not too much resentment. An officer of the Continental army who had just arrived in Kentucky recorded in his diary, "The people take it middling kindly."[11]

When September 10 arrived men began to appear at Clarksville, but two days later there were no more than twelve hundred. Because this was less than had been expected, Clark, who had taken command at that point, asked for the advice of the field officers. They met in council on September 13 with Logan again presiding. The council recommended that Clark proceed to Vincennes with the men at hand. In the meantime one field officer from each county would return home, collect all delinquents and deserters from the first draft, and call out one-half of the remainder of the militia. These additional troops were to meet at Clarksville on September 28 and proceed immediately to Vincennes.[12]

Clark accepted these proposals with one important change. He ordered Logan to take command of all forces that were raised in this way. If he thought them sufficient he was to conduct a separate campaign against the Shawnee, who were continually violating the peace treaty which they had made with the United States. It was Clark's opinion that most of the Shawnee warriors would have gone to the Wabash to help in blocking his expected thrust in that direction. Their villages would be virtually undefended, and a better time to punish them hardly could be found.[13]

[11] Draper MSS. 53 J 42-42(1). Levi Todd to Patrick Henry, August 29, 1786, Draper MSS. 12 S 71-73. "Major Eskuries Beatty's Diary," copied from *Magazine of American History*, April, 1877, Draper MSS. 9 J 240-41.

[12] "Minutes of Meeting of Field Officers," Clarksville, September 13, 1786, *Calendar of Virginia State Papers*, IV, 205, and Draper MSS 12 S 118-19. Bodley, *Clark*, 284-85.

[13] Clark to Logan, September 14, 1786, *Calendar of Virginia State Papers*, IV, 205. Draper MSS. 9 J 243; 11 J 118-21.

Logan experienced some difficulty in carrying out these orders. The country had been combed for provisions, and this second round of impressments met with some opposition.[14] By September 29, however, his men were gathering at Limestone on the Ohio River. On the same day Indians, who evidently had not detected the approach of the white army, were active in the vicinity. At Lee's Station, four miles to the southeast of Limestone, two sons of Moses Phillips were killed and three Negroes were captured. At Clark's Station, six miles to the south of Limestone, Robert Clark, son of George Clark the founder of the station, and two more Negroes were taken. A detachment from the gathering army followed the savages to where they recrossed the Ohio about six miles above Limestone. There the pursuit was abandoned.[15]

Benjamin Logan found upon his arrival that he had about eight hundred men. From these he formed two regiments. Those men from south and west of the Kentucky River were placed in the first regiment, which Colonel John Logan, brother of the county lieutenant, would command. Those from north and east of the Kentucky constituted a second regiment. This would be led by Colonel Robert Patterson of Fayette County. The crossing of the Ohio began on September 30 and continued through much of the night. Logan explained afterward that "a barrel of rum was impressed at Limestone, and [there] being much rain it was given freely to the soldiers, & in consequence of its effect, the army was somewhat delayed in crossing . . . the river." They also had taken the time to kill and dress about twenty head of cattle.

Each regiment marched in three columns, with John Logan's comprising the right wing and Patterson's the left. A rear guard

[14] Robert Patterson to Patrick Henry, December 7, 1786, *Calendar of Virginia State Papers,* IV, 192-93. Levi Todd to Patrick Henry, December 7, 1786, *Calendar of Virginia State Papers,* IV, 196. Draper MSS. 11 CC 6; 1 MM 166-67, 171.
[15] Robert Patterson to Elizabeth Patterson, September 30, 1786, Draper MSS. 1 MM 155. Obadiah Robins to Richard Butler, September 29, 1786, Draper MSS. 1 W 249-50. Draper MSS 9 BB 60(10-12); 9 CC 2-3.

of thirty-five officers and men was led by Major John Hinkston. An advance party consisting of three officers and fifty-three men was led by Benjamin Logan himself. On the night of October 1 camp was made on Eagle Creek, which flows into the Ohio a few miles below Limestone, and on October 2 they turned northward and followed this creek upstream. The pass where this stream breaks through the hills that border the Ohio afterward was commonly spoken of as Logan's Gap.[16] By October 5 the army was within fifty miles of its destination, the Shawnee villages on the upper reaches of the Big Miami. Logan's orders for the day directed his officers to have their men march as quietly as possible. They were not to take any plunder until specific permission was granted. The orders said also that "in case any person, under any description or any color, attempts to come to the army, all persons are forewarned to receive them in a friendly manner."[17]

Logan may have been thinking of the tragic death of Clark's cousin, Joseph Rogers, who during the 1780 Indian campaign was shot down by one of the Kentuckians while trying to escape to the white lines. Further explanation of the order was given later when Logan was a witness at a court martial. He believed that the approach of his army had been discovered by the Indians who committed the murders and took the prisoners in the vicinity of Limestone, and when he and his men reached the Shawnee villages emissaries might come out to sue for peace. Even if this did not happen, prisoners might try to escape to the white army, and these might be mistaken for Indians. George Clark, whose son had been captured only a few days before, and Robert Maffet, who also had a son with the Indians, were in Logan's army. This order, Logan afterward declared, was issued for the protection of such persons as these and "not in favor of any Indian on earth."

[16] Benjamin Logan to Governor Edmund Randolph, December 17, 1786, *Calendar of Virginia State Papers*, IV, 204. Robert Patterson to Elizabeth Patterson, October 1, 1786, Draper MSS. 1 MM 155. See also Draper MSS. 1 MM 155-56; 7 S 114-15; 12 S 139; 19 S 72.

[17] Draper MSS. 11 J 142; 12 S 136-37.

The army marched all of that day and most of the night. On the following day, October 6, about one o'clock in the afternoon, Logan halted his men a short distance from the Indian villages. No peace emissaries had appeared and there was nothing to indicate that any prisoners had tried to escape. Logan began to fear that his orders might prevent his men from fighting as vigorously as would be required. Some might lose their lives in trying to make prisoners of Indians who could have been killed at long range with less risk. Accordingly he rode through the lines and verbally modified his original instructions. His soldiers were told to be careful to spare white persons but were to do as they pleased about Indians.[18]

The army then was divided and several villages were attacked at the same time. As had been expected, many of the Shawnee warriors had gone to the Wabash, where the other Kentucky stroke was expected to fall. Little resistance was encountered, and by the end of the day seven towns—Mackacheck, Wappatomica, New Piqua, Will's Town, McKee's Town, Blue Jacket's Town, and Moluntha's Town—had been destroyed. Ten warriors were killed and thirty-two prisoners, mostly women and children, were taken. Among the prisoners was the old chief Moluntha, sometimes called the Shawnee King. He had headed the delegation which had signed the treaty with the United States earlier in the year. In this treaty the Shawnee had agreed to accept the sovereignty of the United States and to live at peace with the white man. Some had not observed this agreement, but Moluntha evidently believed that he was one of those who had done so. Taking refuge under an American flag which had flown over his village, he had surrendered himself and some women and children who were with him. He was talking with his captors when Hugh McGary, now a lieutenant colonel in the Mercer County militia, approached. He asked Moluntha if he had been at Blue Licks, and it was thought by some in the group that the chief answered that he had. McGary then seized a small ax and

18 Draper MSS. 12 S 137-38.

sank the blade in Moluntha's head. He was bitterly criticized by some of the other officers, especially by James Trotter, lieutenant colonel in the militia of Fayette County. In the course of a heated argument McGary stated, with considerable profanity, that he would chop down Colonel Trotter or anyone else who tried to keep him from killing Indians whenever he liked. Some of the officers wanted an immediate court martial for McGary, but Logan, believing that he could not get a fair trial while feelings were so high, refused to order it.

The Kentucky casualties in the several brief encounters had been light; one killed outright, two mortally wounded, and two slightly wounded. More than two hundred cabins had been burned and an estimated fifteen thousand bushels of corn with them. Plunder valued at nearly one thousand pounds was taken, and a number of hogs, considered too slow to drive back to Kentucky, were slaughtered.

The army was only one day's journey from the ruined villages when it was found that Indians were in pursuit. Logan left a message in a conspicuous place indicating that if any of his men were killed the prisoners would be executed. Nothing more was heard from the pursuers. The horses, cattle, and other plunder were sold at auction as was the custom, and the prisoners were brought to Danville, where they were lodged for the time being in the jail of the District of Kentucky.[19]

Colonel Josiah Harmar, who commanded United States regulars in the Northwest, was critical of Logan's expedition and especially of the killing of Moluntha. He said that the

[19] Logan to Randolph, December 17, 1786, and December 30, 1786, *Calendar of Virginia State Papers*, IV, 204, 212. Caleb Wallace to William Fleming, October 23, 1786, Draper MSS. 9 J 244. Walter Finney to Josiah Harmar, October 31, 1786, Draper MSS. 1 W 243. Wyandot Chiefs to Richard Butler, October 28, 1786, Draper MSS. 1 W 252. W. Ancrum at Detroit to his superiors in London, October 20, 1786, *Michigan Pioneer and Historical Collections*, XXIV, 37-39. Extracts from *Pennsylvania Packet*, November 23, 1786, and December 2, 1786, Draper MSS. 11 J 142-42(1), 144-44(1). See also Draper MSS. 12 C 62(11-15); 5 Q 52; 10 S 125, 128-29; 12 S 133-40, and 18 S 157. (The McKee's Town and Will's Town mentioned here are not the same as the McKee's Town and Willstown which were destroyed in 1782.)

chief "had always been represented as a friend to the United States." He understood that Moluntha had called the attention of Logan's men not only to his American flag but also to a copy of the Miami Treaty of January, 1786. Harmar also had heard that the flag was being displayed as a trophy at the Fayette County courthouse in Lexington. Some of the other tribes, especially the Wyandots, had been so angered by this invasion that some kind of retaliation was a distinct possibility. This had caused the surveyors who were marking off townships in the region to suspend their operations after completing four range lines and starting on a fifth.[20]

While Logan was conducting his successful campaign, Clark was having difficulty on the Wabash. Plagued by a shortage of provisions and by the mutiny of some of the men who had expected to serve under Logan, he failed to engage the Indians in battle or to damage any of their villages.[21]

One aftermath of Logan's expedition was the trial by court martial of three of his officers at Bardstown on March 20, 1787. Alexander Scott Bullitt, the newly appointed county lieutenant of Jefferson, presided, and Logan was one of the principal witnesses. Colonel Robert Patterson and Lieutenant Colonel James Trotter were tried on charges brought by Lieutenant Colonel Hugh McGary. They were said to have delayed the crossing of the Ohio at Limestone by impressing a barrel of rum and distributing it among the men, and to have slaughtered twenty cattle without orders from their commanding officer. McGary charged also that Trotter had ordered his men to "shoot down any man that killed an Indian after he was captured." The court decided that the distribution of the rum was "in some measure irregular." The killing of the cattle, it concluded, had not caused any delay, but "some waste was in-

[20] Josiah Harmar to Arthur St. Clair, December 10, 1786, and Josiah Harmar to Richard Butler, December 16, 1786, Harmar Papers, Letter Book B, 23-24, 27-29, William L. Clements Library, University of Michigan. See also Harmar to Secretary of War Henry Knox, November 15, 1786, in William Henry Smith (arr.), *The St. Clair Papers* (Cincinnati, 1882), II, 19.
[21] Draper MSS. 9 J 134-37, 152-54, 238-38(3); 11 J 58, 79(1-3).

curred thereby." Patterson was sentenced to be reprimanded by his county lieutenant and commanding officer, Levi Todd. The case against Trotter was dropped for lack of evidence.

Patterson and Trotter then presented countercharges against McGary. He was accused of killing the Shawnee chief Moluntha after the Indian had surrendered, with disobeying the order to spare all prisoners, with using abusive and threatening language to Colonel Trotter, and with "conduct . . . unbecoming the character of a Gentleman and an Officer." The court found him guilty of murdering Moluntha. He was found not guilty of the second charge, because Logan testified that he had countermanded that portion of his orders which forbade the killing of Indians who might attempt to come to the Kentucky lines before the action had ended. It was shown at the trial that some of the fighting had taken place after the killing of Moluntha. McGary was found guilty of using abusive and threatening language, but he was declared to be only partially guilty of the fourth charge. The court sentenced him to be suspended from the militia for one year.[22]

Logan believed that some of the witnesses had taken advantage of the opportunity to criticize him. He disliked having their testimony appear on the records of the court martial. "If it tends to my Prejudice," he wrote to the new governor, Edmund Randolph, "I am able to justify my conduct before any court of Justice on earth."[23] There is no evidence to indicate that he was ever called upon to do so.

The prisoners taken by Logan on his Shawnee campaign spent a short period in the district jail and then were turned over to John Crow, who had contracted to feed and house them. The group included a Frenchman, a white woman who had been with the Indians so long that she considered them her own people, and the widow of Chief Moluntha. Among the

[22] Calendar of Virginia State Papers, IV, 258-60. Draper MSS. 12 S 133-40. Levi Todd to Robert Patterson, March 7, 1787, Draper MSS. 2 MM 5.
[23] Logan to Randolph, April 14, 1787, Calendar of Virginia State Papers, IV, 266-68.

children there was a boy about ten years of age, believed to have been at least half white. He became a favorite of some of the Kentucky people, learned English, took the name James Logan, and died fighting with the Americans in the War of 1812.[24]

Regardless of the expense of caring for the Indian prisoners, possession of them was a definite advantage. At least as many white people from Kentucky still were being held by the Shawnee, and now there would be a possibility of some exchanges being made. Soon after he returned from the campaign, Logan assumed the authority that the situation seemed to demand and appointed commissioners to make the necessary arrangements. Selected for this work were Christopher Greenup, Robert Patterson, James Trotter, and Daniel Boone. Having given up his position as county lieutenant of Fayette, Boone now lived at Limestone, the most suitable place for exchanges to be made.

The end of the year came and no representative of the Shawnee had appeared to discuss ways and means of obtaining their people. On the assumption that they were afraid to come, the commissioners decided to send one of the squaws and the Frenchman to the Indian villages to initiate proceedings. This pair reached Limestone on February 2, where Boone supplied them with horses, saddles, bridles, a gun, ammunition, and provisions.

This action soon brought results. On March 4 Noamohouoh, one of the Shawnee chiefs, arrived at Limestone and delivered

---

[24] Robertson, *Petitions*, 165-68. Draper MSS. 12 C 47(1); 8 J 245; 9 J 84; 18 S 170, 174; 13 CC 213-14. Statement of Lewis Wetsell [Wetzel], November 14, 1786, Harmar Papers, Vol. IV.

When Logan returned from his expedition a young Danville blade is said to have congratulated him upon his success, but to have expressed sorrow "that he should have tarnished his well-earned fame by killing Moluntha." Logan is said to have replied, with some indication of anger, that he neither killed the chief nor ordered him to be killed. He then suggested that the young man, who seemed to sympathize so deeply with the bereaved family, prove the sincerity of his emotion by marrying Moluntha's widow. See Draper MSS. 12 C 47(1).

a speech for his people. He brought with him George Clark's son Robert and two other prisoners. The chief asked that two Indians be released in exchange for young Clark and one for each of the others. Noamohouoh had been sent by the head chief of the Shawnee, who expressed his willingness to collect all of the white prisoners and to bring them to Limestone in April.[25]

The idea of exchanging two prisoners for Robert Clark had originated with Logan, at whose fort George Clark and his family had lived during the Indian troubles of 1777. Notices carrying this offer had been posted during the campaign, but the Indians, either because of fear or because they were overly impressed by the value placed upon young Clark, had failed at that time to comply. Logan had promised Margaret Clark that he would do everything in his power to obtain her son, and now the chief was ready to take advantage of the situation. He agreed to accept the squaw who had carried the message proposing an exchange and her two children in lieu of two adults. Boone, who was handling the negotiations, and who had the Shawnee chief as a guest at his tavern for twenty days, gave his word that the desired number of Indian prisoners would be obtained. He wrote to Logan and Greenup about the matter and the exchange soon was completed.[26]

Patterson and Trotter, who had not been consulted, were incensed when they were asked by Boone to send an Indian woman who was in their custody to Limestone for exchanging. They let Boone know that the idea of exchanging two or three Indians for one white man did not have their approval. He replied, with typical Boone spelling: "I am here with my hands full of Bisness and no athority and if I am not indulged in

[25] Greenup to Patterson, December 6, 1786, Draper MSS. 1 MM 162. Patterson to [Alexander] McKee, undated, Draper MSS. 2 MM 9. David I. Bushnell, Jr., "Daniel Boone at Limestone, 1786-1787," in *Virginia Magazine of History and Biography*, XXV (1917), 1-4.
[26] Bushnell, "Daniel Boone," 1-5. Boone to Patterson and Trotter, March 16, 1787, Draper MSS. 26 C 176-76(1). Statement of Solomon Clark, Draper MSS. 9 CC 3-4.

what I do for the best it is not worth my while to put my self to all this trubel."[27]

Before going further with the exchange of prisoners, Logan wrote to Governor Randolph asking for any directions that he might wish to give in regard to a possible treaty with the Shawnee. He told the governor that he had received a "speech" from this tribe and had answered it. It was Logan's belief that most of the people of Kentucky felt that he was the man to handle the negotiations. He told the governor that George Muter, chief justice of the district court, had said that no business with that tribe "could be done by any other person," and that Harry Innes, the attorney general, had added that "no ten men in Kentuckey [sic] would answer as good a purpose to treat with the Shawnies [sic]" as he. Nevertheless, he had learned that Muter and Innes had made a private recommendation of four other men as commissioners to handle all Indian relations for the District of Kentucky. This he considered an unkind action on the part of men who had praised his ability to handle the matter and especially so on the part of Innes, who had offered to serve as his clerk during the negotiations. "But not withstanding these little twists can be made by Indeviduals and Gentlemen of Dis-

[27] Boone to Patterson and Trotter, March 16, 1787, Draper MSS. 26 C 176. (There is a copy of this letter in Draper MSS. 2 MM 7.)

About the middle of March Greenup sent two of the Indian boys from Danville to Lexington in accordance with a request from Patterson. He urged that they be well cared for and made available for the general exchange that was expected to take place in April. On April 30 an officer of the United States army visited Lexington and made the following entry in his diary: "[I] saw two Indian Prisoner boys here, who were brought from Danville, I think for a cruel purpose, which was to be hunted by dogs, to teach them to follow Indians hereafter." The diarist, Lieutenant Eskuries Beatty, may have been correct. It is more probable, however, that he was the victim of a teller of tall tales. He was critical of Logan's invasion of the Shawnee country, and may have been ready to believe anything that he heard about the Kentuckians. (See "Diary of Major Erkuries [Eskuries] Beatty," in *Magazine of American History*, I [1877], 435-36.) Beatty at this time was only a lieutenant. (See Josiah Harmar to Benjamin Franklin, December 23, 1787, Harmar Papers, Letter Book B, 157. See also Greenup to Patterson, March 15, 1787, Draper MSS. 2 MM 6.)

tinktion, let there Reasons Either be self Intrust or prejudice,"
continued Logan, with spelling comparable to Boone's, "it
shall not have that effect on me to neglect any Matter Relative
to Public Business, wherein the Intrust of Kentuckey is so much
depending."[28]

By the end of April more exchanges of prisoners were being
made, but the Indians were brought in only a few at a time
and the process was slow. In the meantime, hostile tribesmen
still were visiting Kentucky. General Charles Scott, a veteran
of the Revolution who had moved his residence to Kentucky,
had a son killed in April, and a man who was accompanying the
boy was slain at the same time. Settlers in the eastern part of
Jefferson County found their position untenable, as did also
those in the northern part of Mercer. The county lieutenant
of Jefferson, Alexander Scott Bullitt, believed that the Shawnee
were in league with the Wabash tribes in the committing of
atrocities. Levi Todd, who held the same position in Fayette
and was closer to the Shawnee, did not think that they were
involved. "I believe," he wrote to the governor, "a door is
open now to bring about a lasting peace with that nation. I
think they might be prevailed upon to move near us, and
depend upon us for the necessaries of Life."

Colonel Josiah Harmar, writing to Secretary of War Henry
Knox, agreed with Todd in placing the blame upon the Wabash
Indians. He suggested the establishment of a military post
"either high up the Wabash or the great Miami," and the
strengthening of his regiment by the addition of four companies of riflemen recruited in Kentucky. If this had been done
it might have promoted better understanding between the
Kentuckians and the United States regulars. Most regular officers felt that Kentucky invasions of the Indian country served
only to aggravate a problem which otherwise might be solved.
The Kentuckians, on the other hand, believed that the regulars

[28] Logan to Randolph, April 14, 1787, *Calendar of Virginia State Papers*,
IV, 266-68. The original is in Executive Papers, Edmund Randolph, April,
1787.

were too few in numbers and too inexperienced in the ways of Indians to provide adequate protection.[29]

Colonel Harmar, stopping at Limestone around the first of May, found Indians camped across the river with six or seven prisoners who were to be exchanged. He crossed over and made a speech to their leader, the Wolf, telling him "that frequent murders were committed in the Kentucky Country by the Indians, & that they would provoke the Thirteen great fires at last to such a degree, that they would send their young warriors & destroy all their nations." The Wolf in his reply insisted that none of these crimes had been committed by Shawnee but "were done by a banditti countenanced by none of the regular tribes."[30]

By the middle of May, Logan was considering going in person to Limestone. He was delayed by an injury, the nature of which he failed to disclose in his letter of May 17 to Governor Randolph. He felt that certain of the Shawnee were involved in some of the raids within the limits of Kentucky, as Bullitt claimed, but agreed with Todd that negotiations would be beneficial. He doubted that the Wabash tribes could be brought to terms until they had tasted defeat.[31]

The proposed meeting with the Shawnee finally was held in the late summer. A message from their leading chief, known to the Kentuckians as Captain Johnny, arrived at Limestone on August 6. On August 10 he appeared in person with some other chiefs, at least fifty braves, and a number of white prisoners. Three days later the Indian prisoners were on their way from Danville to Limestone by wagon. Boone furnished provisions, whisky, and tobacco and kept the Indian guests entertained. There was much feasting and dancing, but care was taken to see that the drinking was not excessive. Boone presented

[29] Todd to Randolph, April 30, 1787, and Bullitt to Randolph, May 16, 1787, *Calender of Virginia State Papers*, IV, 277, 284-85. Harmar to Knox, May 14, 1787, Harmar Papers, Letter Book B, 79.

[30] Harmar to Knox, May 14, 1787, Harmar Papers, Letter Book B, 79-80.

[31] Logan to Randolph, May 17, 1787, *Calendar of Virginia State Papers*, IV, 286-87.

provisions to the Indians in the form of gifts, but careful accounts were kept. These were approved by Logan, paid by the Virginia Council, and charged by that body to the United States.

Among the white prisoners who had been brought for exchanging there was a woman named Sharpe who had been with the Indians for about two years. A person of this sort surely would have rejoiced at the thought of returning to family and friends. Children, on the other hand, might feel differently. One girl, about ten years of age, had been taken when very young. She could not remember her parents and cried when separated from her Indian friends.[32]

When Logan arrived Captain Johnny delivered his speech. He explained that the white prisoners had been widely scattered and that it had required more than two months to collect those whom he had brought with him. Some had been held by Indians who lived as far away as the Wabash, and not all were surrendered at his request. The chief insisted that those of his people who favored a continuation of hostilities against the white man had moved to the Wabash region. "Here [in the old Shawnee country]," he concluded, "[there] will be five little towns of us that will be for peace."

Logan in his reply declared that the Congress had engaged the Kentuckians just as the king of England had engaged the Indians, and that it had been their misfortune to be pitted one against the other. He reminded the red men that the king had lost a war to the Americans and had given away their lands without consulting them. Logan pointed also to the fact that, since the British and Indians together had not been able to defeat the Americans, the Indians alone could not hope to do so. "Brothers," he continued, "let us live in peace, and prevent your old father the king from laughing at us, when we are fighting and destroying one another."

The negotiations that took place at Limestone hardly can be

[32] Extract from *Maryland Journal*, October 2, 1787, Draper MSS. 3 JJ 349. Draper MSS. 29 J 73(3-4); 5 S 190; 6 S 166-67; 7 S 34-38, 55-57; 13 S 158. Bushnell, "Daniel Boone," 5-9.

called a treaty. Nothing more than an exchange of prisoners and expressions of peaceful intentions was involved. The talks, however, were written down and were signed by representatives of both sides. Logan assured the Shawnee that if they remained peaceful their country would never be invaded by Kentuckians. "I am not authorized to treat any further with you," he concluded. "[I] only wish a friendly trade could be carried on between us. I hope what has been said, will be agreeable to you, and you and I will set our names thereto."[33]

All but ten of the Indian prisoners were exchanged. Arrangements were made to send these to Limestone whenever an equal number of white prisoners was brought to that place. The Shawnee were disturbed about not receiving their "prince," probably a nephew of Moluntha, at this exchange. They asked that a young squaw be returned to Danville, and that he be brought to Limestone in her place. Logan refused to comply with this request because of the trouble involved, and also because it would be unfair to the Indian woman to be sent back after having been brought so far on her homeward journey. He assured the Indians that their prince was receiving good treatment and would be sent to Limestone at the next exchange. The meeting ended with Logan secretly doubting the sincerity of the Shawnee and with the tribesmen perhaps equally skeptical about the intentions of the Kentuckians.[34]

[33] *Kentucky Gazette*, August 25, 1787.
[34] *Ibid.* Logan to Randolph, September 24, 1787, *Calendar of Virginia State Papers*, IV, 344.
In addition to his negotiations with the Shawnee, Logan was handed another problem involving an Indian prisoner. Joseph Martin had returned to the Cherokee all of their people who had been taken during the Revolution with the exception of a girl about twelve years old. Her last known residence was with the family of a man named William Whiteside in North Carolina. The Whitesides had moved to Kentucky and presumably had taken the Indian girl with them. Martin, believing their place of residence to be in Lincoln County, asked Governor Randolph to instruct Logan to find the girl in order that she might be returned to her people. When Logan received the governor's message he started an investigation. He found Whiteside, but the girl was not in his possession. He had to report to the governor that, insofar as he could determine, no such Indian had been brought to Kentucky. (See Martin to Randolph, February 10, 1787, and Logan to Randolph, September 24, 1787, *Calendar of Virginia State Papers*, IV, 235, 344.)

CHAPTER XIV

TOWARD STATEHOOD

THE DELEGATES TO THE Fourth Kentucky Convention were elected in August, 1786, according to plan. When September 26, the day set for the opening, arrived, a quorum could not be obtained. Many of the delegates were either with Clark or were preparing to march with Logan. A committee of those present sent a petition to the Virginia Assembly asking for an extension of the time allowed for compliance with the terms laid down in the First Enabling Act. A few delegates met and adjourned from day to day to keep the convention alive.[1]

Lacking anything better to do, some of the delegates decided to conduct an investigation of Clark's recent actions at Vincennes. Forming a committee, they chose Thomas Marshall as chairman. James Wilkinson headed a subcommittee which was to interview Clark. After concluding its work the main committee sent a rather unfavorable report to Governor Edmund Randolph. Clark was charged with enlisting men for a garrison force at Vincennes, with appointing officers to command them, and with seizing the property of three Spanish merchants recently arrived at Vincennes and using this to provision the garrison. All of this, the committee pointed out, he lacked the authority to do. A letter to the governor, written at the same time and signed by some of the members of the committee, approved the idea of a treaty with the Wabash Indians, an idea which had originated with Clark. It was suggested that Clark be removed from the United States Indian Commission because his intemperance had made him unfit for business of that kind. Wilkinson, who is said to have circulated some of the stories about Clark, seems to have been seeking this appointment for himself.[2]

When Logan returned from his Shawnee campaign the Virginia Assembly to which he and John Jouett had been elected as Lincoln County delegates already had convened. After spending a few days putting his personal affairs in order, he set out for Richmond. He carried with him a letter from Caleb Wallace to William Fleming and another from George Rogers Clark to the governor. Clark was reporting on his unsuccessful Wabash campaign and endeavoring to vindicate himself. His letter was addressed to Patrick Henry but, unfortunately for Clark, Henry's term came to an end on November 30. In his place the assembly elected Edmund Randolph, a man who understood less about frontier problems.[3]

While he was in Richmond Logan gave his usual attention to the procuring of ammunition for Kentucky. A commssion composed of Isaac Shelby, Richard Taylor, and Edmund Lyne was established by Virginia to adjust all claims arising out of the expeditions of both Logan and Clark. Logan was named to another commission with James Wilkinson, James Garrard, Green Clay, and Isaac Shelby which was to receive subscriptions for the opening of a road from Lexington to the falls of the Kanawha River.[4]

The assembly received a petition signed by a number of Lincoln County residents asking that their county seat be moved from St. Asaph's to a tract of land less than a mile

[1] Abernethy, *Western Lands*, 324-26. *Bradford's Notes*, 163-66. Green, *The Spanish Conspiracy*, 76. John Logan was one of the delegates who could not be present at this time.

[2] Thomas Green to Governor Telfair of Georgia, December 22, 1786, Draper MSS. 53 J 58-58(2). Draper MSS. 53 J 53, 59-63; 13 S 176-77; 14 S 80-86, 88-91. *Calendar of Virginia State Papers*, IV, 202. Abernethy, *Western Lands*, 322-24.

[3] Draper MSS. 9 J 244. *Calendar of Virginia State Papers*, IV, 213. Hening (ed.), *Statutes*, XII, viii. This was the same Jack Jouett who in 1781 made the famous ride from Cuckoo Tavern to Charlottesville to warn Governor Jefferson and the members of the assembly that the British were near.

[4] *Calendar of Virginia State Papers*, IV, 213. Hening (ed.), *Statutes*, XII, 231-34, 282-83.

away which Benjamin Logan had donated. Although he had
not been present to sign this petition, Logan undoubtedly
agreed with the request which it contained. Having the courthouse and jail so close to his residence must have been annoying. On one occasion the court had ordered that his own house
be used as a temporary prison. Fortunately this order was
rescinded a month later. The assembly complied by incorporat-
ing a town to be called Stanford, a name which the county
court had used several months earlier, and by ordering that a
courthouse and a prison be built in the town. Logan and his
brother John were among the trustees who were named in the
act. It was not, however, until April, 1787, that the court held
its first session at the new location.[5]

While in the assembly Logan served on several committees.
One of these was for the preparation of a bill "directing the
method of taking up estrays in the district of Ky." Another was
to consider a bill for the opening of a wagon road "from State
road to mouth of Little Kanawha." The request from some of
the delegates to the Fourth Kentucky Convention for an
extension of the time allowed for complying with Virginia's
terms for separation was given to a committee of which Logan
was a member. This committee prepared a new enabling act
which was passed by the House of Delegates on December 18
by a vote of 67 to 40. Although the names were not recorded,
it is reasonable to suppose that Logan voted with the majority.[6]

Before Logan started to Richmond he had talked with Clark
about his turbulent Wabash expedition. Soon after his arrival
he made a report to the governor. The garrisoning of Vincennes
by Clark Logan considered a necessary measure if the Indians
were to be kept in a state of fear until a treaty could be

[5] Robertson, *Petitions*, 93-94. Hening (ed.), *Statutes*, XII, 396-97. Draper
MSS. 9 J 185-85(1). Lincoln County Deed Book A, 193-94. Lincoln County
Court Order Book 2, p. 197, and Order Book 3, pp. 2, 5, 81. Logan deeded
twenty-six acres to the county at this time. In 1781 he had offered the county
two tracts, one of ten acres and the other of fifty acres. The former was used
by the court when it met at St. Asaph's, but no deed to it was recorded. The
latter may have included this twenty-six acres.

[6] *Journal of the House of Delegates of the Commonwealth of Virginia, 1786*,
(Richmond, 1828), 8, 97, 106, 123, 125, 129, 137.

arranged. He made no criticism of Clark's seizure of supplies for the use of the garrison troops. Nevertheless, when he was asked by Clark to call a meeting of the field officers of Kentucky and to secure their aid in obtaining provisions for the men at Vincennes, he asserted with perfect justification that he had no such authority.[7]

Logan's service in the assembly caused him to miss an important but by now routine event at home. His sixth child and third son was born on December 16. In honor of one uncle on each side of the family the boy was named John.[8]

Before the information from the Danville committee reached him, Governor Randolph had spoken favorably of the expeditions which Clark and Logan had conducted. He expressed the opinion that they had been necessary for the protection of Kentucky. Randolph had even asked Congress to pay the expenses of both campaigns. They had gone far outside the limits of Virginia, the northwestern boundary of which was now the Ohio River. Congress, however, declined to pay for campaigns which it had not authorized.[9]

In January the convention at Danville finally obtained a quorum and quickly passed a resolution favoring separation on the terms stated in the original enabling act. This scarcely had been completed when the text of the second enabling act arrived. This act extended the time which Kentucky had for deciding upon the question of separation. The new date was January 1, 1789, and the consent of Congress must be obtained by July 4, 1788. The decision was to be made by a new convention whose members would be elected in August and which would meet in September, 1787. This must have been a disappointment to the members of the Fourth Kentucky Con-

---

[7] Logan to Randolph, December 13, 1786, Draper MSS. 12 S 125-26 and *Calendar of Virginia State Papers*, IV, 202.

[8] Draper MSS. 12 C 45(4).

[9] Randolph to President of Congress, January 24, 1787, Draper MSS. 10 S 106-107. There is a copy of this letter in Executive Letter Books, December 1, 1786—December 5, 1788, p. 47. Worthington C. Ford (ed.), *Journals of the Continental Congress* (Washington, 1904-1932), XXXIII, 430n, 441, 449-50. Abernethy, *Western Lands*, 325. Bodley, *George Rogers Clark*, 300-301.

vention, but they could hardly object, for it was they who had asked for the extension. This body immediately dissolved itself and the members returned to their homes.[10]

Before Logan reached home there were Indian troubles in Lincoln County. Horses were stolen and a few settlers were killed. This was believed to be the work of the Chickamauga, a band of Cherokee who had moved farther down the Tennessee but who still were in striking distance of Kentucky. The Kentuckians were confident that it had been these Indians who, in the preceding October, had attacked a company of travelers on the Wilderness Trail between the Big Laurel and the Little Laurel rivers. They had killed twenty-one of the whites and had taken several prisoners. On that occasion the savages had escaped, but this time John Logan, second-in-command in the Lincoln County militia, raised about seventy men and started to follow the trail to their villages. In that part of North Carolina which now is Tennessee he struck a fresh trail. This he followed until he overtook a party of seventeen Indians. John Logan and his men killed seven of these and wounded several more. Although the Kentuckians could not have known it, these Indians were hunters from the friendly Cherokee towns farther up the Tennessee, who believed that they were protected by the Treaty of Hopewell. All of the Cherokee were so angered by this attack that some white traders who were in their towns at the time barely escaped with their lives. Deciding finally to proceed in an orderly manner, the Cherokee registered a complaint with the Indian agent, Joseph Martin, who forwarded it to Governor Randolph.[11]

This news reached the governor before the furor over Clark's

---

[10] Hening (ed.), *Statutes*, XII, 240-43. Abernethy, *Western Lands*, 325-26. Bodley (ed.), *Littell's Political Transactions*, xii-xiv, 17.

[11] Logan to Randolph, April 14, 1787, Draper MSS. 12 S 131-32. Arthur Campbell to William Davies, August 26, 1782, Draper MSS. 11 S 98-103. Campbell to Randolph, March 9, 1787, Draper MSS. 12 S 128-29. Thomas Jackson to Joseph Martin, March 18, 1787, Draper MSS. 12 S 163-65. Martin to Randolph, March 16, 1787, Draper MSS. 12 S 166-67. Martin to Randolph, March 25, 1787, *Calendar of Virginia State Papers*, IV, 261. Draper MSS. 11 J 68-69, 138-39. Green, *The Spanish Conspiracy*, 81-82. *Bradford's Notes*, 183. Draper MSS. 9 J 198(1), 215-216(1); 9 CC 52.

actions at Vincennes had subsided. Randolph wrote to Harry Innes, attorney general for the District of Kentucky, urging him to institute legal proceedings against John Logan. He also notified John Logan that he could expect such action to be taken. "We have reason to believe," Randolph said to Innes, "that the late hostilities committed upon the Indians have roused their resentment." To John Logan he wrote: "The late Expedition against the Indians, said to have been under your Command, has made an impression disadvantageous to the character of this Commonwealth."[12]

Contrary to expectations at the capital, no prosecution of Clark or of John Logan was attempted. In the case of Clark, Harry Innes objected to the fact that an order to take legal action had come from the attorney general of Virginia's eastern district, whom he refused to acknowledge as his superior. He contended that the creation of the District of Kentucky had divided the state into two judicial districts and that neither attorney could give orders to the other. In John Logan's case the order to prosecute had come from the governor. Here Innes sought to show that prosecution would be a mistake. John Logan's action, he contended, had ample justification. The Cherokee who had been attacked had in their possession two horses recently stolen in Lincoln County. They also had a rifle which was identified as belonging to a man who had been killed on the Wilderness Trail. After recounting the crimes which had been committed in Kentucky by the Indians, Innes added a strong statement which later he sought to modify. The western country, he said, if it could not obtain protection from the East, might "revolt from the Union, and endeavour to erect an Independent Government."[13]

[12] Randolph to Innes, May 1, 1787, Harry Innes Papers, Vol. 19, Library of Congress. (Copy in Draper MSS. 10 S 112). Randolph to John Logan, May 1, 1787, Draper MSS. 10 S 112-13. (There are copies of both of these letters in Executive Letter Books, December 1, 1786–December 5, 1788, p. 75.) Randolph to Clark, March 4, 1787, Draper MSS. 53 J 64 or 10 S 107-108.

[13] Innes to Randolph, July 21, 1787, *Calendar of Virginia State Papers*, IV, 321-23. (Copy in Draper MSS. 12 S 151-56). The attorney general at Richmond was James Innes, younger brother of Harry Innes

Except for letters which he wrote to Governor Randolph and to Colonel Arthur Campbell of Washington County explaining and trying to justify his brother's action, Benjamin Logan's only part in the controversy consisted in the sending of a message to the chiefs of the Cherokee nation. This he had been urged by a committee of Lincoln County citizens to do. He made it plain to the Cherokee that John Logan's expedition had not been directed against them but against the Chickamauga. The attack on the Cherokee hunters had been a case of mistaken identity, but the finding of the property of Kentuckians in their possession made it doubtful that they were blameless. Logan warned the Cherokee that they could never live in peace with the white people until they took it upon themselves to restrain the Chickamauga. If this were not done, he concluded, they must expect to suffer the consequences.[14]

About the middle of May, Logan again had occasion to write to the governor about the military situation in Kentucky. He said that twice he had called for a meeting of the county

[14] Logan to Randolph, April 14, 1787, *Calendar of Virginia State Papers,* IV, 266-68. George Muter to Logan, May 10, 1787, *Calendar of Virginia State Papers,* IV, 283. Logan to Campbell, May 18, 1787, *Calendar of Virginia State Papers,* IV, 287. Resolution of Lincoln Committee, *Calendar of Virginia State Papers,* IV, 220-21. Logan's message to the Cherokee as printed in the *Maryland Journal,* August 14, 1787, Draper MSS. 3 JJ 332-34. Draper MSS. 12 S 145-46.

Benjamin Logan's name was used frequently in an argument which continued at intervals for more than a century. In 1806 William Littell attempted to answer charges made by Humphrey Marshall that certain of Kentucky's leaders had sought to separate the District not only from Virginia but from the United States as well. Littell stated that Clark and Logan, who had undertaken their 1786 campaigns for the protection of the people of Kentucky, had been censured by the Virginia executive for so doing. As has been pointed out, it was Clark's actions at Vincennes that were criticized. The only blame that fell upon any member of the Logan family applied to John Logan's Cherokee raid and not to Benjamin Logan's Shawnee expedition.

This may have been an unintentional error on the part of Littell. A later writer, Thomas Marshall Green, took a different view of the matter. He accused Littell of trying to make it appear that Clark and Logan were censured for protecting the people of Kentucky. According to Green, Littell did this in an attempt to show that a separation of Kentucky from the United States might have been justifiable. Benjamin Logan would have been the first to deny that he had been censured, but the charge was not made until four years after his death. See Bodley (ed.), *Littell's Political Transactions,* i, 18-19, and Thomas M. Green, *The Spanish Conspiracy,* 82-95.

lieutenants for the purpose of deciding upon "a place to deposite [sic] the Arms and Ammunition allotted for our Country," but for various reasons no meeting had been held. He hoped that a third attempt, which already was planned, would be more successful. Logan mentioned also the disorder which had accompanied some of the elections for representatives in the assembly. This he viewed as "alarming."[15]

In response to letters from Logan and other Kentuckians the matter of Kentucky's protection was laid before the Virginia Council, and copies of the letters were sent to Virginia's representatives in Congress. On June 5 the council sent a directive to Logan authorizing him to call a meeting of the county lieutenants to consider the question of defense. It was stipulated, however, that Kentucky militiamen must "on no occasion go without the limits of the state except in the immediate pursuit of an invading enemy." In an accompanying letter Lieutenant Governor Beverley Randolph warned Logan to "use the strictest economy in the purchase of such articles as may be necessary for the support of the troops called into service," and to take "no steps which may be recommended by any self erected body of men who may assume Powers unknown to the constitution." Congress was asked by the council to use federal troops to relieve the pressure upon the District of Kentucky or to permit Virginia to solve the problem for herself, but at federal expense.[16]

The meeting of county lieutenants which the Virginia Council had authorized Logan to call was held in Danville on July

[15] Logan to Randolph, May 17, 1787, *Calendar of Virginia State Papers*, IV, 286-87.
[16] Harry Innes Papers, Vol. 19, p. 107. Bodley (ed.), *Littell's Political Transactions*, 22-23, 82-83. Beverley Randolph to Logan, June 5, 1787, Draper MSS 10 S 113-14 and Executive Letter Books, December 1, 1786–December 5, 1788, pp. 102-103. Beverley Randolph to Virginia Delegates in Congress, June 6, 1787, and June 29, 1787, Executive Letter Books, December 1, 1786–December 5, 1788, p. 104 and Draper MSS. 10 S 114. Governor Edmund Randolph was in Philadelphia helping to frame a new constitution for the United States.
The last 'e' in the name 'Beverley' does not appear in the published *Calendar of Virginia State Papers*, but because it does appear consistently in the manuscript Executive Letter Books it will be used throughout.

19. All of the counties except Nelson were represented. Objection was raised to the order forbidding militia action beyond the borders of the state, but it was thought best to comply. This council of officers decided that detachments of militia should be kept on duty for defensive purposes and that provisions for them should be obtained by impressment in cases where they could not be purchased. It was agreed also that an application from two or more of the county lieutenants would authorize Logan to call another meeting.[17]

Two days later Congress passed two resolutions which were intended to improve the military situation in the West. The first required that the Continental troops be placed "in such positions as shall afford the most effectual protection to the frontier inhabitants of Pennsylvania & Virginia." Some numbers and locations were mentioned. The only troops which could possibly be of help to Kentucky were three companies at Vincennes, one on the Miami, and a few men at the Falls of the Ohio. The other resolution requested the Governor of Virginia to order the District of Kentucky to furnish militiamen, up to a maximum of one thousand, to act in conjunction with the United States troops whenever the officer commanding the latter should ask for aid.[18]

The commissioners—Isaac Shelby, Richard Taylor, and Edmund Lyne—who had been named to settle the accounts resulting from Clark's and Logan's 1786 campaigns, spent most of the summer of 1787 holding sessions in the different Kentucky towns. Numerous certificates were issued which were understood to be acceptable for the payment of taxes. There were many items which had been supplied for the troops that were not listed in the law covering the furnishing of supplies for the militia. These the commissioners refused to approve for payment. This situation was laid before the Virginia Assembly in a petition signed by Logan and several other citizens and

---

[17] *Calendar of Virginia State Papers,* IV, 344-45. Draper MSS. 12 S 150-51.

[18] Beverley Randolph to Logan, August 14, 1787, Innes Papers, Vol. 19, p. 108. Harmar Papers, Vol. 6, p. 32. Bodley (ed.), *Littell's Political Transactions,* 23-24, 84.

approved by the commissioners themselves. As a result the assembly in its fall session passed an act adding John Steel, Baker Ewing, and James McDowell to the commission and giving it the authority to decide what claims were justifiable.[19]

While this matter was being settled, the question of who was to pay the cost of Clark's Revolutionary campaigns still was being argued. Late in the summer Logan received a letter from the governor asking him to collect all papers pertaining to these campaigns and to forward them to Richmond. This letter was shown to Clark, who wrote to the governor and assured him that all papers relating to the affairs of the Western Military Department had been turned over to the Fleming Commission of 1783.[20]

While Logan was conducting the exchange of prisoners at Limestone, reports came of Indian atrocities to the south. Colonel James Robertson, ranking military officer in the Cumberland settlements, sent him a message asking for aid. Logan sent his nephew Ben Briggs with the reply that he would come as soon as possible. By the time that men were raised Briggs had returned with the news that the Indians had withdrawn and little damage had been done. Instead of forty-three families having been wiped out, as was reported in some of the newspapers, only two persons were killed.

Incidents comparable to this still occurred within the limits of Kentucky. In September, a woman and four children were killed and two persons were captured near English's Station in Lincoln County. In Bourbon County two boys were killed at Limestone and one at Blue Licks.[21]

---

[19] Hening (ed.), *Statutes*, XII, 231-32, 521-22. Robertson, *Petitions*, 100-102. Peter Tardiveau to Beverley Randolph, —————, 1789, *Calendar of Virginia State Papers*, V, 70.

[20] Edmund Randolph to Logan, August 20, 1787, Executive Letter Books, December 1, 1787–December 5, 1788, pp. 150-52. Clark to Edmund Randolph, October 8, 1787, *Calendar of Virginia State Papers*, IV, 346-47.

[21] *Kentucky Gazette*, August 18, 1787, August 25, 1787. Extract from *Virginia Independent Chronicle*, September 5, 1787, Draper MSS. 3 JJ 346-47. Draper MSS. 3 JJ 349-50; 9 J 201. Samuel McDowell to Arthur Campbell, September 23, 1787, Draper MSS. 9 DD 46. Logan to Edmund Randolph, September 24, 1787, *Calendar of Virginia State Papers*, IV, 344.

The years 1786 and 1787 were filled with activity, but Benjamin Logan did not neglect his obligations to the Transylvania Seminary. In 1786 he served on a committee which recommended terms under which the lands of that institution were to be leased. In the following year he was a member of another committee which drew up a petition to the assembly asking that one-sixth of all surveyors' fees paid within the District of Kentucky be set aside for the support of Transylvania instead of going to William and Mary as then was the case. This brought quick action from the assembly, which in December passed the desired measure.[22]

The elections for delegates to the Fifth Kentucky Convention had been held in August, 1787. The members, including Ben and John Logan, assembled at Danville on September 5. The two acts of the Virginia Assembly relating to separation, a letter of June 5, 1787, from Lieutenant Governor Beverley Randolph to Benjamin Logan regarding the use of the militia, and various other papers pertaining to the District of Kentucky were laid before the committee of the whole. The Cumberland settlements sent two representatives to investigate the possibility of joining Kentucky. Some of the members of the convention discussed the matter with them privately, but no official action was taken.

On September 22, with only one absent, all of the members present voted in favor of separation from Virginia in accordance with the terms of the Second Enabling Act. It was recommended that another convention be elected in April, 1788, for the purpose of drafting a constitution. This convention would meet at Danville on the fourth Monday in July. December 31, 1788, was named as the day when the authority of Virginia over the District of Kentucky should cease. Congress was petitioned for the admission of Kentucky to the Union. Upon the recommendation of the Fifth Convention, the Virginia Assembly elected John Brown, then a member of the state senate, as Kentucky's first representative in Congress.

[22] Hening (ed.), *Statutes*, XII, 642. "Proceedings of the Transylvania Board," 8-13.

One member of some of the previous conventions must have been conspicuous by his absence from the fifth. James Wilkinson had gone to New Orleans with a cargo of tobacco and other Kentucky produce. While there he made an agreement with the Louisiana governor Esteban Miró whereby Wilkinson would promote Spain's interests in the West. He would try to persuade the Kentucky leaders to separate the district not only from Virginia but from the United States as well. The resulting new nation would then make a commercial treaty with Spain and would probably become a Spanish satellite.

Wilkinson had selected a favorable time for launching his scheme. On August 3, 1786, the American Secretary of Foreign Affairs John Jay reported to Congress that a commercial treaty which would benefit the people east of the Appalachian divide was being discussed with the Spanish minister, Diego de Gardoqui. However, the United States would have to forgo the privilege of navigating the Mississippi. Jay thought that if a twenty-five or thirty year restriction upon the use of this river were accepted by the United States, a treaty could be arranged. This proposal was not made public immediately, and it was not until the spring of 1787 that the news reached Kentucky. Protest meetings were held, and feeling ran high. Many Kentuckians looked upon the use of the Mississippi as a natural right, as the cost of transporting their produce across the mountains was so great that generally no profit could be made.[23]

In 1788 Virginia was to hold a convention to consider ratification of the proposed federal constitution. A number of the

[23] Samuel McDowell to William Fleming, September 23, 1787, Fleming Papers, Washington and Lee University. Samuel McDowell to Arthur Campbell, September 23, 1787, Draper MSS. 9 DD 46. Beverley Randolph to Logan, June 5, 1787, Executive Letter Book, December 1, 1786–December 5, 1788, pp. 102-103. Extract from *Maryland Journal,* March 14, 1788, Draper MSS. 3 JJ 364-65. *Kentucky Gazette,* November 17, 1787, March 1, 1788. Abernethy, Western Lands, 321-31. Bodley (ed.), *Littell's Political Transactions,* xiv-xvi, xxi-xxii, xl-xliv, 17-18, 24-26, 84-85, 87. Collins, *History of Kentucky,* I, 354. William R. Shepherd, "Wilkinson and the Beginnings of the Spanish Conspiracy," in *American Historical Review,* IX (1903-1904), 494. Draper MSS. 11 J 79, 82, 157.

leading men in Kentucky saw objections to this document and feared its effect upon the West. One member of this group was Benjamin Logan. On February 29 Logan, Samuel McDowell, Caleb Wallace, George Muter, Benjamin Sebastian, Harry Innes, Christopher Greenup, and Thomas Allin addressed a letter upon this subject to the county court of Fayette. It was suggested that at the March court the people of that county elect three representatives to meet with the representatives of the other counties at Danville on the first Monday in April "to consider the proposed Federal Constitution, & if necessary to instruct our delegates to the state convention."

It is probable that copies of this letter were sent to the courts of the other counties and that it had the desired effect. Delegates to the Virginia convention, including John Logan and Henry Pawling from Lincoln County, were elected in April. In Richmond on June 25 they had their opportunity to express themselves upon the new constitution. It was ratified by a vote of eighty-eight to seventy-eight, but ten of the fourteen Kentucky delegates had voted against it, and one, Notley Conn of Bourbon County, had failed to vote. The only Kentuckians who favored the document were the two delegates from Jefferson County, Robert Breckinridge and Rice Bullock, and Humphrey Marshall of Fayette.

The reasons which Logan, McDowell, and the other signers of the letter gave for their opposition to the constitution are worthy of some consideration. They feared that with the federal government empowered to regulate commerce the right to use the Mississippi as a commercial outlet would never be gained. As a result the value of Kentucky land would decrease, and people would cease to move west of the mountains. They disliked also the clause forbidding a state to place a duty on goods imported from another state. They believed that without this right Kentucky, when she became a separate state, would be unable to encourage manufacturing within her borders, and her wealth would flow to other states. There was also in the minds of the letter writers the fear that this document gave the central authority too much power over the militia. At times Kentucky might be at the mercy of the Indians while her men were being forced to do duty elsewhere. A fourth objection was to the establishment of a supreme court, which would sit at a great distance from Kentucky and before which it was believed that land titles might have to be defended. The establishment of lower federal courts evidently was not expected in the near future. Although they did not say so in their letter, some of the signers believed that the constitution should contain a bill of rights. The new constitution did not injure Kentucky, but those Kentuckians who feared that it might do so were quite right in pointing out their objections.[24]

It was also on February 29 that Kentucky's progress toward statehood was furthered by the presentation to the Congress of the Fifth Convention's petition for statehood. The matter was referred to the committee of the whole, which registered its approval. A smaller committee was then assigned the task of preparing a bill. Thus, when Benjamin Logan and the other delegates to the Sixth Kentucky Convention were elected in April, it appeared that statehood was assured and that the principal work of this convention would be the writing of a constitution.

When the members assembled on July 28, no news of further action by Congress had arrived. This information, however, was not long delayed. A message was received by the president of the convention, Samuel McDowell, stating that Congress, after several postponements, had decided to leave the question of Kentucky's statehood to the government soon to be established under the new constitution. This was a blow to most of the delegates. There was, however, one member of the

---

[24] McDowell, *et al.* to Court of Fayette, February 29, 1788, Draper MSS. 11 J 182-82(2). Draper MSS. 31 S 342. Abernethy, *Western Lands,* 346. Collins, *History of Kentucky,* I, 21, 355. Mrs. W. T. Fowler, "Captain John Fowler of Kentucky and Virginia," in *Register of the Kentucky State Historical Society,* XXXVII (1939), 264. Charles Gano Talbert, "Kentuckians in the Virginia Convention of 1788," in *Register of the Kentucky Historical Society,* LVIII (1960), 187-93.

convention who must have been well pleased. James Wilkinson, whether he expected to detach Kentucky from the United States or merely to keep the Spanish officials believing that he would do so, now had a more fertile field to cultivate.

While this convention was still in session, its president gave the members some information which he had received from Kentucky's representative in Congress, John Brown. According to Brown, the Spanish minister Gardoqui had stated that he was empowered to grant to the Westerners the much desired use of the Mississippi. This, however, he would be prevented from doing by Spain's commercial treaties with other nations so long as Kentucky remained a part of the United States.[25]

In the light of all of the information which it had received, the convention on July 31 passed a resolution calling for the election in October of five delegates from each county to meet at Danville on the first Monday in November. This new convention was authorized to "take such measures for obtaining admission of the District as a separate and independent member of the United States of America, and the navigation of the River Mississippi, as may appear most conducive to these important purposes." The convention was empowered also to "form a Constitution of Government for the District and organize the same when they shall Judge it necessary." Then came a clause which, for those who believe that a movement to make Kentucky a separate and independent nation was underway, is full of sinister meaning. The delegates to the next convention were to have the power to "do and accomplish whatever on a consideration of the State of the District may in their opinion promote its interests." This was broad authority, and it was impossible to say what the outcome would be.[26]

Although Logan was in favor of Kentucky's obtaining the

<hr />

[25] Abernethy, *Western Lands*, 347-49. Bodley (ed.), *Littell's Political Transactions*, xxiv-xxxviii, xlvii-l, 26-27. *Bradford's Notes*, 202-205. Collins, *History of Kentucky*, I, 21-22, 355.

[26] "Journals of the Kentucky Conventions, 1788-1792," bound MSS., 106 pp., Kentucky Historical Society, Frankfort, Kentucky, p. A, 4. The page numbers are preceded by letters, A for the Sixth Convention, B for the Seventh, and so forth.

use of the Mississippi, there is little evidence that would connect him with an attempt to separate Kentucky from the Union. It is true that his name is on a list which Wilkinson later sent to Governor Miró indicating the use which he might make of $18,700 he had asked of the Spaniard for bribes, but so are the names of several other prominent Kentuckians. These men were classified according to what Wilkinson said was their feeling about separation and a Spanish treaty. Logan was listed as one who favored "separation from the United States and a friendly connection with Spain." It should be remembered, however, that Wilkinson was in the pay of Spain. He therefore was under an obligation to keep the Spanish authorities thinking that he could deliver Kentucky, if not into their hands, at least to a point where it could be tied by treaties to the Spanish economic system.[27]

Benjamin Logan's time usually was occupied with family, county, and military duties. Early in 1788 he received instructions from the governor to call a meeting of the field officers of the district to consider means of defense against the Indians. This meeting was held in Danville on April 16, but only four of the seven counties were represented. Lincoln sent Colonel John Logan and Major Baker Ewing. Bourbon was represented by her county lieutenant, James Garrard, and her lieutenant colonel, Benjamin Harrison. Fayette sent Levi Todd, who was county lieutenant, and James Trotter, a lieutenant colonel. Mercer was represented by Gabriel Madison, now county lieutenant, and Major Joseph Lewis. Christopher Greenup agreed to serve as clerk.

This council decided that, in line with Virginia's existing

[27] Wilkinson to Miró, September 18, 1789, in William R. Shepherd (ed.), "Papers Bearing on James Wilkinson's Relations with Spain, 1787-1789," in *American Historical Review*, IX (1903-1904), 765. Another copy of this letter has Logan, Isaac Shelby, and James Garrard listed as men who favored "separation from Virginia and an amicable agreement with Spain." (See Bodley [ed.], *Littell's Political Transactions*, xlvi.) It is likely that the Shepherd quotation is the correct one. Bodley has a different group of men listed as favoring "separation from Virginia." His copy also described Logan as "lately a major of militia," while Shepherd's calls him a "recent commander of the militia," which Wilkinson undoubtedly knew to be the case.

militia law, scouts should be ordered out to watch for signs of
Indians and that they should be under the direction of the
county lieutenants of their own counties. Fayette, Jefferson,
and Nelson Counties were to furnish twelve each, Lincoln,
Bourbon, and Madison were to furnish eight each, and Mercer
was to have only six. In order that a force might be ready to
strike on short notice, it was ordered also that one-twelfth of
the militia of each county should be placed on active duty as
rangers. These men would be stationed wherever the county
lieutenants should direct. The counties which were less exposed
or which had larger numbers of militiamen were to furnish
extra rangers for those which were not so favored. It would be
the duty of the county lieutenants to contract for provisions for
the men who were placed on duty. At a special session of the
Virginia Assembly in June, the state treasurer was authorized
to use any required amount up to a maximum of six thousand
pounds per year for the payment of the scouts and rangers.[28]

Even with this system in effect Indians entered Kentucky to
steal and sometimes to kill. Early in May a party was discovered in Fayette and pursued for a long distance. One
member of the party was captured. He was the Shawnee chief
Blue Jacket, who had assisted Captain Johnny with the negotiations at Limestone. The chief made his escape in a few days,
but the incident caused many to doubt the sincerity of the
Shawnee, as Logan had done immediately after his meeting
with them.[29]

About a month later Indians came within a few miles of
Logan's home and killed James Burton and his son Ben, who
were working in a field. A party of twenty-one men, including
Logan's nephew Ben Briggs and Mrs. Logan's brother William
Montgomery, went in pursuit. Crossing the Knobs and entering
the upper Green River valley, they overtook the savages, killed

28 Edmund Randolph to County Lieutenants of the counties comprising the
District of Kentucky, January 8, 1788, Executive Letter Books, December 1,
1786–December 5, 1788, 186-87. Calendar of Virginia State Papers, IV,
427-28. Hening (ed.), Statutes, XII, 645-46.
29 Levi Todd to Edmund Randolph, May 12, 1788, Calendar of Virginia
State Papers, IV, 438.

two of them, and obtained two horses, two guns, and some blankets and kettles.[30]

The greatest difficulty with the system of scouts and rangers was the inability of the officers to obtain provisions. The county lieutenants tried to make contracts as the council of militia officers had directed, but no one could be found who would furnish supplies at the figure of six pence per ration which the government had set. This was partly because a rapid increase in Kentucky's population had put a strain upon the available food supply and thus had forced up the price. At least eighteen thousand people were said to have arrived during the last nine months of 1787, and in the first six months of 1788 over six thousand more came by the river route alone. There were reports of single parties of immigrants which totaled more than one thousand. The total population was estimated at sixty-two thousand. Before the end of the summer, Logan, evidently becoming disgusted with the way the system was functioning, dismissed most of his scouts.[31]

About the same time the field officers of the district held another meeting in Danville and instituted a plan which had been formulated by the assembly. A cavalry troop of thirty-six men was to be attached to each militia regiment. Blank commissions which had been sent out were to be filled by the county lieutenants on the basis of recommendations made by their field officers.[32]

Logan still was faithful in his duties to the Transylvania Seminary. The April meeting of the board of trustees came at the same time as the meeting of the field officers of the district. Both were held in Danville, so that he was able to divide his time between them. At this time John Brown, Robert Todd,

[30] Statement of Ben Briggs, Draper MSS. 9 J 200(1). Extract from *Maryland Journal*, Draper MSS. 3 JJ 390-91.

[31] Josiah Harmar to Henry Knox, June 15, 1788, Harmar Papers, Letter Book C, p. 61. *Calendar of Virginia State Papers*, IV, 456. Extracts from *Maryland Journal*, January 29, 1788 and November 25, 1788, Draper MSS. 3 JJ 362-63, 414. Draper MSS. 18 J 103-104. Barnhart, *Valley of Democracy*, 254-56.

[32] Printed copy of the act of the assembly, Draper MSS. 2 MM 30. Levi Todd to Robert Patterson, August 12, 1788, Draper MSS. 2 MM 46.

and William Ward were elected to fill the places made vacant by the deaths of William Christian, Isaac Cox, and Edward Taylor. Two of the trustees, Samuel McDowell and Caleb Wallace, who also were judges of the supreme court of the District of Kentucky, resigned from the board on the ground that suits involving the seminary might be brought before that court.

On June 9 Logan and five other trustees met in Danville. There not being a quorum, they adjourned until July 29. At the July meeting the chairman of the board was requested to write to the principal surveyors of the District of Kentucky requiring them to turn over to him one-sixth of the fees which they had collected since December 13, 1786. This was in accordance with an act which the Virginia Assembly had passed on that date.

Pursuant to a previous agreement the trustees held their October meeting in Lexington, county seat of Fayette, now the most populous county in the district. Logan arrived on the appointed day, October 13, and was unanimously elected temporary chairman. This was a longer meeting than usual, and he was not in attendance after October 14. It does not appear, however, that he returned to his home. He had just resigned the office of county lieutenant, which he had held for seven years, and the county court had recommended John Logan for the position. This left Benjamin Logan more nearly free of responsibility than he had been at any time since the organization of Kentucky County in 1777.[33]

In spite of the fact that trading with New Orleans supposedly was limited to Wilkinson or to those to whom he gave permission to trade in his name, prices of Kentucky produce were rising. A Spanish merchant arrived in the summer and purchased about fourteen thousand hogsheads of tobacco, which

---

[33] "Proceedings of the Transylvania Board," 13-19. Lincoln County Court Order Book 3, p. 297. Governor Randolph was at this time still writing to Logan as county lieutenant. (See Randolph to Logan, October 20, 1788, Executive Letter Books, December 1, 1786–December 5, 1788, 272.) This would seem to indicate that his resignation had not yet been accepted or was not known to the governor.

he had agreed to furnish to his government. By fall the price of tobacco had risen from twelve shillings to twenty-five shillings per hundred pounds. Wheat was bringing a dollar per bushel and beef was selling unusually well.[34]

It was thought that if produce could be delivered to New Orleans the price would be even greater. It may have been this belief which caused Benjamin Logan to take the risk which he assumed in the fall of 1788. Another determining factor may have been a desire to investigate for himself the possibility of using the Mississippi as an outlet for Kentucky produce.

Whatever the reason, Logan purchased about ninety head of cattle and had them driven to Louisville and slaughtered. He traded the hides for salt and for barrels in which to pack the meat. The exact date of his departure is uncertain, but it seems likely that after doing his duty as a trustee of Transylvania, he went directly to Louisville to supervise the packing of the beef and the loading of the flatboat.

Logan went to New Orleans with his cargo, but accounts given many years later by his relatives and friends differ as to exactly what happened when he arrived. According to one story, his cargo was seized and Logan was thrown into the calaboose, but the more common account is that his beef was purchased at a price which was ruinous to him. Nevertheless, there is general agreement upon one fact. He was asked by some Spaniards when he would bring them another cargo, and Logan replied rather angrily that when he came down the Mississippi with another load of beef he would have with him enough men to eat the entire cargo. The agreement of the various stories would seem to indicate that this was the account which Logan gave upon his return to Kentucky. If it happened as he seems to have related it, it is not surprising that he left New Orleans without further delay.[35]

Logan's trip to New Orleans prevented him from being a member of the Seventh Kentucky Convention which opened

[34] Extracts from *Maryland Journal,* June 24, 1788, and November 25, 1788, Draper MSS. 3 JJ 378-79, 415.
[35] Draper MSS 12 C 45(4); 9 J 203-203(1); 18 S 158; 29 S 103.

at Danville on November 3, 1788. Lincoln County was represented by John Logan, William Montgomery, Baker Ewing,
Nathan Huston, and Willis Green. Samuel McDowell again
was elected president, and James Wilkinson was made chairman of the committee of the whole. Wilkinson read to the
convention a paper which he said was his memorial to the
Spanish government. Actually it was an expurgated copy which
dealt chiefly with the advantages of trade between Kentucky
and Louisiana and said nothing about a separation of Kentucky
from the United States. Naturally, the convention endorsed it.
Wilkinson evidently was expecting someone else to make the
first move, probably John Brown, who had returned from
Congress in time to be one of his county's delegates. Brown
had indicated to Gardoqui that such was his intention, but, as
he later wrote to James Madison, he had a change of heart.
When questioned about his talks with the Spanish minister
Gardoqui he replied in a cautious manner. He then shifted
the attention of the members away from a possible connection
with Spain by moving the adoption of a resolution which stated
that "it is the wish and interest of the good people of this
District to seperate [sic] from the State of Virginia and that
the same be erected into an Independent Member of the
Federal Union." After some discussion, this resolution was
passed and Virginia was asked for a new act providing for a
constitutional convention and extending the time for obtaining
admission to the Union. Wilkinson continued his efforts for
several years, but after the Seventh Convention the likelihood
that Kentucky would become the nucleus of a new nation was
greatly diminished.[36]

Late in December the Virginia Assembly responded with an
act providing for the election of an eighth convention to
consist of five delegates from each of the nine counties, Mason

[36] "Journals of the Kentucky Conventions, 1788-1792," B, 1-15. Abernethy,
Western Lands, 347-50. Extract from *Maryland Journal*, February 6, 1789,
Draper MSS. 3 JJ 435-36. John Mason Brown, *Political Beginnings of Ken-
tucky*, Filson Club Publications Number 6 (Louisville, 1889), 138, 194, 209,
257. Bodley (ed.), *Littell's Political Transactions*, lv-lxiv, cxv-cxvi. Shepherd,
"Wilkinson and the Beginnings of the Spanish Conspiracy," 490-91.

and Woodford having been recently created. It was to meet at Danville on July 20, 1789. This third enabling act differed from the preceding ones in at least two respects. Kentucky was to assume a share of Virginia's public and domestic debt, and land in Kentucky which had been reserved for veterans of the Revolution but which had not been claimed was to remain at the disposal of Virginia. If the terms of the new act were accepted by the July convention, that body was to name a day after November 1, 1790, when the authority of Virginia over the District of Kentucky should come to an end. There was the additional requirement that before September 1, 1790, Congress must have agreed to accept the new state as a member of the union.[37]

When elections for delegates to the Eighth Kentucky Convention were held, Lincoln County chose Benjamin Logan, Isaac Shelby, William Montgomery, Nathan Huston, and James Davis. The men who assembled at Danville on July 20, 1789, had varying views regarding the terms of the Third Enabling Act. There was no reason why Kentucky should not assume a share of Virginia's public debt. Earlier enabling acts carrying this stipulation had been approved. It seems to have been the insertion of the term "domestic debt" which created opposition. If this referred to that part of the state's debt which was owed to her own people, the objections of some of the Kentuckians are understandable. Enough of the state's bonds could have fallen into the hands of speculators to create opposition to helping enrich such men.

In spite of the two objectionable clauses in the act, there were some delegates who wanted it accepted in order to obtain an objective which had been sought for almost five years. To this group Benjamin Logan belonged. Other members either disliked the changed terms or believed that separation should be postponed until the attitude of the new Congress toward the navigation of the Mississippi could be determined. When a vote was taken, separation under the terms of the Third

[37] Draper MSS. 53 J 79. Hening (ed.), *Statutes*, XII, 788-91. Abernethy, *Western Lands*, 351. Bodley (ed.), *Littell's Political Transactions*, 33.

Enabling Act was rejected, the count being twenty-five to thirteen. Logan was placed on a committee which drafted an address to the Virginia Assembly asking for a new act more nearly in line with the first and second.

The system of scouts and rangers, for reasons which already have been given, had not worked well, but it is doubtful if many Kentuckians were ready to discard it. This, however, was done for them in a Virginia order dated June 1, 1789, under which the county lieutenants were to discharge all men who were on active duty in either capacity. In case of an Indian attack in the future, word was to be sent to the nearest commander of Continental troops, who would be somewhere north of the Ohio River. Realizing the worthlessness of protection of this kind, the convention appointed another committee to send a remonstrance to the governor and to direct an address to the President of the United States, pointing out the impracticability of the proposed system. It is not surprising that Logan, a veteran of so many Indian engagements and a former county lieutenant, was placed on this committee. The Ordinance of 1787 had provided a plan of government for the Northwest Territory. In January, 1789, its governor, Arthur St. Clair, had negotiated the Treaty of Fort Harmar in which several of the northern tribes had confirmed their earlier cession of much of what is now the state of Ohio to the white man. Nevertheless, it would take several years for the settlement of this region to progress to such a degree that it could provide for Kentucky a buffer against the Indians.[38]

The same committee that prepared the remonstrance to the

[38] Beverley Randolph to County Lieutenants, June 1, 1789, Executive Letter Book, 1788-1792, p. 19. Extract from *Maryland Journal*, October 13, 1789, Draper MSS. 3 JJ 465. *Kentucky Gazette*, August 29, 1789, September 5, 1789. "Journals of the Kentucky Conventions, 1788-1792," C, 1-18. Abernethy, *Western Lands*, 351-52. Bodley (ed.), *Littell's Political Transactions*, 33-34.

Virginia felt that the United States should assume the responsibility for defense against the Indians. A step in this direction was taken when Governor St. Clair and General Harmar were authorized to direct the county lieutenants in Kentucky to employ at federal expense a maximum of eight scouts per county. This was to be done only in time of danger. See Henry Knox to Arthur St. Clair, March 3, 1790, Innes Papers, Vol. 19, no. 111.

governor and the address to the President was asked to consider several resolutions which had been presented to the convention protesting against the use of foreign luxuries. Its members signed an agreement to cease, as of February 1, 1790, to purchase "any imported gauze, silk or lace of any kind." They also would refuse to buy any "imported broadcloth which shall cost more than thirty shillings a yard, or any narrow cloth which shall cost more than fifteen shillings a yard." They agreed to "promote, increase and use the manufactures of the District." This agreement was signed by the fifteen members of the committee, which included in addition to Logan such men as Samuel McDowell, George Muter, George Nicholas, Harry Innes, and David Rice. The group passed seven resolutions of its own urging strict economy, abstention from the use of foreign luxuries, and the manufacture of "the coarser woolens, cottons, linens, tobacco cordage, leather and iron, and the production of salted pork and beef, butter, cheese, soap, tallow, and candles." The resolutions advocated also "the distilling of spirits . . . in such quantities as would be sufficient for general consumption." Four of the resolutions dealt with the proposed formation of county associations, each with an executive committee of seven members. The purpose of these associations would be to further the aims which this committee of the convention had set forth. It was suggested that each executive committee send two of its members to annual meetings which were to be held in rotation at Danville, Lexington, and Bardstown on the fourth Monday in November. Thus it would appear that Logan and the other Kentuckians who had worked so long for political independence favored economic independence as well.[39]

[39] *Kentucky Gazette*, August 29, 1789.

CHAPTER XV

STATEHOOD ACHIEVED

THE VIRGINIA ASSEMBLY complied with the request of the Eighth Kentucky Convention and approved on December 18, 1789, a fourth enabling act which was more to the liking of the Kentuckians. Another convention was to meet at Danville on July 26, 1790, to register the feeling of the people toward separation on these latest terms. If favorable action were taken, this convention was to name a day after November 1, 1791, when Virginia's authority over Kentucky should come to an end. The assent of Congress still was required. If that should be obtained, a constitutional convention was to sit sometime between November 1, 1791, and the day set for the cessation of Virginia's control.[1]

When the Ninth Kentucky Convention met at Danville on July 26, 1790, Logan again was a member. After selecting George Muter as president and Thomas Todd as clerk, the delegates discussed the question of separation under the provisions of Virginia's act of December 18, 1789, at some length. On July 28 the matter came to a vote and was carried. The count was twenty-four to eighteen with Logan voting in the affirmative. It then was agreed that Congress should be petitioned for admission to the Union. If this were granted, new elections were to be held in December, 1791. Each county would choose five delegates and these forty-five would meet on the first Monday in April, 1792, for the purpose of writing a constitution. June 1, 1792, was named as the day on which

Virginia's authority should cease and the new state government should begin to function.[2]

The requests that the Eighth Convention had sent to the governments of Virginia and of the United States for a better system of control over the Indians brought results of varying value. The response of the Virginia executive was an order forbidding the Kentuckians to take any action against the Indians beyond the repelling of "an attack of an enemy within the limits of the State." The county lieutenants were instructed to "issue the most positive orders that no such party shall . . . enter either into the territory of the United States or any Indian tribe." General Arthur St. Clair, governor of the Northwest Territory, was authorized by President Washington "to call upon the nearest counties of Pennsylvania and Virginia for militia not exceeding in the whole 1500 to act in conjunction with the federal troops in such operations offensive and defensive as the said governor and the commanding officer of the Troops conjointly shall judge necessary."[3]

Fortunately for the safety of Kentucky the government of the United States had under consideration measures which eventually were to prove more effective. In the meantime it authorized the reemployment at federal expense of scouts to keep watch along the frontiers. Harry Innes, now judge of the federal district court in Kentucky, was the official to whom this order was sent. In his reply to the secretary of war, Innes gave some figures on damage done by Indians in the district. He estimated that in his period of residence, which was of less than seven years' duration, they had killed fifteen hundred people either in Kentucky or on the routes connecting it with

[1] Hening (ed.), *Statutes*, XIII, 17-21. *Kentucky Gazette*, February 14, 1789. Abernethy, *Western Lands*, 352. Bodley (ed.), *Littell's Political Transactions*, 34-35.

[2] *Kentucky Gazette*, February 12, and April 16, 1791. "Journals of the Kentucky Conventions of 1788-1792," D, 1-16. Abernethy, *Western Lands*, 352. Bodley (ed.), *Littell's Political Transactions*, 35, 113.

[3] Governor Beverley Randolph to County Lieutenants, March 10, 1790, Draper MSS. 10 S 116-117. *Kentucky Gazette*, May 24, 1790. Josiah Harmar to Henry Knox, January 14, 1790, Harmar Papers, Letter Book G, pp. 6-12.

the East. He believed that no less than twenty thousand horses had been stolen, and other property taken or destroyed he valued at fifteen thousand pounds.[4]

The use of scouts was not considered by most Kentuckians to be sufficient so long as they could not meet the Indians on the latter's ground. On July 2 a meeting of interested citizens was held at Danville to consider the question of defense. There may have been no connection, but shortly thereafter the United States decided to replace the scouts with rangers— militiamen who would be on active duty only in time of extreme danger, but who would hold themselves in readiness to move on short notice.[5]

By this time the United States was planning an invasion of the Indian country on the upper Miami and the Maumee. General Josiah Harmar was to plan and to lead the expedition, and the Kentucky militia was to assist and to act under Harmar's direction. Friction between the regulars and the militia was anticipated, but very little was done to prevent it. The Kentuckians, although many of them lacked the military experience acquired by the first settlers in that region, considered themselves superior at Indian fighting to regular United States soldiers and even to the regular officers who commanded them. One Kentuckian said later that at this time it was believed that it took four regulars to equal one Indian, but that one man from Kentucky was more than a match for two Indians.[6]

There was one measure which might ease the tension. Secretary of War Henry Knox had heard that the influence of Benjamin Logan and Isaac Shelby with the Kentucky militiamen was so great that their presence on the expedition, even

[4] Henry Knox to Arthur St. Clair, March 3, 1790, Henry Knox to Harry Innes, April 13, 1790, and Harry Innes to Henry Knox, July 7, 1790, Innes Papers, Vol. 19, nos. 111 and 113.

[5] Henry Knox to County Lieutenants, July 29, 1790, Innes Papers, Vol. 19, no. 116. Bodley (ed.), Littell's Political Transactions, pp. 37, 116.

[6] Statement of John Graves to John D. Shane, Draper MSS. 11 CC 124. Bodley, History of Kentucky, 456-57.

as volunteers, might promote closer cooperation with the regulars and avert possible disaster. Knox wrote to Governor Randolph asking him to use his influence with these gentlemen in regard to their joining the other Kentuckians. On the following day he wrote to General Harmar suggesting that he communicate with Logan and Shelby. Knox outlined to Harmar the trouble which might arise and this possible way of avoiding it. "I therefore submit the idea," he wrote, "that the Governor and you invite those characters to accompany you in the expedition, and that you treat them with the greatest cordiality." Knox enclosed a letter from Congressman John Brown to Logan which presumably contained the same request.[7]

Knox's letter to Harmar did not reach Fort Washington until that officer was on his way to meet the Indians. Governor St. Clair probably did not see the letter. He had left for New York and would not have known of this request unless Knox made it personally there. James Wood, lieutenant governor of Virginia, did write to Logan and Shelby on September 14, 1790. In behalf of the Virginia executive, Wood said, "It has been suggested to the President of the United States, that the intended Expedition may be liable to miscarriage from a Jealousy between the militia and regular troops; but he hopes that such suggestions may be entirely unfounded." Wood went on to say that the President had great confidence in both of them and believed that their presence, even as volunteers, would be important to the success of the campaign. "I am induced to make this communication," he continued, "by the desire of the President, who wishes it to be made through the executive of the state."

This letter may not have reached Logan and Shelby in time for them to join the expedition. Whatever the reason, the fact remains that they did not do so. To the expected trouble

[7] Knox to Randolph, September 2, 1790, *Calendar of Virginia State Papers*, V, 204-205. Knox to Harmar, September 3, 1790, Harmar Papers, Vol. 13, p. 84. See also Draper MSS. 2 W 287; 13 S 2.

between regulars and militia there was added a dispute between two of the ranking militia officers, Colonel John Hardin, county lieutenant of Nelson, and Colonel James Trotter of Fayette. Harmar, after sustaining heavy losses in an engagement with the enemy, was forced to retreat.[8]

This disaster brought some changes in the methods employed in opposing the Indians. The Kentucky delegates to the Virginia assembly sent a petition to President Washington in which they expressed the opinion that neither regulars nor a mixture of regulars and militia was satisfactory. "The confidence of the militia in their own officers," said the petitioners, "can never be . . . transferred to or Reposed in those in the Regular Service." They then suggested the appointment of some militia officers to higher ranks than any then existing in Kentucky. Charles Scott, who had served as a brigadier general in the Continental army and who had settled in Kentucky after the war, was recommended for the rank of major general. It was thought that there should be two brigadier generals, and for this rank Benjamin Logan and Isaac Shelby were suggested.

Washington may have passed this suggestion on to Governor Randolph with some modifications of his own. On December 30 the governor sent to Charles Scott a commission as a brigadier general of militia and placed him in command of the entire District of Kentucky. Thus was achieved a unity of organization which had not existed since George Rogers Clark retired from the Virginia Line more than seven years before. Even in Clark's time it had not been complete, and his lack of direct authority over the militia had at times impaired his efficiency. In the interim Logan, so long as he remained a county lieutenant, was authorized on several occasions to

<hr/>

[8] James Wood to Logan and Shelby, September 14, 1790, Executive Letter Book, 1788-1792, pp. 155-56. Harmar to Knox, July 15, and December 4, 1790. Harmar Papers, Large Letter Book A, pp. 7, 29-37. Extract from *Maryland Journal*, February 4, 1791, Draper MSS. 3 JJ 491-92. Bodley, *History of Kentucky*, 458-61. Kerr (ed.), *History of Kentucky*, I, 381-83. Harmar to John Hardin, Harmar Papers, Letter Book H, 36-37.

convene the field officers of the district, but no constant unifying factor had been in existence. The appointment of Scott must have seemed to most Kentuckians to be a step in the right direction.[9]

One of the leading citizens of the district, George Nicholas, who may have been speaking for others as well as for himself, wrote to John Brown asking that he seek permission from the United States for the Kentuckians to conduct a campaign of their own against the Indians of the Northwest. Nicholas stated that the men would be willing to furnish their own horses and would be satisfied with "about half a dollar a day . . . for everything." He added that he had "reason to believe that all the better kind of people in the district would go, particularly Shelby and Logan."

On March 9, 1791, further unification of Kentucky's military strength was achieved with the creation by President Washington of a Board of War for the district. The President named as its members Charles Scott, John Brown, Harry Innes, Benjamin Logan, and Isaac Shelby. He gave to this board authority to take whatever steps its members felt were necessary to achieve security.

The Board of War held its first meeting at Danville on April 8, with all of the members present. It ordered General Scott to draft any number of militiamen up to a total of 326 privates for a period of sixty days or less and to station them at the most advantageous points along the frontiers of the district. These men were to be obtained according to the percentages usually accepted as being proper for the various counties. An expedition to the north of the Ohio was proposed, and the militia officers were asked to enlist volunteers for this purpose, reporting to the board on the numbers obtained. At another meeting held on May 2 these volunteers were ordered to meet

[9] Draper MSS. 10 S 118. *Kentucky Gazette*, February 5, 1791. Levi Todd to Robert Patterson, March 24, 1791, Draper MSS. 3 MM 31. For the petition of the Kentucky delegates see Charles Scott Papers, University of Kentucky Library.

May 15 at Frankfort on the Kentucky River, where General Scott would take command.[10]

The men of Kentucky responded readily to the suggestion of a campaign against the Indians. On May 17, General Scott with James Wilkinson as second-in-command left Frankfort and marched down the Kentucky River with about eight hundred troops. Logan and Shelby did not go along as Nicholas had predicted, but John Brown, who had been instrumental in getting the Board of War created, went along as a private.

There is some reason for believing that both Logan and Shelby had desired the commission which had gone to Scott. It was not the first time that this sort of thing had happened to Benjamin Logan. When Lincoln County was created he had seen the colonel's commission go to a new arrival, Stephen Trigg, while he had been offered and had refused a commission as lieutenant colonel. In that case it was only six months until Logan, as the new county lieutenant, outranked Trigg.

Governor Arthur St. Clair, who visited Kentucky just before Scott's expedition, said that Shelby had swallowed his pride and was doing "everything to forward the business while Logan has thrown much cold water upon it." Although Logan may have been disappointed, no evidence has been found to indicate that he tried to discourage or hamper Scott's campaign. St.

---

[10] George Nicholas to John Brown, December 31, 1790, in Huntley Dupre (ed.), "Three Letters of George Nicholas to John Brown," in *Register of the Kentucky State Historical Society*, XLI (1943), 6-7. Bodley (ed.), *Littell's Political Transactions*, 38, 117-18. Innes, Logan, and Shelby to Henry Knox, May 20, 1791, copy in Innes Papers, Vol. 19, no. 136. Minutes of Board of War, Charles Scott Papers.

Two days before the members of the Board of War were named, Thomas Jefferson wrote to Harry Innes expressing the wish that George Rogers Clark could be rescued from the obscurity into which his now well-known addiction to liquor had helped to drive him, and brought forward as a military leader in the West. "I know the greatness of his mind," said Jefferson, "and am the more mortified at the cause which obscures it. Had not this unhappily taken place, there was nothing he might not have hoped. Could it be surmounted, his lost ground might yet be recovered. No man alive rated him higher than I did, and would again, were he to become again what I knew him." Unfortunately for Clark, and perhaps for his country as well, the difficulty was not surmounted and the lost ground was not regained. See Jefferson to Innes, March 7, 1791, Draper MSS. 11 J 191.

Clair also remarked that "from what I have heard of Logan's conduct when he was formerly at the head of an enterprise, from persons who were with him, he appears to be as little qualified for command as it is possible [to be]." Here he was referring to Logan's 1786 Shawnee expedition. The killing of Moluntha had been criticized by regular officers such as Harmar, but it was something which Logan could hardly have prevented. Harmar and St. Clair assumed that Scott, who had served both in the Virginia Line and in the Continental army, would be superior to Logan, whose only experience had been with the militia. In the matter of fighting Indians this would not necessarily have been true.[11]

On May 23 Scott's army left its camp opposite the mouth of the Kentucky and headed for the Indian villages on the upper Wabash. The main engagement took place at the village of Ouiatenon on June 1, and the entire campaign was a success. Thirty-two Indian braves were killed, fifty-eight prisoners were taken, and several villages were destroyed.[12]

Although they had been willing to participate in a campaign, most Kentuckians did not enjoy garrison duty. The Board of War soon suggested the erection of two blockhouses on the Wilderness Trail for the protection of travelers, but these and other strategic points would need to be manned, the pay was small, and, as one of the county lieutenants pointed out, a man with a family to support would risk a court martial rather than spend two months in a blockhouse.

On one occasion Innes, Logan, and Shelby, who handled most of the board's work, wrote to the county lieutenant of Mercer, Christopher Greenup, asking why a lieutenant and

[11] Innes, Logan, and Shelby to War Department, May 20, 1791, and Innes to War Department, May 30, 1791, Innes Papers, Vol. 19, no. 136. St. Clair to Secretary of War, May 26, 1791, in William H. Smith (arr.), *The St. Clair Papers* (Cincinnati, 1882), II, 214. Josiah Harmar to Robert Elliott, August 5, 1790, Harmar Papers, Letter Book H, p. 32.

[12] Charles Scott to Arthur St. Clair, June 20, 1791, Scott Papers. *Kentucky Gazette*, June 25, 1791. Bodley, *History of Kentucky*, 466-68. Bodley (ed.), *Littell's Political Transactions*, 38. Dupre (ed.), "Three Letters of George Nicholas to John Brown," 6n.

sixteen privates had not been sent to a new post on the Ohio River, sixteen miles below the mouth of the Kentucky. In this case the report of the lieutenant showed that he and his men did go to the place in question. On their arrival they found that the Jefferson County officers had no orders to provide them with provisions and ammunition, and the people did not seem to want them; so they returned to Mercer County after having been on active duty for seventeen days. Greenup in his reply to the board admitted that he had experienced some difficulty in getting his militiamen to serve along the Ohio and at Drennon's Lick. He doubted, however, if there was any legal basis for punishing those who refused. It was his belief that the authority which had been granted to General Scott had applied only to the campaign and had already expired. This opinion was incorrect.[13]

Toward the end of June, General Arthur St. Clair, who in addition to being governor of the Northwest Territory had replaced General Harmar as commander of the army, wrote to Kentucky's Board of War stating that the President had authorized one or more additional campaigns if the commanding officer considered them necessary. He directed the board to dispatch a maximum of five hundred officers and men to Fort Washington, opposite the mouth of the Licking, for another Wabash expedition. At the same time he suggested that no more guards be sent to the frontiers.

General Scott, who was ill at the time, could not meet with the board but sent his opinion in writing. He doubted that five hundred men would be enough for such an expedition and opposed the plan to remove the frontier guards, at least until the results of the intended campaign were known.

The board, however, ordered that all guards be discharged by July 15 except for those Bourbon militiamen stationed at

[13] Todd to Innes, Shelby, and Logan, June 14, 1791, Innes Papers, Vol. 19, no. 121. Report of Lieutenant Ebenezer Corn, June 6, 1791; Innes, Shelby, and Logan to Greenup, June 11, 1791; and Greenup to Innes, Shelby, and Logan, June 22, 1791; Innes Papers, Vol. 19, nos. 119-123. Draper MSS. 12 C 63.

the ironworks in that county and some Woodford militiamen at Big Bone Lick. At the same time the expedition to the Wabash was ordered to be prepared in accordance with St. Clair's directions. James Wilkinson was to command as a lieutenant colonel and his subordinates, Colonels John Hardin and James McDowell, were to rank as majors. Wilkinson was to be in Lexington on July 12 to appoint the captains. Men who volunteered for this campaign were to furnish their own arms, horses, and provisions for thirty-three days and were to meet at Fort Washington on July 20. However, Wilkinson and some of his men did not start to Fort Washington until July 26.[14]

Wilkinson with his army of about five hundred volunteers left Fort Washington on August 1, made a feint toward the Miami villages, and then marched to the Wabash. Again the Kentuckians were successful. Although only nine warriors were known to have been killed, thirty-two prisoners were taken, two villages were burned, and five hundred acres of corn were destroyed. The returning army reached the Ohio at Louisville on August 21, with only two Kentuckians having lost their lives on the campaign.[15]

In three letters written during the summer and fall of 1791 Secretary of War Knox praised the work of the Kentucky Board of War. He relayed the congratulations of President Washington upon the board's very able planning of Scott's and Wilkinson's campaigns.[16]

[14] St. Clair to Board of War, June 24, 1791, in *St. Clair Papers*, II, 222-23. Scott to Innes, Brown, Logan, and Shelby, June 29, 1791, Innes Papers, Vol. 19, no. 125. Board of War to County Lieutenants of Lincoln, Madison, Fayette, Bourbon, Mason, and Woodford, July 6, 1791, Draper MSS. 3 MM 38-39. Scott, Innes, Brown, and Logan to Greenup, July 5, 1791, Innes Papers, Vol. 19, no. 128. *Kentucky Gazette*, July 16, 1791. Scott, Innes, and Brown to Henry Knox, August 30, 1791, Innes Papers, Vol. 19, no. 137. Draper MSS. 9 J 208.

[15] Extract from *Maryland Journal*, October 7, 1791, Draper MSS. 4 JJ 199. Draper MSS. 11 CC 123-24. Wilkinson's Report, quoted in Bodley, *History of Kentucky*, 469-71. Bodley (ed.), *Littell's Political Transactions*, 38.

[16] Knox to Innes, Logan, and Shelby, June 30, 1791, Innes Papers, Vol. 19, no. 127. Knox to Innes, Brown, Logan, and Shelby, August 3, 1791, and Knox to Scott, Innes, and Brown, September 29, 1791, in Bodley (ed.), *Littell's Political Transactions*, 120-21.

The success of the Kentucky militia against the Indians should have indicated to United States authorities that if another expedition were needed that year it would be better to allow the Kentuckians to operate independently. This, however, was not to be. On November 4, General St. Clair at the head of a force consisting of regulars and Kentucky militiamen was surprised by an Indian army between the Maumee and the Wabash and suffered a crushing defeat. As soon as this was known in Kentucky, General Scott went to Fort Washington with about two hundred volunteers and with the promise that more were to follow. There was a feeling that the Indians might try to capitalize upon their advantage, but this did not occur.

That Logan accompanied these volunteers is uncertain, but St. Clair, who evidently had revised his estimate of Logan, expressed the hope that he would do so. "Should Colonel Logan be of the party," he wrote to the secretary of war, "there will be no doubt as to numbers."[17]

It is not likely that Logan's work with the Board of War required so much of his time as had his duties as county lieutenant. Thus he must have been able to give more attention to his family and his farms. Two more sons had been born, Benjamin on January 3, 1789, and Robert on August 30, 1791. The family now included five boys and three girls. By the time of Robert's arrival, David, the oldest son, was seventeen and William was almost fifteen. Jane, the oldest of the girls, lacked a month of being twelve. A list of taxpayers in the census of 1790 shows that Logan's four brothers, Hugh, John, William, and Nathaniel, and his mother Jane, who must have been about seventy years of age, were living in Lincoln County.[18]

---

[17] Scott to County Lieutenants, November 11, 1791, in *Kentucky Gazette*, November 12, 1791. St. Clair to Knox, November 24, 1791, in St. Clair Papers, II, 269-71. Collins, *History of Kentucky*, I, 23. Dupre (ed.), "Three Letters of George Nicholas to John Brown," 6n.

[18] Draper MSS. 12 C 45(4); 18 S 167-68. Charles B. Heinemann and Gains M. Brumbaugh, *First Census of Kentucky, 1790* (Washington, 1940), 59.

By 1792 Logan was reporting to the tax assessor the owner-ship of eight slaves, six of whom were over sixteen years of age, nine horses, ninety head of cattle, and twenty-five hun-dred acres of Lincoln County land. Some of the land lay along the Hanging Fork of Dick's River. In the summer of 1790 Logan, who had been operating a small grist mill on St. Asaph's Branch, decided to erect another mill on the larger stream. While he may have supervised the construction and later the milling, it is probable that by this time most of the work was done by employees or slaves.[19]

In addition to his own settlement and preemption Logan had purchased claims of various types in Lincoln and other counties totaling more than ten thousand acres. Occasional tracts of land were sold, including, in addition to those already listed, twenty-six acres to the justices of Lincoln County in 1786, fifty-two acres to William Montgomery in 1787, two hundred acres to Jane Montgomery in 1789, thirty acres to Joel Atkins in 1790, two hundred fifty acres to Ben Pettit in the same year, and seventy-two acres to William Montgomery in 1791.[20]

Logan did not give the same attention to the Transylvania Seminary after the trustees began to meet in Lexington in-stead of in Danville. The meeting that he attended in Oc-tober, 1788, was his last. At the board meeting in October, 1792, he was declared to have forfeited his seat under a pro-vision which allowed a member to be absent from no more than three consecutive meetings. James Trotter of Fayette County was elected to fill the vacancy.[21]

Benjamin Logan was fortunate in being able to relax when the opportunity came. Even when the Indian menace was at its height, he loved to join his friends at a dance. One of his

[19] Lincoln County Tax Lists, 1792, Kentucky Historical Society. Lincoln County Court Order Book 3, p. 505. Draper MSS. 29 S 104.

[20] Willard R. Jillson (ed.), *The Kentucky Land Grants*, Filson Club Publica-tions Number 33 (Louisville, 1925), 78-79, 202. Lincoln County Deed Book A, pp. 193, 360, 412, 455-56, 512-13, 515-17.

[21] "Proceedings of the Transylvania Board," 20-22, 49.

militiamen, Hugh Leeper, provided the music with his fiddle. At times these affairs would be ended abruptly by news of Indians being in the vicinity, and the pursuit would start without delay.

Logan was described by those who knew him as a man of great physical strength, just over six feet in height and weighing about one hundred eighty pounds. He showed no hesitation about engaging in the rough-and-tumble fighting which was popular on the frontier, and he usually emerged the winner. His black hair had a tendency to curl as it fell over his slightly rounded shoulders, his complexion was rather dark, and his features were sharp but regular. He generally was quiet, and except on a few occasions exhibited coolness and prudence. John Logan, his brother, is said to have been more polished but also more impetuous.

On Sundays Logan read the Bible and taught the catechism to his children. He had been baptized as a Presbyterian, but one of his children many years after Logan's death expressed the belief that he had not belonged to any church. This would seem to indicate that even after the church reached the Kentucky frontier, he was not very regular in attendance. Ann Logan, on the other hand, seems to have been a very faithful Presbyterian.[22]

So long as the people of Lincoln County alone were making the decision, Logan seems to have been able to win any election that he chose to enter. The selection of delegates for the Tenth Kentucky Convention did not alter the pattern. These elections were held in December, 1791, and Lincoln County chose Benjamin Logan, John Bailey, Isaac Shelby, Benedict Swope, and William Montgomery. The approval of Congress, which several conventions had sought, had been obtained at last, and this was to be the constitutional convention. The act providing for the entry of Kentucky into the Union on

[22] Draper MSS. 12 C 10(10-11), 46(2); 18 S 157, 159, 176-77; 29 S 103-104.

June 1, 1792, had been signed by President Washington on February 4, 1791.[23]

This convention opened at Danville on April 2, 1792. Once again Samuel McDowell was selected as president and Thomas Todd as clerk. Logan again was placed on the committee of privileges and elections, where he had become almost as much a fixture as was Todd at the clerk's table. There were five delegates from each of the nine counties. Among the outstanding members were George Nicholas of Mercer County, Robert Breckinridge, Alexander Scott Bullitt, and Richard Taylor of Jefferson, James Garrard of Bourbon, Isaac Shelby of Lincoln, and Caleb Wallace of Woodford.

Nicholas usually is considered to have been the author of Kentucky's first constitution, but numerous suggestions were made and resolutions offered by the other members. The first draft of this document was reported by the committee of the whole on April 13. After some debate the convention again resolved itself into a committee of the whole, which reported a revised draft on April 18. An attempt to remove Article IX, which protected the institution of slavery, was defeated by a vote of twenty-six to sixteen. Benjamin Logan voted with the majority. Final approval of the constitution was obtained on April 19.[24]

In the convention Logan seems to have belonged to a group that occupied the middle ground between the conservative large landowners, many of them speculators, and the more democratic smaller farmers. The constitution as written does not indicate a complete victory for either extreme, but rather

[23] *Kentucky Gazette*, April 16, 1791, and January 14, 1792. Bodley, *History of Kentucky*, 489n. Bodley (ed.), *Littell's Political Transactions*, 37, 39, 116.

[24] "Journals of the Kentucky Conventions, 1788-1792," E, 1-2. Bodley, *History of Kentucky*, 489. H. V. McChesney, "Sidelights on Kentucky Constitutions," in *Register of the Kentucky State Historical Society*, XLV (1947), 11, 14, 16. George L. Willis, Sr., "History of Kentucky's Constitutions and Constitutional Conventions," in *Register of the Kentucky State Historical Society*, XXVIII (1930), 313, 316. Mann Butler, *A History of the Commonwealth of Kentucky* (Cincinnati, 1836), 207. Pratt Byrd, "The Kentucky Frontier in 1792," in *Filson Club History Quarterly*, XXV (1951), 288-91.

a compromise in which moderate men like Logan, Shelby, McDowell, and Caleb Wallace certainly played a part. The new state was to have a bicameral general assembly with the lower house chosen by the people. In this house the counties would have representation in proportion to their populations. When the people chose their representatives they also were to choose an equal number of electors. These electors would name the governor and the members of the senate. There would be a court of appeals which, as the conservatives desired, would have original jurisdiction in cases involving the ownership of land.[25]

The people of Lincoln County chose William Montgomery, Henry Pawling, James Davis, and Jesse Cravens as their representatives in the general assembly, and Benjamin Logan, John Logan, Isaac Shelby, and Thomas Todd as electors. On May 15, 1792, the electors met at Lexington and selected Isaac Shelby to be the first governor of the state. Among the senators who were elected at the same time was John Logan. Benjamin Logan was soon being discussed as a good prospect for congressman. It may be that it was an understanding of his own limitations which prevented him from becoming a candidate. It is probable also that he objected to spending away from his family the long periods which service in Congress would have required.[26]

The first session of the Kentucky General Assembly opened at Lexington on June 4, 1792. Among the acts which were passed was one which divided the state into military districts. These districts were to furnish such militia units as divisions, brigades, regiments, battalions, and companies. Governor Shelby named Logan as major general in command of the first division. Charles Scott was given the same rank and

---

25 Marshall, *History of Kentucky*, I, 396-98, 401-402. Barnhart, *Valley of Democracy*, 77-79, 82, 91-92, 104-105.
26 *Kentucky Gazette*, May 12, 19, 1792. Hubbard Taylor to James Madison, May 17, 1792, quoted in James A. Padgett, "The Letters of Hubbard Taylor to President James Madison," in *Register of the Kentucky State Historical Society*, XXXVI (1938), 109.

placed in command of the second division. Each division consisted of two brigades. Logan's brigadier generals were John Hardin and Thomas Kennedy, but by the end of the year both of these officers had resigned their commissions. They were replaced by Robert Breckinridge and Thomas Barbee. The brigadier generals in the second division were Robert Todd and Benjamin Harrison. Governor Shelby hardly could have made more suitable choices for his major generals than Logan and Scott. Both were capable military leaders, and both had acquired valuable experience against the Indians which still might be needed.

Logan also was given civil commissions, one as a justice of the peace in Lincoln County, a position which he long had held under Virginia, and the other as a judge of that county's court of quarter sessions. The county court was to consist of five justices, and the court of quarter sessions would have three members. Logan resigned the latter position on November 9 of the same year.[27]

On June 18, 1792, by a joint ballot of both houses of the general assembly John Logan was elected to the office of state treasurer. One week later he resigned from the senate, and that body chose Henry Pawling, then a member of the lower house, to replace him. At a special election ordered by the house on June 27 and held on the third Tuesday in August, Benjamin Logan was chosen to replace Pawling as a Lincoln County representative.

When the second session of the First General Assembly opened on November 5, Logan was present. It was not until November 15 that the committee of privileges and elections got around to the matter of certifying his right to be there, but prior to that time he had been added to this committee

---

[27] William Littell (ed.), *The Statute Law of Kentucky* (Frankfort, 1809-1819), I, 59-62. "Executive Journal, 1792-1796, Commonwealth of Kentucky," 80 pp., bound MSS., Kentucky Historical Society, pp. 2-3, 8, 20, 40. *Kentucky Gazette*, July 7, 1792. Lincoln County Court Order Book 4, p. 95. Logan to Shelby, November 9, 1792, Shelby Family Papers, Vol. 2, no. 771, Library of Congress.

and also to the committee of courts of justice. He served also on committees to prepare an answer to the governor's speech, to prepare a bill "giving further time to the owners of lots in the Town of Stanford to improve the same," and to prepare a bill amending "the act establishing a permanent Revenue."[28]

Shortly after Kentucky became a state, seven more counties were formed. One of these, which was carved out of Lincoln County and which included most of that part of the state which lay west of the Green River, was named in honor of Benjamin Logan.

Kentucky at the time it was founded was allowed four presidential electors. On November 30, 1792, Governor Shelby appointed Richard C. Anderson, Benjamin Logan, Charles Scott, and Notley Conn to serve in that capacity for the choice of a President and a Vice President.[29]

Logan's duties as a major general in the Kentucky militia were comparable to those of the position of county lieutenant, which he had held for so long under Virginia. He now was in charge of the military affairs of half of the state, but the area was little greater than that of Lincoln County at the time of its formation. The population of course had increased, so that there were more militiamen to supervise. This was balanced in part by a decrease in the ferocity of some of the Indian tribes and the gradual migration of others.

Included in Logan's military district was a new settlement on Russell's Creek, a tributary of Green River, which his brother-in-law William Casey had established in 1791. Casey, who had taken part in the rescue of the captives who were taken at Montgomery's Station in February, 1781, later had

[28] Journal of the Senate of the Commonwealth of Kentucky, June, 1792, 31 pp. bound manuscript, Louisville Public Library, pp. 13-14, 21. Journal of the First Session of the House of Representatives of the Commonwealth of Kentucky, 31 pp. bound manuscript, Louisville Public Library, p. 30. Journal of the House of Representatives at the Second Session of the General Assembly for the Commonwealth of Kentucky, 193 pp. bound manuscript, University of Kentucky Library (microfilm), pp. 3, 12, 20, 28, 31, 39.

[29] Kerr (ed.), History of Kentucky, II, 1100-1102, 1109. Collins, History of Kentucky, II, 479. Kentucky Gazette, December 1, 1792.

married Ann Logan's sister, Jane Montgomery. Casey's settlement was located between the Green River and the Cumberland. Being at least fifty miles from the nearest settlement to the north, it sometimes was visited by parties of Indians from some of the southern tribes. Logan believed that a blockhouse on the Cumberland would provide this settlement with some protection and brought the matter to the attention of Governor Shelby. He discussed it also with Casey, who dispatched a letter to the governor expressing his approval of the idea of building such a fortification. "If you can Spare time from Business of a greater moment," he wrote, "I would be under many oblagations [sic] to you if you wod [sic] transmit a line to me by the bearer to Inform me whether there is a probability of it being Erected or not."

Shelby in his reply made no definite commitment. He agreed that such a post had been considered but pointed also to some of the difficulties which would be involved. Chief among these was the existing militia law, under which he was empowered to place militia units on active duty for no more than thirty days at a time. "At least one third . . . of that time," he reminded Casey, "would be spent in Traveling to and from the post." In the following April, when it seemed that the danger to Casey's settlement was increasing, Shelby ordered Logan to send a guard to that vicinity and to make any other arrangements for the protection of Lincoln, Green, and Madison counties that seemed necessary. In compliance with this order Logan had three officers and thirty-nine men on duty for thirty days, one officer and ten men for fifteen days, and fifteen men for twenty days.[30]

On April 8, 1793, Logan reported to Shelby that the northern part of Mercer County, through which the road from Frankfort to Louisville passed, was so thinly settled that the portion of

---

[30] Casey to Shelby, February 12, 1793, Draper MSS. 16 DD 30(1). Shelby to Casey, n.d., Draper MSS. 16 DD 30. "Executive Journal, 1792-1796," p. 26. Bayless Hardin (ed.), "Governor Shelby's Militia Report to the General Assembly of Kentucky—1792," in *Register of the Kentucky State Historical Society*, XXXVI (1938), 355.

the road between Frankfort and Brashear's Creek was unsafe for travelers. He suggested that a guard be placed on the road for the protection of those who had to pass that way as well as for the benefit of the few people who lived in the vicinity.

Shelby immediately ordered Brigadier General Thomas Barbee to "call into service of the State for the term of thirty days, one Ensign, one Sergeant and fifteen privates and to station them amongst the most exposed families on the frontiers of Mercer County."[31]

Indians still were a menace along the Wilderness Trail. It was believed that in most cases they were Chickamauga, and Logan may have talked of a volunteer expedition against their villages in the spring of 1793. One resident of Kentucky, a man named Buford, claimed that preparations for such a campaign were in progress. He circulated the story that Logan was ready to march to the Chickamauga or Lower Cherokee Towns with between 150 and 250 men and that William Whitley, who already had gone in pursuit of some Indian marauders, would join him with a company of unknown size. This story was picked up by William Macklin and carried to Knoxville, where it was communicated to the territorial governor William Blount.

Blount, who was contemplating a treaty with the Chickamauga, wrote to Governor Shelby asking that he stop the expedition if there were yet time. In another letter, addressed to General James Robertson, he asked that Logan be intercepted if he should come through the Nashville region and that he be warned to desist. Blount explained to Robertson that his order of March 28 was still in effect. Under the terms of this order Logan or anyone else might treat any adult male Indian found within fifty miles of a white settlement as an enemy, but beyond that limit they were not to be molested. Shelby in his reply branded the report as having little or no basis in fact. Blount then notified the secretary of war and a representative of the Indians, with both of whom he seems

31 Logan to Shelby, April 8, 1793, in *Register of the Kentucky State Historical Society*, I (1903), 33. "Executive Journal, 1792-1796," p. 26.

to have communicated before, that the report was not well founded.[32]

By the fall of 1793, General Anthony Wayne, who had replaced General St. Clair as commander of the United States Army, was calling for mounted volunteers from Kentucky to take part in another campaign against the Indians. The Kentuckians, lacking confidence in regulars and regular officers, did not rush to volunteer. Wayne then wrote to Governor Shelby urging a draft. Logan and Scott, armed with Shelby's orders, soon had the desired one thousand men ready. "As to proper characters to command them," said Shelby, "Major Generals Scott and Logan stand equally alike in the esteem of the people and have both had considerable experience in Indian wars." By the time these men, under Scott's leadership, had joined Wayne it was so late in the season that nothing could be attempted. The regulars went into winter quarters, and Scott and his men were sent home to wait until spring.[33]

The first session of the Second General Assembly opened at Frankfort on November 4, 1793, with Logan as a representative from Lincoln County. A capitol building not being ready, the meetings were held in the house of Andrew Holmes. Robert Breckinridge was unanimously elected speaker of the house, and Thomas Todd was named as clerk. Logan was placed on the committee of privileges and elections and also on the committee for courts of justice. The former committee made its report on November 7, and on the basis of this report the house of representatives decided that those members who had accepted appointments from the United States as commanders

[32] Blount to Robertson, [April 12, 1793], Draper MSS. 31 S 125. Blount to Secretary of War, May 9, 1793, in Clarence E. Carter (comp. and ed.), *The Territorial Papers of the United States*, IV, *The Territory South of the River Ohio, 1790-1796* (Washington, 1936), 255. Young Ewing to Shelby, May 11, 1793, Draper MSS. 11 DD 19. *American State Papers, Indian Affairs*, I, 448, 451. J. G. M. Ramsey, *The Annals of Tennessee* (Kingsport, Tenn., 1926), 576.

[33] Wayne to Scott, September 18, 1793, in *Kentucky Gazette*, September 28, 1793. Wayne to Scott, September 26, 1793, *ibid.*, October 5, 1793. *Ibid.*, November 16, 1793. Shelby to Wayne, May 27, 1793, Scott Papers, University of Kentucky Library (Extract).

of volunteers had vacated their seats by so doing. This eliminated John Adair of Mercer, Horatio Hall and Notley Conn of Bourbon, William Shannon of Shelby, Charles Ewing of Washington, and David Walker of Fayette. New elections were ordered to be held in these counties.

On November 6 the assembly heard Governor Shelby's message. In a joint ballot taken on November 11, John Logan was unanimously reelected state treasurer. On Friday, November 15, Benjamin Logan was granted a leave of absence until the following Wednesday. A week after his return the house in committee of the whole passed a resolution stating: "That an intermediate court, with general Jurisdiction, civil and criminal, ought to be established . . . and that the Court of Oyer and Terminer ought to be abolished." The House passed this measure by a vote of twenty-one to thirteen, with Logan voting in the affirmative. The representatives suggested also that the courts of quarter sessions should be replaced by circuit courts which should meet quarterly in the respective counties. These should be presided over by one of three judges who should be appointed for the state as a whole. Logan and the other members of the committee on courts of justice prepared a bill to this effect, but no agreement with the senate could be reached at this session. Logan served also on a committee which brought in a bill to prevent the further importation of slaves, but this measure failed to pass to its third reading. The assembly adjourned on December 21.[34]

Several constructive acts were passed at this session of the assembly. Provision was made for clearing a wagon road from Frankfort to Cincinnati, representation of the different counties was reapportioned according to population, and militiamen who served in the blockhouses on the Wilderness Trail were granted the same pay as those called into the service of the United States.

[34] Kentucky General Assembly, House Journal, 1793, 183 pp., bound manuscript, Kentucky Historical Society, pp. 1, 5, 7, 9, 16-18, 26, 41, 59-60, 63-64, 75-77, 88, 183. *Kentucky Gazette*, November 23, 1793.

When the question of salaries for the proposed circuit judges was being discussed, Logan was one of those who favored one thousand dollars per year. This was as much as the governor received, and the figure was soon trimmed to three hundred dollars. A relative of Logan later quoted him as having remarked on the floor of the house that "a judge should be a gentleman . . . [and] few men . . . would be found . . . [who would] agree to behave themselves like gentlemen for $300 a year."[35]

[35] Littell (ed.), *Statute Law*, I, 185, 217-18. Draper MSS. 12 C 47(1-2). Collins, *History of Kentucky*, I, 23.

CHAPTER XVI

INTRIGUES AND INDIANS

THE DESIRE OF THE PEOPLE of Kentucky for the free and unrestricted use of the Mississippi River made some of them willing to listen to any scheme which appeared to have that end in view. On April 27, 1789, Dr. James O'Fallon, a representative of the South Carolina-Yazoo Company, arrived at Lexington. The intention of that company was to acquire and settle a tract of land at the mouth of the Yazoo River. It was expected that it would become independent of the United States and closely allied with Spain. This plan, which contained little promise of a solution to the Mississippi problem, came to nothing, but O'Fallon was not one to be easily discouraged. He married a younger sister of George Rogers Clark, and by the end of 1792 he and Clark were at work on a scheme which might or might not be beneficial to Kentucky, but which was distinctly unfriendly to Spain.[1]

At the time of his marriage O'Fallon was corresponding with the Spanish authorities and claiming to be sympathetic to their interests. While stopping at Crab Orchard on February 18, 1791, he received a dispatch which indicated that the Spanish commandant at Natchez had arrested a man named Phelan in the belief that he was O'Fallon. The doctor was shocked to learn that this would certainly have happened to him if he had gone down the Mississippi. In a letter to Governor Miró, he requested that he be granted a passport "not unworthy [of] the station I hold, and [of] the gratitude which, from every true Spaniard, is due me, for my friendly views." He then added a sentence which deserves some consideration in the light of both past and future events. "This intelligence has reached me . . . while at table with Col. Logan, and such are the sentiments it has excited in me that . . . I judged it becoming of me to disclose them to yourself confidentially." This would seem to indicate that Logan was known to Miró. If such were not the case it is probable either that his first name would have been included or that he would not have been mentioned at all. It is possible that his visit to New Orleans with a boatload of beef in 1788 had attracted sufficient attention to gain him the notice of Miró. If there were no other connection at the time, O'Fallon may have known that Logan's name was on the list of Kentucky leaders and their alleged prices which Wilkinson had sent to the Spanish governor.[2]

It would be interesting to know just what O'Fallon and Logan said while they were "at table," but apparently no records have survived. This may have been their only meeting, but it is more likely that it was one of several in which the two men exchanged views upon the question of how the Mississippi could be opened to the commerce of Kentucky. It may well be that O'Fallon already was thinking of resorting to force. In that case Logan, whose name could rally a considerable band of followers and who had not been too well treated on his own trip down the river, might be a very useful man.

The United States authorities soon became suspicious. On March 19, 1791, President Washington issued a proclamation warning all citizens against any association with James O'Fallon who was "levying an armed force in that part of the state of Virginia which is called Kentucky [which] disturbes the . . . peace and sets at defiance the treaties of the United States with

[1] John Carl Parrish, "The Intrigues of Doctor James O'Fallon," in *Mississippi Valley Historical Review*, XVII (1930-31), 240, 252, 258.

[2] James O'Fallon to Esteban Miró, February 18, 1791, in Lawrence Kinnaird (ed.), *Spain in the Mississippi Valley, 1765-1794, Annual Report of the American Historical Association, 1945* (Washington, 1949), III, 401-402. Shepherd (ed.), "Papers Bearing on James Wilkinson's Relations with Spain, 1787-1789," 765.

the Indian Tribes."[3] If O'Fallon had hostile intentions against the Indians alone, Logan undoubtedly would have been interested, and he might not have been averse to leading men against the Spaniards. At this time Charles Scott had just received his commission as a brigadier general. This would have been known to Logan, who may have felt that Virginia was treating him very shabbily in not giving this commission to him in recognition of his long militia service on the frontier. Washington's proclamation was issued ten days after he named Logan to the Board of War, and the appointment may have changed Logan's attitude and made him hesitant about participating in any scheme that was not approved by the United States.

Whether or not O'Fallon was "levying an armed force" at the time of this proclamation, there is ample evidence to show that he later advocated doing so. He and George Rogers Clark devised a plan in which Clark was to raise an army under the auspices of the newly created French Republic and liberate the French people, who constituted most of the population of Louisiana, from Spanish rule. The plan was transmitted to the French government, where it was favorably received. France already had given some attention to the possibility of regaining Louisiana or at least of aiding the establishment of a republic which would be bound by treaties to France.

When the French minister Edmond Genêt arrived in America, he received a letter from Clark dated February 2, 1793. The former general expressed the belief that he could take the upper regions of Louisiana with four hundred men, and that eight hundred would be sufficient for the capture of New Orleans. He estimated the expenses at three thousand pounds and urged that some naval assistance be provided by France.[4]

For a time Genêt devoted his attention to the dispatching of

[3] *Kentucky Gazette*, May 17, 1791.

[4] Thomas Paine to James O'Fallon, February 17, 1793, Draper MSS. 12 J 60-60(3). Draper MSS. 12 J 59. Frederick J. Turner, "The Origin of Genêt's Projected Attack on Louisiana and the Floridas," in *American Historical Review*, III (1897-98), 653-54, 665.

ships from American ports to attack the enemies of his country. When this practice was rendered hazardous by Washington's neutrality proclamation of April 22, 1793, he sought to further Clark's plan, which could be executed at a safer distance from the seat of government.[5]

Genêt called upon Secretary of State Thomas Jefferson, who was considered friendly to France, and tried to obtain from Jefferson acceptance of the botanist, André Michaux, as a French consul in Kentucky. In this he was not successful, but he showed little hesitation about divulging some of his plans to Jefferson. Genêt even went so far as to say that in Kentucky there were two generals who would be willing to head the expedition. He was careful, however, to give the secretary of state the impression that the men would gather beyond the Mississippi and hence not on American soil.[6]

Even without accreditation as consul, Michaux was sent to Kentucky by Genêt. He carried a letter of introduction to Governor Shelby from Senator John Brown dealing chiefly with his reputation as a botanist. Michaux's instructions, however, directed him to visit the "two generals," Clark and Logan. He was to deliver to them a sum of money which was to be used in making preparations for an expedition against New Orleans.[7]

On September 11, with the French merchant Peter Tardiveau as his interpreter, Michaux called upon Benjamin Logan. It is not possible to know everything that was said, but Logan definitely expressed interest in the enterprise. However, he had just received a letter from John Brown indicating that the

[5] Archibald Henderson, "Isaac Shelby and the Genêt Mission," in *Mississippi Valley Historical Review*, VI (1919-20), 452. Copy of Washington's proclamation in Shelby Family Papers, Vol. 2, no. 858, Library of Congress.

[6] Richard Lowitt, "Activities of Citizen Genêt in Kentucky, 1793-1794," in *Filson Club History Quarterly*, XXII (1948), 256-57, 266n. Justin Winsor, *Westward Movement* (Boston, 1897), 536-38.

[7] Brown to Shelby, June 24, 1793, Draper MSS. 11 J 200-200(1). Affidavit of Charles De Pauw, Draper MSS. 12 J 29-30. Genêt's instructions to Michaux in *Annual Report of the American Historical Association, 1896* (Washington, 1897), I, 934, 995-96.

United States had opened negotiations with Spain on the question of the use of the Mississippi. Brown advised against any hostile action for the present and suggested waiting at least until December 1, 1793, to see what the government might be able to accomplish by diplomatic means. Logan indicated that he was in favor of accepting this advice. He was preparing to visit a farm which he was developing along Bullskin Creek in the newly formed county of Shelby and suggested that other meetings be held after Michaux had visited Clark.

It is very probable that Michaux was carrying a commission for Logan and failed to present it because of Logan's stated desire to await developments. When Michaux called upon Clark he delivered Genêt's letter of July 12, 1793, accepting his services. He also handed him a commission as a major general in the proposed French Legion.[8]

Preparations were made so openly that word of what was going on reached the ears of Spanish officials. Through her representatives at Philadelphia, Spain complained to President Washington about this attempt to persuade citizens of Kentucky to attack the possessions of Spain. As a result Jefferson asked Shelby to warn any persons who might become active in furthering the plan of the illegality of their actions, and to "take those legal measures which shall be necessary to prevent any such enterprise." He spoke also of the impropriety of such a movement at a time when the United States was negotiating with Spain in the interest of the people of the West. Shelby replied that he would "be particularly attentive to prevent any attempts of that nature," but that he was "well persuaded, at present, none such is in contemplation."[9]

By this time Genêt had dispatched Charles De Pauw, whose home was in Kentucky, and three other Frenchmen—La Chaise,

[8] Draper MSS. 12 J 68; 18 S 158-59. "Journal of André Michaux in Reuben G. Thwaites (ed.), *Early Western Travels, 1748-1846*, III (Cleveland, 1904), 38-41, 39n, 40n, 41n.

[9] Jefferson to Shelby, August 29, 1793, and Shelby to Jefferson, October 5, 1793, *Kentucky Gazette*, July 19, 1794.

Gignoux, and Mathourin—on a mission similar to that of Michaux. They were to promote the project in all parts of Kentucky. To Clark they brought blank commissions which he might issue to those whom he selected as his subordinate officers. It was generally understood that Logan, if he would accept, was to be second-in-command with the rank of brigadier general.[10]

Jefferson wrote to Shelby again on November 9, calling these French agents by name, describing them, and relaying the request of President Washington that their activities be stopped. The secretary of state suggested the use of some civil process such as "binding to the good behavior these, or any other persons exciting or engaging in these unlawful enterprises." He reminded the governor that, if other methods should fail, "suppression by the militia of the state has been ordered and practiced in the other states."[11] If Governor Shelby had resorted to the latter method Benjamin Logan would have been in a peculiar position. As a major general of the Kentucky militia he might have been asked to lead a force against men who were engaged in a project in which he himself was somewhat interested.

There are indications that the governor was not opposed to the methods that were being contemplated. When he wrote again to Jefferson on January 13, 1794, he admitted that Clark had accepted a French commission and that De Pauw and La Chaise were declaring that an army would move down the river as soon as sufficient funds had arrived. At the same time Shelby expressed doubt that he had the authority to restrain Kentuckians who might wish to leave the state, adding that he would never "assume a power to exercise it against men who

[10] Shelby to W. Worsley, July 2, 1812, Draper MSS. 12 J 22-22(1). Draper MSS. 11 J 201-208(1). Extract from *Maryland Journal*, January 3, 1794, Draper MSS. 4 JJ 443-45. Affidavit of Charles De Pauw, Draper MSS. 12 J 29-30. Draper MSS. 12 J 25-26. E. Merton Coulter, "The Efforts of the Democratic Societies of the West to Open the Navigation of the Mississippi," in *Mississippi Valley Historical Review*, XI (1924-25), 378. "Journal of André Michaux," 40n.

[11] Jefferson to Shelby, November 9, 1793, *Kentucky Gazette*, July 19, 1794.

I consider as friends and brethren, in favor of a man whom I view as an enemy and a tyrant." He was referring to the king of Spain, using him as a symbol as Jefferson had once used George III of England.[12]

It is not difficult to see that an expedition against Louisiana would have a double appeal for Kentuckians. They could help to liberate the French population from Spanish rule, and in return these people, once they were in control of their own affairs, surely would show their appreciation by opening the Mississippi to Kentucky commerce.

It was on the last day of the year that this joint cause of liberation and navigation gained another recruit. Benjamin Logan, who had waited upon the outcome of the negotiations with Spain until well past the date which John Brown had suggested, wrote to Clark and offered his services. "I have taken my leave of appointments in this state of the United States," said Logan, "and do presume I am at liberty to go to any foreign country I please and intend to do so." There is in this statement a suggestion of bitterness that is unexplained. Logan may have concluded that the United States was never going to accomplish the desired end by diplomatic means. He may have come to believe that the federal government's main interest was in the region east of the Appalachian divide and that the people of Kentucky would have to shift for themselves. How much his decision was based on a feeling that his past services had not been properly recognized it would be impossible to say. In Clark's case this was undoubtedly a major factor.[13]

It was not until January 13, 1794, that Logan's resignation as a major general in the Kentucky militia was accepted, but obviously he considered himself free at the close of the year. No record of the commission that he received has been found. It is likely that this and other significant papers were lost years later when his last residence, then the home of Benjamin

12 Shelby to Jefferson, January 13, 1794, Draper MSS. 55 J 9.
13 Logan to Clark, December 31, 1793, Draper MSS. 55 J 9.

Logan, Jr., was destroyed by fire. He is said to have been made a brigadier general in the French Legion which was then forming in Kentucky. In view of his experience and the rank which he had attained it would hardly be reasonable to believe that he would have accepted less. A dispatch from a friend of Spain to a Spanish official, dated February 1, 1794, treated Logan as second-in-command to Clark.[14]

By this time it was said that one thousand men had been engaged for the enterprise. Clark, however, was advertising in *The Sentinel of the Northwestern Territory*, a newspaper published in Cincinnati, for additional recruits. He offered to those who would enlist 1,000 acres of any unappropriated land which might be conquered. Two thousand acres was offered to "those that engage for one year," and 3,000 acres to those who served for two years or for the duration of France's current war, whichever was less. Those who were not interested in land were promised one dollar per day instead.[15]

Logan, who now made frequent trips to his land on Bullskin Creek, sometimes traveled the additional twenty-five miles to Louisville to confer with Clark about the raising of men and the gathering of provisions. April 15 was being mentioned as the probable day for the army to start down the Ohio.[16]

Governor Shelby's letter of January 13, 1794, to Jefferson was answered on March 29, 1794, by Edmund Randolph, who had replaced Jefferson as secretary of state. Randolph criticized the governor's hesitation and implied that if Kentucky had no law to cover such a situation she had better enact one. He reminded Shelby that Congress recently had empowered the President of the United States to call out the militia of a state for the purpose of suppressing an insurrection or subduing

[14] "Executive Journal, 1792-96," pp. 2-3. Draper MSS. 12 J 25-26. Bodley, *George Rogers Clark*, 346-47. James White to Gayoso De Lemos, February 1, 1794, quoted in Kinnaird (ed.), *Spain in the Mississippi Valley, 1765-1794*, 252-53.

[15] Reprinted in *Kentucky Gazette*, February 8, 1794.

[16] Draper MSS. 11 J 240. Clark to Charles De Pauw, February 7, 1794, Draper MSS. 11 J 241. Extracts from *Maryland Journal*, March 17, 1794, April 16, 1794, and June 6, 1794, Draper MSS. 4 JJ 475-76, 489.

"any combination against the laws which may be too powerful for ordinary judicial proceedings."[17]

The Washington administration had its share of problems in this year 1794. General Anthony Wayne would have to be more effectively supported if his planned drive into the Indian country were not to be the failure that those of Harmar and St. Clair had been. In western Pennsylvania the growing opposition to the whisky tax was attaining dangerous proportions. The situation in Kentucky, however, needed to be corrected at once if trouble with Spain were to be avoided.

On March 31, the secretary of war sent specific orders to General Wayne. He was to reactivate Fort Massac on the Ohio River just below the mouth of the Tennessee. It was to be garrisoned with whatever force he could spare, a blockhouse was to be constructed, and a few cannon were to be sent from Fort Washington. The officer who was to be placed in command must be carefully selected, "a man of approved integrity, firmness and prudence." He was to be given a copy of Washington's recent proclamation forbidding the proposed attack upon Louisiana, and if armed men should appear who were believed to be engaged in that enterprise he was to stop them, by peaceful means if possible, but in any event to stop them.[18]

Fortunately the attempt was not made, and no blood was shed. On May 24 La Chaise, one of the French agents, informed the Lexington Democratic Society that "unforseen events had stopped the march of 2000 brave Kentuckians."[19]

These "unforseen events" seem to have been three in number: the opposition of the federal government, the failure of sufficient funds to arrive from France, and the disavowal of the enterprise by the French Republic through Genêt's successor,

[17] Randolph to Shelby, March 29, 1794, *Kentucky Gazette*, July 19, 1794. *Kentucky Gazette*, July 26, 1794.

[18] Secretary of War to Wayne, March 31, 1794, Draper MSS. 4 JJ 489-92. Bodley, *George Rogers Clark*, 347.

[19] Draper MSS. 12 J 70. The assembled citizens sent a lengthy remonstrance to the President and Congress protesting against Spain's closing of the Mississippi and Britain's incitement of the Indians. See *Kentucky Gazette*, May 31, 1794.

Joseph Fauchet. The new minister was authorized to approve accounts for supplies which had been purchased, but not the bills that might be presented for time or services contributed to the cause.

There is no reason for believing that Benjamin Logan had lost anything but a little time. Certainly his reputation would not have suffered in Kentucky where the double purpose of freeing the French inhabitants of Louisiana and of opening the Mississippi was extremely popular. The long-desired use of the river was obtained with the ratification of the Treaty of San Lorenzo in 1796 and made even more secure by the purchase of Louisiana by the United States in 1803.[20]

Kentucky in 1794 had not been completely relieved from Indian troubles, and John Bradford was carrying a column of Indian news as a regular feature in his *Kentucky Gazette*. On March 11 a company of travelers on the Wilderness Trail was attacked near Richland Creek with the loss of four of its members. By May 15 Governor Shelby had found it necessary to order Major William Whitley, who lived near Crab Orchard, to place some of his militiamen on active duty for a period of thirty days to protect the residents of that area. In August the situation with the northern Indians was improved considerably by their defeat in the Battle of Fallen Timbers. The regulars of Anthony Wayne were assisted by sixteen hundred Kentuckians under General Charles Scott.[21]

A lesser blow was struck at the southern Indians in September. William Whitley with one hundred Kentucky volunteers and Major James Orr with about four hundred militiamen, some from around Nashville and others from the Holston region, fell upon the Chickamauga towns of Nickajack and Running Water and destroyed both. The plunder secured contained enough stolen articles to connect the Chickamauga

[20] Draper MSS. 12 J 71, 75. Bodley, *George Rogers Clark*, 347. Bodley (ed.), *Littell's Political Transactions*, lxxv-lxxvi. Winsor, *Westward Movement*, 541, 554-56.

[21] *Kentucky Gazette*, March 22, 29, July 19, 1794. "Executive Journal, 1792-1796," p. 54. Collins, *History of Kentucky*, I, 24.

with much of the damage that white settlers and travelers had suffered. They were such evident enemies of the United States and so deserving of punishment that the expedition drew very little criticism.[22]

Opinions differed as to what the next step should be. Logan did not believe that the Chickamauga had received sufficient punishment to bring them into a sincere and lasting peace arrangement. On October 11 he inserted in the *Kentucky Gazette* a notice of his intention to lead a volunteer expedition against them. His force was to leave Kentucky on October 25, and he hoped to reach Nashville by November 1. Those who wished to join him were asked to provide their own horses, provisions, and arms. Logan's next step was to send William Whitley and six other men to the Holston country, where they were to obtain canoes, descend the Holston and a portion of the Tennessee, and wait for Logan's arrival.[23]

On October 20 Double Head, a chief of the Chickamauga, sent a peace talk to the territorial governor William Blount. The governor replied that because the tribe wished peace the people of the United States would exhibit no further signs of hostility. Two days later Blount learned of Logan's plans and considered it his duty to warn the Indians. Logan's expedition, he told them, was not authorized by the government. Logan's reasons for his intended action, according to Blount, were that the Chickamauga had caused much blood to be shed along the frontiers and that the Indians had in their possession Negroes and horses that had been stolen from the whites.

Blount advised the Indians that if Logan advanced to their

[22] Valentine Sevier to John Sevier, August 9, 1794, Draper MSS. 11 DD 118. Draper MSS. 31 S 162-63. Extract from *Maryland Journal*, October 31, 1794, Draper MSS. 4 JJ 609. *Kentucky Gazette*, October 4, 1794. James Robertson to William Blount, October 8, 1794, in Ramsey, *Annals of Tennessee*, 617-18. Richard Taylor to James Madison, October 11, 1794, in James A. Padgett, "The Letters of Colonel Richard Taylor and Commodore Richard Taylor to James Madison . . . ," in *Register of the Kentucky State Historical Society*, XXXVI (1938), 333. Winsor, *Westward Movement*, 547.

[23] *Kentucky Gazette*, October 11, 18, and 25, 1794. Draper MSS. 12 C 62(2). John Magill, *The Pioneer to the Kentucky Emigrant*, ed. by Thomas D. Clark (Lexington, Ky., 1942), 67-68.

towns after being warned to desist it would be well for them to remove their families and property to the woods. He urged them to allow their towns to be destroyed rather than to cause additional loss of life and suggested that they deliver immediately to the blockhouse at Tellico all prisoners and stolen property in their country.[24]

The governor then wrote to Logan and to Whitley warning them to turn back. To each he sent copies of Double Head's peace talk and of his own reply, explaining also that he had warned the Indians of the possible attack. The message for Logan was given to Sergeant McClellan, who was sent from Knoxville to the trace leading from Nashville to the Tennessee River which had been followed by Orr and Whitley several weeks earlier and which it was expected that Logan would take.[25]

Logan, however, experienced earlier difficulties. Only thirty volunteers appeared on the appointed day, and he saw that it would be useless to make the attempt. A few men reached Nashville intending to join him there, but they obeyed Blount's orders to return to their homes and seemed pleased to learn of the prospect of peace. Whitley reached the point where he and Logan were to meet without having learned that the enterprise had been abandoned. Blount's letter had not been delivered. He waited a few days, left a note for Logan, and started home. Game being scarce, Whitley and his men experienced great hardship. A man who lived in Lincoln County at the time claimed afterward that the seven had nothing to eat for three days but one raccoon.[26]

Governor Blount met with representatives of the Cherokee

[24] *American State Papers, Indian Affairs,* I, 532-34.

[25] Blount to Logan, November 1, 1794, and Blount to Whitley, November 1, 1794, *Kentucky Gazette,* January 10, 1795. Blount to McClellan, November 1, 2, 1794, and Blount to Secretary of War, November 3, 1794, *American State Papers, Indian Affairs,* I, 533-35. *Territorial Papers of the United States,* IV, 361-62. Draper MSS. 31 S 152.

[26] [James] Winchester to Blount, November 9, 10, 1794, and James Robertson to Blount, November 15, 1794, *American State Papers, Indian Affairs,* I, 539-42. Statement of William Whitley, Jr., Draper MSS. 12 C 62(2-3). Magill, *The Pioneer to the Kentucky Emigrant,* ix-x, 67-68.

and the Chickamauga on November 7 and arranged for an
exchange of prisoners. At that time he had not learned that
Logan had been thwarted. He promised the Indians that if
they did not offer any resistance the United States would pay
them for any damage which Logan might do. By this time,
however, Logan was in Frankfort for the meeting of the general
assembly to which he had been reelected in the spring.[27]

Several acts of importance were passed at this session. One
of these provided for the establishment of the Kentucky
Academy. Another made provision for the opening of a road
from Madison Courthouse to the Hazel Patch, where it would
join the Harrodsburg branch of the Wilderness Road. A third
act repealed all former laws governing the importation of
slaves and forbade them to be brought directly from a foreign
country to Kentucky. Those Negroes brought from other
states must have entered the United States prior to January 1,
1789. This act made possible also the emancipation of slaves
on the death of their owner if the desire was stated in his will.[28]

Prior to the establishment of Kentucky, Virginia had given
some attention to the improvement of the Wilderness Road,
and John Logan had been named as one of the commissioners
to superintend the work. The road still was not suitable for
wagon traffic, and at this session a committee was named to
prepare a bill for its further improvement. Its chairman was
John Adair and two of its members were the Logan brothers,
Benjamin and Hugh. The bill was presented by the committee
but was not passed at this session.

Logan served also on the committee of privileges and elections, the committee for courts of justice, and the committee on
religion. When a member of the house proposed that a record
of the voting on each measure be inserted in the *Kentucky
Gazette* he was one of those who was opposed, although his
reason is not apparent. The motion was defeated by a vote of

---

[27] *Kentucky Gazette*, January 17, 1795, May 17, 1794. Kentucky General
Assembly, "House Journal, 1794," 225 pp. bound MSS., Kentucky Historical
Society, pp. 5, 20.

[28] Littell (ed.), *Statute Law*, I, 228, 231, 241-47.

twenty-eight to eleven. By a joint vote of the senate and house, John Logan was retained in the office of state treasurer. It is to be assumed that two of his votes were contributed by his brothers, Benjamin and Hugh.[29]

[29] Hening (ed.), *Statutes*, XIII, 184-85. "House Journal, 1794," pp. 2-3, 20, 41, 84, 91.

CHAPTER XVII

DISAPPOINTMENT
AND DEATH

BENJAMIN LOGAN LIVED FOR almost twenty years on or near the site of the original settlement of St. Asaph's. He acquired land in other parts of Kentucky, but apparently it was not until 1794 that he gave serious consideration to making a change in his residence. On Bullskin Creek in Shelby County he had purchased the 1,000-acre preemption of Jacob Myers and the 1,400-acre preemption and settlement of Thomas Gibson, the latter from Roger Topp.[1] In 1794 he built some cabins and a grist mill on Bullskin, and at a nearby spring he began to construct a house for his family.

By 1795 Benjamin and Ann Logan were the parents of five sons and four daughters. Their last child, Ann, was born on April 9, 1794, just one day before the twentieth birthday of David, the first son and eldest child. They now were the owners of fourteen slaves, ten horses, and seventy cattle.

The removal to Shelby County was made in March, 1795. The Lincoln County Court in its meeting on March 17 granted to Thomas Johnson "a license . . . to keep a Tavern at the Plantation lately occupied by Genl. Logan."[2] Although Logan was a recent arrival in their county, some of the people of Shelby must have known him personally, and others certainly knew him by reputation. On May 5 they chose him to represent their county in the general assembly.[3]

The first session of the Fourth General Assembly opened at Frankfort on November 2, 1795. Acts were passed to establish district courts which would relieve the court of appeals of all original jurisdiction, to reapportion the seats in the assembly, and to raise the pay of the members of the assembly to nine shillings per day for each day in session. A bill which Logan had helped to prepare in the preceding assembly, providing for the establishment of a wagon road from Crab Orchard to Cumberland Gap, was passed by both houses. In the fall of 1796 the commissioners who were appointed to supervise this work announced that the road had been completed. Wagons carrying up to a ton, if pulled by four horses, could travel the entire distance with little difficulty.[4]

Logan's removal from Lincoln County to Shelby may have been related to his announcement in 1796 of his candidacy for the office of governor. Under Kentucky's first constitution the chief executive was chosen by electors selected by the people. Each county was allowed as many electors as it had representatives in the lower house of the general assembly. In 1792 the electors had chosen a resident of Lincoln County, Isaac Shelby, as governor. Although the Kentucky constitution did not forbid a second term for the governor, the idea might not have been looked upon with favor, and it is not likely that the electors would have selected another Lincoln County man in 1796. If Logan were a resident of another county his chance for the governorship would be greater. He could reasonably expect to gain the support of his new county, and he might retain the allegiance of Lincoln County and of those counties which once were a part of Lincoln.

Logan was a Republican, but so were the other candidates,

[1] Shelby County Deed Book B, pp. 41-42, 196-97, 242-44. *The* [Frankfort] *Palladium*, April 25, 1799. Jillson (ed.), *The Kentucky Land Grants*, 78-79, 202.

[2] Lincoln County Court Order Book 3, p. 130. Shelby County Tax Lists, 1795, Kentucky Historical Society. Draper MSS. 12 C 45(3-4); 18 S 159.

[3] *Kentucky Gazette*, May 16, 1795.

[4] Kentucky General Assembly, "House Journal, 1795," 185 pp., bound MSS., Kentucky Historical Society, pp. 2-17. Littell (ed.), *Statute Law*, I, 275, 298-300, 354-55. *Kentucky Gazette*, November 7, 1795, December 26, 1795, October 15, 1796.

James Garrard and Thomas Todd, and in fact, a majority of Kentuckians. Garrard and Todd had come to Kentucky later than Logan, and both were better educated than he. Todd had served as clerk of nine of the conventions leading to separation and usually performed the same function in the lower house of the general assembly. Garrard, now a Baptist lay preacher, had been county lieutenant of Bourbon and had served under Logan in the Shawnee expedition in 1786.[5]

An interesting question was whether a poorly educated pioneer such as Logan could hold his own against the type of leader who came to Kentucky after the Revolution. Others had fallen behind. Boone had left the state. Harrod had disappeared and presumably was dead. Both Garrard and Logan had prospered economically, but even in this there was a difference, as Garrard owned 38,000 acres of land while Logan now held only 6,000 acres.

The practice of campaigning for office had not been developed to the heights which it was to reach in the days of popular elections. Logan, however, was not averse to expressing his views to the people of a doubtful area. On one occasion he was traveling to the town of Winchester to address a gathering. He came upon one of his own wagons which he had sent to the Knobs region near Mount Sterling to obtain millstones. The wagon had broken down or was mired down. Logan, whose political ambitions had not replaced his interest in his farm and his mill, dismounted and sought to help. Accounts of the event differ. One story indicates that he removed his coat before trying to raise one wheel of the wagon and ruined his shirt in the process of lifting. In another version he removed his shirt as well as his coat and the shirt was so badly chewed by a cow that it was unwearable. Regardless of the

[5] Draper MSS. 12 C 1(10), 45(3); 12 S 139. Allen Johnson, Dumas Malone, and Harris E. Starr (eds.), *Dictionary of American Biography* (New York, 1928-44), VII, 159-60; XVIII, 574-75. Edward Channing, *A History of the United States* (New York, 1917), IV, 164-69. See also Kentucky's first constitution in Humphrey Marshall, *The History of Kentucky* (Frankfort, 1824), I, 396 ff.

accuracy of either story, they agree that Logan "lost his shirt," and that he solved the problem by making his speech with his coat buttoned almost to his chin.[6]

Both Logan and Garrard were named as electors for their counties. Bourbon County had six electors, Shelby only two. Fifty-three electors met at Frankfort on May 17 and cast their ballots. Logan received twenty-one votes, Garrard sixteen, Todd fourteen, and one went to John Brown. Since Brown was not a candidate it is probable that the vote which he received was that of either Garrard or Logan. One or the other may have been just as hesitant about voting for an opponent as about voting for himself.

No candidate had received a majority. Although the constitution did not say that this was necessary, most of the electors felt that such was the intent of its framers. They proceeded to drop the names of Todd and Brown and to take a second ballot. This time Garrard received a majority and was declared elected.[7]

One of Logan's daughters stated many years later that there had been a bargain between the supporters of Garrard and the supporters of Todd. It is true that Garrard appointed Todd to the court of appeals, but this was more than four years later. By that time Garrard had been the winner in a popular gubernatorial contest.[8]

Logan did not claim that a deal had been made by his opponents, but he did feel that he had been wronged, and he was not the man to accept this without a fight. On May 28 he inserted in the *Kentucky Gazette* a notice of his intention to

[6] Draper MSS. 11 CC 92-93. Bessie T. Conkwright, "A Sketch of the Life and Times of General Benjamin Logan," in *Register of the Kentucky State Historical Society,* XIV (1916), 32.

[7] *Kentucky Gazette,* May 14, 21, 28, June 4, 1796. Ethelbert D. Warfield, "The Constitutional Aspects of Kentucky's Struggle for Autonomy, 1784-1792," in *Papers of the American Historical Association, 1890* (New York and London, 1890), IV, 363. Ethelbert D. Warfield, *The Kentucky Resolutions of 1798* (New York, 1887), 61.

[8] Draper MSS. 12 C 45(3). *Dictionary of American Biography,* XVIII, 574-75.

contest the election. Logan declared that the constitution gave the electors no authority to take a second ballot. In this he was correct. Such a provision was made only for the case of a tie. Logan published also a question which he was submitting to Kentucky's attorney general, John Breckinridge: "Had the electors a right under the constitution to proceed to a second ballot, and is James Garrard legally elected?"[9]

The same issue of the *Gazette* carried Breckinridge's reply. The attorney general denied that, in his official capacity, he had any legal or constitutional authority for answering the question. Nevertheless, he was willing to give his private opinion as a lawyer. The electors, he believed, were meant to express the will of the people. They had no right to do anything which would not have been done by the people themselves, unless the constitution expressly gave them such authority. The people, Breckinridge reasoned, would have had no authority for voting a second time. Instead, the person with the highest number of votes would have been declared elected. The constitution said nothing about the electors having the right to do otherwise. He concluded that "Logan was constitutionally elected Governor upon the first ballot, and ought to have been declared and returned as such by the electors."[10]

Nevertheless, the electors had named Garrard, and on June 1 he began to perform the duties of the office. On May 27, Isaac Shelby in a letter to Garrard had congratulated him on being "called forth by your country to succeeed me in office."[11]

The *Kentucky Gazette* devoted much of its space to letters relating to the election. "A Constitutionalist" agreed with Breckinridge's interpretation. George Nicholas, one of the authors of the constitution, writing under the pseudonym "a citizen," implied that Logan had paid Breckinridge for his favorable opinion. Nicholas agreed that the constitution was "silent as to the numbers of electors necessary to elect a

[9] *Kentucky Gazette*, May 28, 1796.   [10] *Ibid.*
[11] *Ibid.*, June 4, 1796. "Executive Journal, 1796-99," Kentucky Historical Society, p. 81. Shelby to Garrard, May 27, 1796, Shelby Family Papers, Vol. 3, No. 1215. Library of Congress.

governor," but approved their action when "in conformity to a practice long established, they determined that a majority of the electors present should concur. . . . Our electoral body have solemnly adopted the rule," he continued, "and why shall an innovation be attempted to gratify the spleen of a disappointed and ambitious man."

"Another Constitutionalist" reminded the other debaters that the First General Assembly had passed a law making the senate, in committee of the whole, the arbiter of disputed elections. The argument continued until August 6, when "A Constitutionalist" wrote the last letter.[12]

The Kentucky senate in 1796 had fifteen members selected at large. They were Alexander Scott Bullitt of Jefferson County, William McClung of Nelson, James Knox of Lincoln, James Davis of Logan, David Standiford of Shelby, Benjamin Helm of Hardin, Green Clay of Madison, John Campbell of Fayette, Hubbard Taylor of Clark, Robert Mosby of Mercer, John Machir of Mason, William Henry of Scott, John Edwards of Bourbon, Robert Alexander of Woodford, and Matthew Walton of Washington. No senators lived within the borders of the four remaining counties, Green, Harrison, Franklin, and Campbell. On November 10, with Edwards, Alexander, and Walton absent, the senate resolved itself into a committee of the whole and Henry was selected as chairman. Bullitt presented a letter from Logan in which he stated his intention to contest Garrard's election under the provisions of the statute which had made the senate the determining body.

The discussions which followed were printed at great length in the *Kentucky Gazette*. The senators did not seek legal advice. According to one Kentuckian, "they thought a Lawyer would not handle the subject fairly."[13]

Bullitt opened the debate with a long speech in support of

[12] *Kentucky Gazette*, June 4, 11, 18, 25, July 9, August 6, 1796. Breckinridge MSS. Vol. 14, pp. 2297-98. Library of Congress.

[13] *Kentucky Gazette*, December 3, 1796. (The Kentucky Historical Society has a copy of Logan's letter attested by the clerk of the senate.) See also Kerr, II, 1100, and James Blair to John Breckinridge, December 10, 1796, Breckinridge MSS. Vol. 14, p. 2367.

Logan's case, reading the twelfth section of the first article of the constitution, which stated the method to be followed in the selection of a governor. It was evident that there was no authorization for the taking of a second ballot except in the case of a tie. Bullitt anticipated the argument that, although the constitution did not empower the electors to proceed to a second ballot in the event of no candidate having a majority, it did not forbid their doing so. He could recall but one precedent. At the first election held after the separation from Virginia he and two other candidates were being considered for the senate. Bullitt received the largest number of votes, but not a majority. The electors "unanimously agreed that he was duly elected to the office of senator."

Bullitt admitted that the practice of taking a second ballot in such cases had once been followed in Virginia. It was abandoned in favor of certifying the candidate who received the most votes. Bullitt then turned to Samuel McDowell, a witness to the proceedings, and asked him to verify the opinion that had just been expressed. Before McDowell could answer, Green Clay interrupted to say that he considered the whole proceeding irregular. Clay insisted correctly that Logan's letter was not a petition, but merely a notice of his intention to petition. The petition itself had been filed with the clerk. This should have been known to Logan's friends in the senate, but apparently it was not. The petition was never brought before the committee.[14]

It was not on the ground of an improper petition that the issue was ended. Clay, Mosby, Taylor, and Campbell argued that the senate had no right to decide a gubernatorial election. McClung, like Bullitt, contended that such a right did exist and that the senate should declare Logan to have been elected. It was brought out in the discussions that even if the proceedings had no constitutional basis they did have a legal basis. A statute which had been enacted by the First General Assem-

14 *Kentucky Gazette,* December 3, 1796.

bly placed contested elections in the hands of the senate for decision. "Another Constitutionalist" had called attention to this law in a letter to the *Kentucky Gazette,* which appeared on June 18, 1796. Clay opposed this point of view with vigor. He admitted the existence of the law in question but declared that it was unconstitutional. He referred to the last section of article twelve in the state constitution. This section read: "All laws . . . contrary to this constitution shall be void." Clay explained that the constitution had forbidden any department of the government to encroach upon the affairs of any other department. This, he thought, was exactly what the disputed law attempted to sanction. It sought to allow the legislative department to interfere in the affairs of the executive department. The logical conclusion to Clay's reasoning would have been to allow a man to decide for himself whether or not he had been constitutionally elected.

His argument, however, may have had some effect, especially upon those members who had not entered into the discussion. When the question was put to a vote the senate in committee of the whole decided that it had no authority to decide a disputed election, and Garrard remained in office. One Kentuckian reported that Logan, who was in Frankfort when this decision was reached, "cursed them all and went home."[15]

Logan believed that he had been denied his legal and constitutional rights. Through the medium of the *Kentucky Gazette* he suggested to the people of the state that they "pursue their own method of proceeding for redress on similar occasions." He listed the names of the senators who had opposed his cause. This information he may have obtained from a favorable member of the senate. If Logan's list is correct it would seem that the senators were diverted from the legal and constitutional aspects of the question by other considerations. The senators who voted to avoid the issue came

[15] *Ibid.,* November 12, December 3, 1796. Constitution of 1792 in Marshall, *Kentucky,* I, 396 ff. Robert Barr to John Breckinridge, December 9, 1796, Breckinridge MSS., Vol. 14, p. 2365.

from counties which lay in a solid block in the eastern portion
of the state, and those senators who wanted to decide the
dispute came from the counties of Shelby, Jefferson, Nelson,
Hardin, and Logan, which lay in a comparable block in
the west. That the views of these men upon a legal or a
constitutional problem would divide them on a strictly geographical basis is highly improbable. Hence it must be assumed
that the senators, instead of answering the question that had
been referred to them, actually had elected a governor. In
doing so they must have voted either for the man whom they
personally favored or whom they believed their constituents to
favor.

One writer has viewed the 1796 election as a struggle
between the conservative planters of the Bluegrass region, who
are said to have favored Garrard, and the more liberal and
democratic small farmers of the Green River country, who are
said to have favored Logan. The outcome is then said to have
been "widely interpreted as an outrageous bit of political deceit
perpetrated by the conservatives who favored Garrard." This
opinion has considerable merit but may involve an over-
simplification. The views of Logan and Garrard were not so
different that the former could be classed as a liberal and the
latter as a conservative. In the constitutional convention
Logan had voted to protect the institution of slavery, a stand
which appealed to the big planters. Garrard had voted against
slavery, which should have endeared him to the small farmers.
The senators did divide geographically on the issue of the
disputed election, but the line of demarcation left planters
such as Bullitt and McClung supporting Logan. To accept this
interpretation it would also be necessary to explain why John
Breckinridge, a leader of the planter group, seemed to favor
Logan. Of course in the case of Breckinridge it may have
been merely a feeling that Logan had been legally elected,
rather than a matter of personal preference.

If Logan had moved to Shelby County because of his desire
to be governor, and if he thought that in so doing he would

retain the support of his old region while gaining that of a new, he had made a mistake. Even James Knox, the senator from Lincoln and over a long period of years the occasional associate of Logan, had voted with the opposition.

Logan's cause undoubtedly was injured by the time that elapsed between the election and the consideration of the matter by the senate. Garrard had by that time been in office more than five months. To have turned him out in favor of Logan would have produced a feeling of unrest which the senators probably wished to avoid.[16]

Although Logan was disappointed he was not through with politics. In the spring of 1797 he again was elected to represent Shelby County in the lower house of the general assembly. At the second session of the preceding assembly the date for the convening of a new assembly had been changed from the first Monday in November to the first Monday in January. Governor Garrard, however, found it necessary to call a special session in November, 1797. As usual Logan was placed on the committees of privileges and elections and courts of justice. A law extending the time for having land grants surveyed and entered was about to expire, and there was a general feeling that this would work a hardship on some Kentuckians. The law had originated in the Virginia Assembly in 1785 and there had been several extensions. Kentucky had followed this example, granting sometimes one-year extensions and sometimes two. At this special session the time limit was advanced another year. A final one-year extension was granted in November, 1798.

The regular session of the Sixth General Assembly was held in January, 1798. The legislators registered their disapproval

---

[16] *Kentucky Gazette*, November 26, 1796. Barnhart, *Valley of Democracy*, 102. Pratt Byrd, "The Kentucky Frontier in 1792," in *Filson Club History Quarterly*, XXV (1951), 289. Lowell H. Harrison, "John Breckinridge and the Kentucky Constitution of 1799," in *Register of the Kentucky Historical Society*, LVII (1959), 210-11. John D. Barnhart, "Frontiersmen and Planters in the Formation of Kentucky," in *Journal of Southern History*, VII (1941), 26. Jillson (ed.), *The Kentucky Land Grants*, 214.

of the new time of meeting and decided to return to the old practice of beginning the sessions on the first Monday in November.[17]

There was at this session an extended debate upon the question of calling a constitutional convention. The eleventh article of the first constitution provided that this question should be submitted to the people at the general election in 1797. If a majority of those who voted for representatives in the assembly were in favor of a convention the assembly was to provide for the taking of a second vote on the same question a year later. If again a majority should be obtained the assembly must call a convention. If in either year the issue should fail to receive a majority vote a convention should not be called until two-thirds of each branch of the legislature should register approval.

Most of the argument centered around the question of whether or not the required majority had been gained in the vote which had been taken in May, 1797. The sheriffs of some of the counties had not understood that a vote was to be taken on the convention issue and thus had not advertised this fact. Returns indicated that 5,820 out of a total of 10,839 people had voted for a convention, but there was doubt as to the accuracy of these figures.

The senate decided to conduct an investigation. This body was believed by the advocates of a convention to be hostile to reform, as its members were chosen by electors and thus did not feel so responsible to the people as did the members of the lower house.

The senate was the main hope of the people of property, many of whom feared a convention. This group saw in the convention movement a desire to emancipate their slaves or even to divide large estates for the benefit of the poor. "Where is the difference," asked John Breckinridge, "whether I am

17 Littell (ed.), *Statute Law*, I, 115, 173-74, 288, 673, 695-96 and II, 44, 185-86. Kentucky General Assembly, "Journal of the House of Representatives at the First Session of the Sixth General Assembly for the Commonwealth of Kentucky," 26 pp., bound MSS., Kentucky Historical Society, pp. 3, 8, 22.

robbed of my house by a highwayman, or of my slaves by a set of people called a convention?"

The senate called several witnesses from the various counties, and their opinions on the vote for a convention and on the total vote cast were sought. From these the senators concluded that a convention had been approved by only 5,576 of the voters and that the total vote cast for representatives in the assembly had been 11,970. On this basis the senate opposed the calling of a convention.

There were also many in the lower house of the assembly who were against a convention. They introduced a resolution to the effect that all those who voted for a representative and did not vote on the convention issue should be counted as voting against it. This would have been constitutional, but it also would have been unfair. Some had failed to vote because they did not know that such a vote was being taken. Logan was among the representatives who defeated this resolution. A bill was then introduced to allow another popular vote to be taken in 1798. On February 10 this bill was passed by a vote of twenty-eight to fourteen. Logan voted in the affirmative. After proposing several amendments, which the members of the house refused to accept, the senators reluctantly agreed to the measure. When a second popular vote was taken in May, a convention was demanded by 8,804 voters out of the 11,853 who voted for representative.[18]

The opponents of a convention should have realized that the required majority of those voting for representatives either had been obtained or it had not. If it had been obtained, then no possible combination of those voting against a convention and those not voting on that issue could have changed that majority by even one vote. This fact seems to have escaped the members of the legislature and some historians as well.

At the same time that the people of Shelby County were voting on the convention issue they elected Logan to another

[18] *Kentucky Gazette*, January 31, February 14, March 7, 1798. Collins, *History of Kentucky*, I, 24-25. Kerr (ed.) *History of Kentucky*, I, 390-400. Harrison, "John Breckinridge and the Kentucky Constitution of 1799," 212-13.

term in the assembly.[19] When this body convened in November it provided for a constitutional convention to meet on July 22, 1799. The delegates were to be elected at the same time as the members of the general assembly, and each county was to have the same number of delegates as it had representatives in the lower house. Two-thirds of the total number of delegates would constitute a quorum. They were to consider "the propriety of altering, amending or re-adopting" the existing constitution.[20]

Several acts providing for the formation of new counties were passed at this session. One of these, carved out of Logan's county, was named in honor of Patrick Henry. Another, formed partly from Shelby County and partly from Franklin County, was named for Albert Gallatin.

A merger of the Transylvania Seminary and the Kentucky Academy, favored by a majority of the trustees of each institution, was approved. The new school was to be known as Transylvania University. Another measure which received final approval on December 22, the last day of the session, provided for the establishment of several secondary schools or academies. Among these was the Shelby Academy, with Logan as one of the trustees.[21]

It was at this session of the general assembly that a set of resolutions criticizing certain acts of Congress commonly known as the Alien and Sedition Acts were introduced by John Breckinridge. These resolutions were passed by the house with only one dissenting vote and by the senate unanimously. The Republican point of view and opposition to President John Adams were very strong in Kentucky.[22]

The protection or abolition of slavery was the most lively topic of discussion just prior to the election of delegates to the

[19] *Kentucky Gazette*, May 2, November 28, 1798.
[20] *Ibid.*, December 26, 1798. Littell (ed.), *Statute Law*, II, 211. *The Palladium*, February 12, 1799.
[21] Littell (ed.), *Statute Law*, II, 200-203, 234, 240-46. *The Palladium*, December 25, 1798. *Kentucky Gazette*, December 26, 1798.
[22] *The Palladium*, November 13, 1798. Bodley, *History of Kentucky*, 549-58. Collins, *History of Kentucky*, I, 25.

constitutional convention. One slave owner, writing in the *Kentucky Gazette,* had this advice to offer to the voters: "Trust none but those who have property of their own to protect, and then we shall not be in danger from the new-fangled doctrines of our noisy emancipators." Benjamin Logan's stand on slavery and his having voted for its protection in the First Constitutional Convention must have been known to his constituents in Shelby County. In May, 1799, they selected him as one of their delegates to the Second Constitutional Convention.[23]

Moving to a new county had not made Benjamin Logan governor, but separation had benefited the Logan family politically. John Logan's position as state treasurer had caused him to move to Franklin County. Benjamin Logan's second son, William, who was now a lawyer, had remained in Lincoln. William Casey, a brother-in-law of Benjamin Logan, was a resident of Green County. All four were elected as delegates to the constitutional convention. This would not have happened if they had remained in the same county.[24]

The delegates met at Frankfort on July 22 and selected Alexander Bullitt as president. Benjamin Logan, who often had served on committees of privileges and elections in the assembly, was given the same assignment in the convention. The existing constitution was read and considered section by section. The changes which were agreed upon included popular election of the governor and the senators. The new constitution also provided for a lieutenant governor. The action of the senate in regard to the preceding gubernatorial contest may have been a factor in causing the election of the governor to be placed in the hands of the people.

Some of the delegates had favored keeping the electoral system but requiring a majority for election. The electors would also have been prohibited from choosing one of their own number as governor or senator. Another suggestion was

[23] *Kentucky Gazette,* December 26, 1798, March 7, May 16, 1799.
[24] *The Palladium,* May 16, 1799. Littell (ed.), *Statute Law,* I, 57-58.

that the governor be chosen by a majority vote of the house of representatives.

William Logan was more active in this convention than his father, his uncle John, or his uncle by marriage, William Casey. He was a leader in the movement to have the senators elected by the people, but he opposed Felix Grundy's suggestion that if no candidate for governor obtained a popular majority the decision should be made by the lower house.

Although he had led the opposition to the calling of a convention and had lost, John Breckinridge had gained in popularity because of his opposition to the Alien and Sedition Acts. He had been elected to the convention and had become one of its principal leaders, exerting himself to see that no drastic changes were made. George Nicholas, one of the authors of the first constitution, had aided Breckinridge in opposing a second convention. Nicholas, however, died in June, about a month before the convention met.

State elections, which formerly had been held during the first week in May, were to be held during the first week in August. The question of another constitutional convention was to be submitted to a popular vote whenever two-thirds of the members of each house of the assembly, within the first fifteen days of any annual sesion, should vote in favor of so doing. Article IX of the original constitution, which provided for the protection of slavery, was retained. The second constitution went into effect on June 1, 1800, just eight years after Kentucky had begun to function as a separate state.[25]

Benjamin Logan may have believed that in 1796 he was favored by more people than any of the other candidates for

[25] Harrison, "John Breckinridge and the Kentucky Constitution of 1799," 225-32. (Harrison confuses Benjamin Logan with his son, William, and thus he credits to the father some accomplishments which were actually the work of the son.) Breckinridge MSS., Vol. 17, p. 2975, and Vol. 18, pp. 3017, 3031. *Dictionary of American Biography*, XIII, 482-83. *The Palladium*, July 25, 1799, August 8, 1799, August 22, 1799. *Thomas Todd* (clerk), *Journal of the Convention* . . . (Frankfort, 1799), 1-50. *Kentucky Gazette*, August 1, 1799, August 8, 1799. Draper MSS. 27 S 55-56. (For the full text of the second constitution see Marshall, *History of Kentucky*, II, 294-316. Collins, *History of Kentucky*, I, 25.)

governor. If the electors provided a true reflection of the general sentiment he had some grounds for such a belief. On the first ballot he had received twenty-one electoral votes as compared to sixteen for Garrard, fourteen for Todd, and one for Brown.[26] Nevertheless, the second ballot, although taken without legal or constitutional authority, indicated that a majority of Todd's supporters had Garrard rather than Logan for a second choice. In a popular election there would be no second ballot. The candidate with the highest number of votes would be declared elected. This thought must have been uppermost in the mind of Benjamin Logan when he decided to become a candidate in Kentucky's first popular gubernatorial election.

After an illness in the winter of 1799-1800, the nature of which he did not disclose, Logan addressed printed copies of his announcement to an undetermined number of voters. "From my long state of indisposition," he said, "I forbore to inform you and others of my fellow citizens in this particular manner, that I am a candidate for the office of Chief Magistrate at the ensuing Election; but having recovered my health, I feel myself now at liberty to give such information. I trust you will communicate it to your acquaintances."

The clause in the new constitution which prevented a governor from succeeding himself would not prevent Garrard from serving one term under the 1799 document. He took advantage of the possibility by announcing his candidacy. Thomas Todd again was a candidate. The fourth contender for the governorship was Christopher Greenup. He had served for seven years as clerk of the supreme court for the District of Kentucky and for five years as one of Kentucky's representatives in Congress. Greenup and Todd each had an advantage over Logan in education. Garrard could point also to four years of experience as governor.[27]

[26] *Kentucky Gazette,* May 28, 1796. Warfield, *The Kentucky Resolutions of 1798,* 61.
[27] Breckinridge MSS., Vol. 18, pp. 3172-73. *Dictionary of American Biography,* VII, 159-60, 589-90; XVIII, 574-75.

Logan's chief political assets were his status as one of the earliest settlers in Kentucky and his leadership in the long struggle against the Indians. These were things which decreased in value with the passage of time. New people constantly were moving to Kentucky, and many young men had reached the voting age since Logan's last Indian campaign in 1786. To these groups his contributions were virtually unknown.

The election was held in May. Garrard received 8,391 votes, Greenup received 6,745, Logan polled 3,995, and Todd got 2,166. Alexander Scott Bullitt won the lieutenant governorship by a plurality of more than 2,400 votes. The returns seem to indicate that Garrard had increased in popularity during his four years as governor.

Although Logan may have forfeited the support of Lincoln and the adjacent counties in 1796 by his removal to Shelby County, he now regained it in part. The seven counties which he carried were Garrard, Harrison, Lincoln, Madison, Ohio, Pulaski, and Shelby. The question of what kind of a governor Benjamin Logan would have made can of course not be answered with finality. He undoubtedly would have required the help of subordinates better educated than he, but so, for that matter, did James Garrard. Harry Toulmin, former president of the Transylvania Seminary who served as secretary of state under Garrard, had great influence in the administration. Writing to Secretary of War Henry Dearborn in 1803, General Charles Scott said of Garrard: "His Secretary is an Englishman and in a very considerable degree our Govorner [sic]." Another Kentuckian said of Garrard in 1802: "The Governor is as unpopular with our Assembly as John Adams would be with congress if now President."[28]

This was Benjamin Logan's last attempt in the political arena. Although he must have been disappointed, he had his family

---

[28] *Kentucky Gazette*, May 29, 1800. *The Palladium*, May 22, 1800. Charles Scott to Henry Dearborn, May 9, 1803, copy in Charles Scott Papers, University of Kentucky Library. James Morrison to John Breckinridge, December 20, 1802, Breckinridge MSS., Vol. 23, pp. 3901-3902.

and his farms to occupy his mind. His eldest son, David, married Nancy McClelland on May 28, 1800. On September 4, of the same year his second daughter, Mary, was married to Abraham Smith, and on January 28, 1802, his second son, William, married Priscilla Wallace, daughter of Judge Caleb Wallace. The Logan family produced one winner in the election of 1800. Hugh Logan was selected as senator from Lincoln County.[29]

Logan continued to buy and sell land. On April 14, 1801, he purchased 4,500 acres on Indian Camp Creek in Ohio County from Nicholas Merriwether.[30] He disposed of some of his Lincoln County land on March 15 of the next year. Three and one-half acres were given to the Buffalo Spring Presbyterian Congregation to be held by that body so long as a house of public worship was maintained thereon. If this requirement were not fulfilled the land was to revert to Logan's sons David and William. At the same time Logan sold 21 acres of land to Samuel Davidson and 115 acres to James Gilmore.[31]

The Logan name still was prominent in Lincoln County politics in 1801 and 1802. Benjamin Logan's brother Hugh was a state senator and his son William was one of the county's representatives in the lower house of the general assembly.[32]

On December 11, 1802, when Logan was in his sixtieth year, he attended a sale at the home of a man named Owen not far from Shelbyville. He and several others remained for supper. While seated at the table Logan suffered a stroke of apoplexy and died instantly.[33]

Benjamin Logan was buried with military honors on a hill overlooking Bullskin Creek in what later became a family

[29] Hattie M. Scott, "The Logan Family of Lincoln County, Kentucky," in *Register of the Kentucky State Historical Society*, XXX (1932), 174. *Kentucky Gazette*, May 22, 1800.

[30] Shelby County Deed Book E, 240-41.

[31] Shelby County Deed Book E, 19, 61-62, 125.

[32] *Kentucky Gazette*, November 6, 1801, August 20, 1802. *Palladium*, August 12, 1802.

[33] Arthur Campbell to Charles Cummings, December 25, 1802, Draper MSS. 9 DD 76. Draper MSS. 12 C 45; 7 S 18; 18 S 43, 144-45, 175, 177. *Kentucky Gazette*, December 14, 1802.

cemetery. The general assembly, which was in session when he died, passed a resolution in favor of the wearing of mourning "in token of that high regard and respect which the people of Kentucky entertain for the memory of the deceased General Benjamin Logan, the firm defender of his country."[34]

In addition to his land, Logan left personal property valued at $3,395. This included nine slaves, nine horses, and forty-one cattle. He left no will, but at a sale held on February 4, 1803, for the purpose of settling the estate, the greater part of the personal property was purchased by his widow.[35]

At the time of his death Logan's children ranged in age from eight to twenty-eight. Ann Logan was fifty-one. Three years later she married James Knox, whom she is said to have rejected more than thirty years earlier. Knox lived until December 24, 1822, and his wife until October 18, 1825.[36]

Although the children of Benjamin and Ann Logan all reached maturity, four of them died before their mother. The youngest son, Robert, was killed in the Battle of Frenchtown on January 22, 1813. David died on September 16, 1816, Jane on February 27, 1821, and William on August 9, 1822. William Logan had been elected to the United States Senate in 1820 but resigned to make what proved to be an unsuccessful race for the governorship. Martin D. Hardin, husband of Logan's daughter Elizabeth, also served as a United States senator.[37]

If Benjamin Logan came to Kentucky to obtain land, he did extremely well. If it were adventure that he sought, he experienced a full share. He was one of a large number of pioneers who brought their families to Kentucky at the earliest opportunity and sought to establish homes as like as possible to those which they formerly had known. As a woodsman and a hunter he had few superiors in Kentucky. As a commander of

[34] Draper MSS. 18 S 175, 177; 12 C 48. *Kentucky Gazette*, December 21, 1802. *Palladium*, December 16, 1802.

[35] Shelby County Will Book 3, pp. 6-7.

[36] Draper MSS. 12 C 45(4); 18 S 164, 174-75. Waddell, *Annals*, 321.

[37] Draper MSS. 12 C 45(4). 18 S 167. *Biographical Encyclopaedia of Kentucky* (Cincinnati, 1878), 69, 658-59. Scott, "The Logan Family of Lincoln County Kentucky," 174.

men in engagements with the Indians he was second only to George Rogers Clark.

Between 1783 and 1788 Logan was looked upon as the leading military man in the District of Kentucky. He was called upon to preside whenever a meeting of the county lieutenants and field officers was held. By 1785 positions of leadership in the civil affairs of the district were being filled by men of more education than Logan had been able to obtain. Most of these men came to Kentucky after the Revolution had ended. Many of them had held positions of importance in the eastern portion of Virginia or in other states. Logan alone, among those pioneers who had little or no education, continued to make his influence felt in public affairs. Nevertheless, it was as a protector of the people that he made his greatest contribution. The members of the Kentucky General Assembly realized this when they rendered him tribute, not as a great leader in the legal, political, or constitutional realms, but as "the firm defender of his country."

BIBLIOGRAPHICAL NOTES

MANUSCRIPT SOURCES for a biography of Benjamin Logan are adequate but are scattered over a wide area. With patience a large amount of information can be gleaned from the Draper Manuscript Collection owned by the State Historical Society of Wisconsin. The search must not be limited to the portion known as the Kentucky Papers. This section is valuable, but of almost equal value are the Preston and Virginia Papers, the George Rogers Clark Papers, and Lyman C. Draper's extracts from newspapers.

Other collections which have been drawn upon are the John Breckinridge Papers, the Harry Innes Papers, and the Shelby Family Papers in the Library of Congress, the Josiah Harmar Papers at the University of Michigan, the William Fleming Papers at Washington and Lee University, and the Durrett Collection at the University of Chicago.

The archives department of the Virginia State Library at Richmond has the state's Executive Papers, which contain a number of letters written to state officials by Logan and some of his associates, and the Executive Letter Books in which copies of letters from the governor to Logan and other county and militia officers may be found.

The House Journal for the first session of the 1792 Kentucky General Assembly was used at the Louisville Free Public Library, while that for the second session is available on microfilm at the University of Kentucky Library. The journals of the other sessions of which Logan was a member were used at the Kentucky Historical Society, as were in addition the journals of five of the conventions leading toward the separation of Kentucky from Virginia. The journal of the first of this series of conventions is in the Fleming Papers at Washington and Lee University. The Kentucky Historical Society has the manuscript Executive Journals for the period during which Logan was in the general assembly and commander of the first division of the Kentucky militia.

County court records are invaluable in tracing the actions and movements of any individual. This is true not only of deed books and will books but also of the order books of the county courts. The court records which yielded the most information on Logan and his family were those of the Virginia counties of Augusta, Fincastle, and Lincoln, and the Kentucky counties of Lincoln and Shelby.

Two newspapers provided a wealth of information, *The Kentucky Gazette,* published at Lexington, and *The Palladium,* published at Frankfort.

A large quantity of useful primary source material has been published. Ranking especially high in value for this study were William W. Hening (ed.), *The Statutes at Large . . . of Virginia,* 13 vols. (Richmond, 1810-1823); James A. James (ed.), *George Rogers Clark Papers, 1771-1784,* 2 vols. (Springfield, Illinois, 1912-1926); *Journals of the House of Delegates of the Commonwealth of Virginia . . . 1776-1787,* 12 vols. (Richmond, 1827-1828); William Littell (ed.), *The Statute Law of Kentucky,* 5 vols. (Frankfort, 1809-1819); *Michigan Pioneer and Historical Collections,* Vols. IX, X, XI, XIX, XX, and XXIV (Lansing, 1908-1912); William P. Palmer and others (eds.) *Calendar of Virginia State Papers, 1652-1869,* 11 vols. (Richmond, 1875-1893); James R. Robertson (ed.), *Petitions of the Early Inhabitants of Kentucky to the General Assembly of Virginia, 1769 to 1792* (Louisville, 1914); and William Henry Smith (ed.), *The St. Clair Papers,* 2 vols. (Cincinnati, 1882).

Articles in some of the journals constitute another valuable primary source. In the *Journal of Southern History* (Baton Rouge, 1935-   ) there is a unique contribution, Thomas P. Abernethy, "Journal of the First Kentucky Convention," I (1935), 67-78. The existence of this journal was not known until Abernethy discovered it among the William Fleming Papers. In the *American Historical Review* (New York, 1895-   ) some light is thrown upon the Spanish Conspiracy by William R. Shepherd (ed.), "Papers Bearing on James Wilkinson's Relations with Spain, 1787-1789," IX (1903-1904), 748-766.

The *Filson Club History Quarterly* (Louisville, 1926-   ) and the *Register of the Kentucky State Historical Society* (Frankfort, 1903-   ) have made available source materials gathered mainly from court records and from the Draper Manuscripts. In the *Quarterly* are "The Henderson Company Ledger," XXI (1947), 22-48; "Reverend John D. Shane's Notes on Interviews in 1844, with Mrs. Hinds and Patrick Scott of Bourbon County," X (1936), 166-177; "Reverend John Dabney Shane's Interview with Mrs. Sarah Graham of Bath County," IX (1935), 222-241; and "A Sketch of the Early Adventures of William Sudduth in Kentucky," II (1927-1928), 43-70, all edited by Lucien Beckner. The same journal has carried "John D. Shane's Interview with Ephriam Sandusky," VIII (1934), 217-228; Louise P. Kellogg, "A Kentucky Pioneer Tells Her Story of Early Boonesborough and Harrodsburg," III (1929), 223-236; "Reverend John D. Shane's Interview with Pioneer William Clinkenbeard," II (1927-1928), 95-128; and Mabel C. Weaks, "Memorandum Book of Governor Isaace Shelby, 1792-1794," XXX (1956), 203-231.

Charles R. Staples, "History in Circuit Court Records," began in the *Register* in 1930 and continued through the third issue in 1935. Other contributions of this nature in the *Register* are Lucien Beckner, "History of the County Court of Lincoln County, Va.," XX (1922), 170-190, and "Lincoln County Records," XII (1914), No. 34, 119-124, No. 35, 77-78, No. 36, 89-99; Mrs. Jouett Taylor Cannon, "Index to Military Certificates,

1787, etc.," XXII (1924), 2-20, and "State Archives—General Expenditures—1792-1798," XXXI (1933), 201-215; "Certificate Book of the Virginia Land Commission of 1779-80," XXI (1923), 3-168, 175-347; Huntley Dupre (ed.), "Three Letters of George Nicholas to John Brown," XLI (1943), 1-10; Bayless Hardin (ed.), "Governor Shelby's Militia Report to the General Assembly of Kentucky—1792," XXXVI (1938), 353-358, and "Whitley Papers, Volume 9—Draper Manuscripts—Kentucky Papers," XXXVI (1938), 189-209; "Kentucky State Papers," XXVII (1929), 587-594; "Kentucky's Active Militia—1786," XXXII (1934), 224-243; "Lincoln County Militia, 1780-1783," XXV (1927), 310-312; James A. Padgett, "The Letters of Colonel Richard Taylor and Commodore Richard Taylor to James Madison Together with a Sketch of Their Lives," XXXVI (1938), 330-344; and "Roll of Lincoln Militia," XXX (1932), 173-178.

Some of the general histories of Kentucky are lacking in objectivity, especially in their treatment of the Spanish Conspiracy. They also have suffered from the fact that many of the essential documents were carried away by Lyman C. Draper, and these have been used slightly or not at all. As a result, errors in one work have often been accepted as fact and repeated by later authors. Among the better histories of Kentucky are Temple Bodley, *History of Kentucky*, Vol. I (Chicago and Louisville, 1928), which carries the story to 1803; Thomas D. Clark, *A History of Kentucky* (New York, 1937); and Charles Kerr (ed.), *History of Kentucky*, 5 vols. (Chicago, 1922). Bodley presented a considerable amount of new material, but because his use of it was not that of a trained historian, he has never received the credit he deserves.

Biographies of Benjamin Logan's contemporaries contain much pertinent information. This is especially true of those of George Rogers Clark, with whom Logan was often associated. The best of these is James A. James, *The Life of George Rogers Clark* (Chicago, 1928). Two others which may be classed as good are John Bakeless, *Background to Glory, the Life of*

George Rogers Clark (Philadelphia and New York, 1957), and Temple Bodley, *George Rogers Clark, His Life and Public Services* (Boston, 1926). Among the other biographies of Kentucky pioneers are John Bakeless, *Daniel Boone* (New York, 1939); Edna Kenton, *Simon Kenton: His Life and Period, 1755-1836* (Garden City, New York, 1930); and Kathryn H. Mason, *James Harrod of Kentucky* (Baton Rouge, 1951).

Although they do not agree upon the extent to which democracy existed upon the frontier, two indispensable works for the student of Kentucky's state-making period are Thomas P. Abernethy, *Western Lands and the American Revolution* (New York, 1937) and John D. Barnhart, *Valley of Democracy* (Bloomington, Indiana, 1953).

Now that a reprint is available, John Bradford, *Historical Notes on Kentucky* (San Francisco, 1932) deserves more attention than it has received. Bradford was a participant in some of the events which he describes and a close observer of others. Two books by Thomas M. Green, *Historic Families of Kentucky* (Cincinnati, 1889) and *The Spanish Conspiracy* (Cincinnati, 1891) are helpful but must be used with caution and checked against other sources. Considerably better in quality are Robert L. Kincaid, *The Wilderness Road* (Indianapolis, 1947), and William S. Lester, *Transylvania Colony* (Spencer, Indiana, 1935).

William Littell, *Political Transactions in and Concerning Kentucky* (Frankfort, 1806) contains valuable material, but allowance must be made for the fact that Littell was writing a defense of men accused of conspiracy by Humphrey Marshall. Temple Bodley's reprint of Littell's work, one of the publications of the Filson Club (Louisville, 1926), has a lengthy and informative introduction. Among the other Filson Club Publications, which have been used with caution but also with increased respect, are John Mason Brown, *Political Beginnings of Kentucky* (Louisville, 1889); Reuben T. Durrett, *Bryant's Station* (Louisville, 1897); Willard R. Jillson (ed.), *The Kentucky Land Grants* (Louisville, 1925) and *Old Kentucky*

Entries and Deeds (Louisville, 1925); George W. Ranck, *Boonesborough* (Louisville, 1901); Thomas Speed, *The Wilderness Road* (Louisville, 1886); and William H. Whitsitt, *Life and Times of Judge Caleb Wallace* (Louisville, 1888).

In addition to primary source materials published in the historical journals there have been a large number of articles which have some bearing upon Benjamin Logan and pioneer Kentucky.

In the *American Historical Review* William R. Shepherd, "Wilkinson and the Beginnings of the Spanish Conspiracy," IX (1903-1904), 490-506, deals with an affair with which James Wilkinson attempted to associate Logan's name. In the same journal Frederick J. Turner, "The Origin of Genêt's Projected Attack on Louisiana and the Floridas," III (1897-1898), 650-671, covers the initial stages of the French Conspiracy, a movement in which Logan played a prominent role. Turner's "Western State-Making in the Revolutionary Era," I (1895-1896), 70-87, treats some early steps toward an objective which was finally attained in Kentucky in 1792.

The *Mississippi Valley Historical Review* (Cedar Rapids, 1914-   ) contains several articles which have been drawn upon either for specific information or for background. Among these are Clarence W. Alvord, "Virginia and the West: An Interpretation," III (1916-1917), 19-38; E. Merton Coulter, "The Efforts of the Democratic Societies of the West to Open the Navigation of the Mississippi," XI (1924-1925), 376-389; Huntley Dupre, "The Kentucky Gazette Reports the French Revolution," XXVI (1939-1940), 163-180; Leonard C. Helderman, "The Northwest Expedition of George Rogers Clark, 1786-1787," XXV (1938-1939), 317-334; Archibald Henderson, "Isaac Shelby and the Genêt Mission," VI (1919-1920), 451-469, and "Richard Henderson and the Occupation of Kentucky, 1775," I (1914-1915), 341-363; James A. James, "An Appraisal of the Contributions of George Rogers Clark to the History of the West," XVII (1930-1931), 98-115; Anthony Marc Lewis, "Jefferson and Virginia's Pioneers, 1774-1781," XXXIV (1947-

1948), 551-588; John Carl Parrish, "The Intrigues of Dr. James O'Fallon," XVII (1930-1931), 230-263; and Wilbur H. Siebert, "Kentucky's Struggle with Its Loyalist Proprietors," VII (1920-1921), 113-126.

The *Journal of Southern History* has carried articles by three of the leading authorities on pioneer Kentucky, Thomas P. Abernethy, "Democracy and the Southern Frontier," IV (1938), 3-13; John D. Barnhart, "Frontiersmen and Planters in the Formation of Kentucky," VII (1941), 19-36; and Robert S. Cotterill, "The Virginia-Chickasaw Treaty of 1783," VIII (1942), 483-496.

E. Merton Coulter, coauthor of the *History of Kentucky* edited by Charles Kerr, has published a very good article entitled "Early Frontier Democracy in the First Kentucky Constitution," in the *Political Science Quarterly* (Boston, 1886-   ), XXXIX (1924), 665-677.

The *Virginia Magazine of History and Biography* (Richmond, 1893-   ), the *Filson Club History Quarterly,* and the *Register of the Kentucky State Historical Society* all have articles which contribute to an understanding of Kentucky and Kentuckians in the period when the frontier was advancing westward across the region. The most useful of the articles from the *Virginia Magazine of History and Biography* is David I. Bushnell, Jr., "Daniel Boone at Limestone, 1786-1787," XXV (1917), 1-11. A few other articles from this journal are cited in the footnotes.

Articles by the author in the *Register* and in the *Filson Club History Quarterly* have, with the permission of their editors, been drawn upon freely. Papers of exceptional value published in the *Quarterly* are Pratt Byrd, "The Kentucky Frontier in 1792," XXV (1951), 181-203, 286-294; Thomas D. Clark, "Salt, a Factor in the Settlement of Kentucky," XII (1938), 42-52; Robert S. Cotterill, "Battle of Upper Blue Licks," II (1927-1928), 29-33; Richard Lowitt, "Activities of Citizen Genêt in Kentucky, 1793-1794," XXII (1948), 252-367; Milo M. Quaife, "When Detroit Invaded Kentucky," I (1926-1927), 53-57;

Hambleton Tapp, "Colonel John Floyd, Kentucky Pioneer," XV (1941), 1-24; and Elizabeth Warren, "Benjamin Sebastian and the Spanish Conspiracy in Kentucky," XX (1946), 107-130.

Among the most helpful of the articles published in the *Register* are Bessie T. Conkright, "Estill's Defeat or the Battle of Little Mountain," XXII (1924), 311-322, and "A Sketch of the Life and Times of General Benjamin Logan," XIV (1916), No. 41, 21-35, and No. 42, 21-33; Lowell H. Harrison, "John Breckinridge and the Kentucky Constitution of 1799," LVII (1949), 209-233; Willard R. Jillson, "Bibliography of Lincoln County," XXXV (1937), 339-359; and Hattie M. Scott, "The Logan Family of Lincoln County, Kentucky," XXX (1932), 173-178.

INDEX